PONTNEWYDD CAVE

A LOWER PALÆOLITHIC HOMINID SITE
IN WALES

THE FIRST REPORT

H. Stephen Green

National Museum of Wales Quaternary Studies Monographs, No. 1.

Frontispiece: Pontnewydd Cave. Excavations in progess, 1983. The view is taken from the inner entrance to the Guard Chamber. Excavations in the East Passage are shown far left. The Deep Sounding is centre right.

PONTNEWYDD CAVE

A LOWER PALÆOLITHIC HOMINID SITE IN WALES

THE FIRST REPORT

H. Stephen Green

with contributions by

M.J. Aitken, R.E. Bevins, P.A. Bull, C. Clayton, S.N. Collcutt, A.P. Currant,
N.C. Debenham, C. Embleton, J. Huxtable, M. Ivanovich, D.A. Jenkins,
T.I. Molleson, M.H. Newcomer, H.P. Schwarcz, C.B. Stringer,

Amgueddfa Genedlaethol Cymru

National Museum of Wales

Cardiff

1984

ISBN 0 7200 0282 6

Produced by
Alan Sutton Publishing Ltd.,
Gloucester

Printed in Great Britain by
REDWOOD BURN LIMITED
Trowbridge

I went full of curiosity and the faint, unrecognized apprehension that here, at last, I should find that low door in the wall . . which opened onto an enclosed and enchanted garden.

Evelyn Waugh

for Miranda
who has shared the enchantment
of Pontnewydd

FOREWORD

The National Museum of Wales has always taken an active part in archaeological excavation, but generally in latter years of a rescue nature. In 1974, the creation of four Archaeological Trusts, who now take full responsibility for dealing with threatened sites, has made it possible for the Museum to consider adopting its own programme of excavation. In 1978 the Museum instituted *The Palaeolithic Settlement of Wales* research-project under the direction of Dr. Stephen Green, F.S.A., Assistant Keeper of Prehistoric Archaeology. The initial results from the first site to be excavated, Pontnewydd Cave, have been extremely promising. The antiquity of man's presence in Wales has been more than doubled, and now extends to a quarter of a million years. Furthermore, the site has yielded not only the tools made by the Palaeolithic hunters who occupied the cave, but also remains of the hunters themselves.

The story is complex, as may be seen from the chapters that follow, but the outlines are clear. The cave itself fronts on to a cliff face in the Carboniferous limestone of the Elwy river-valley not far from Denbigh and St. Asaph in Clwyd. Before the early investigations of the cave took place over a century ago, it was filled up nearly to its roof by a succession of deposits which had, for the most part, slumped and flowed in from near the cave-entrance at a time when the valley floor was still 50m. above the present level, a striking index of the majestic age of the period under study. This infill is related, ultimately, to the climatic events of the last Ice Age which began over 500,000 years ago. It is doubtful whether glacial ice covered areas of Wales for more than a small part of this time, and so, for the remainder, the country would have been habitable, seasonally at least, during the cooler periods and all the year round during the warmer climatic phases.

For much of the Ice Age, Britain was joined to Europe, and settlement was largely confined to the southern and eastern areas of England. Indeed, Wales has only two known sites which predate the arrival of Modern Man in Europe, some 35,000–40,000 years ago, in comparison with dozens of such sites in England. The rarity of early sites in Wales probably reflects both the small size of the human population at this time and, also, the destructive power of glaciation which has no doubt scoured out most traces of early settlement from northern England and Wales, although the infrequency and haphazard nature of scientific research hitherto may also have had an influence.

The earliest deposits in the cave pre-date the known record of human beings in the area and reflect the action of just such glacial processes, for the basal layers are full of erratic pebbles moved by ice from Snowdonia. These pebbles, of the very hard igneous rocks, still lay around when the earliest hunters moved into the area and were selected by them for making into implements during, in all probability, the interglacial period which lasted from about 250,000 to 230,000 years ago, and perhaps also during the period of cooler climate which followed it. Some time around 230,000 years ago natural debris–flows bodily moved the refuse discarded by the Palaeolithic hunters into the cave to become incorporated in the deposits of the Intermediate complex and the Lower Breccia described in this book. This refuse included the bones of wild animals, tools made by the human occupants of the site, and human skeletal fragments as well. The implements include handaxes and spear-points and suggest the use of the original cave-entrance for butchering products of the chase. The species hunted by Early Man cannot, however, be determined exactly, for his food-bones are inextricably mixed with bones belonging to a different period when bears used the cave as a den for winter hibernation. What can be said is that the hunters selected their prey from species which included horse, roe deer, red deer, lion, bear, rhinoceros and bison or wild cattle.

The most exciting finds from the cave are the actual fragments of early humans, so far from at least three individuals – an adult, a child aged about 8–9 years and a possible adolescent. Only jaw fragments are represented so far, but are enough to suggest the identification of the visitors as Early Neanderthals. The discovery of such remains of this antiquity is important, for the *classic* Neanderthals of Europe – so grossly misrepresented in horror films – belong to the much more recent period of 70–35,000 years ago. The finds from Pontnewydd, taken with evidence from elsewhere, then, suggest a long period of stable development before the sudden disappearance of the Neanderthals, perhaps as a consequence of the arrival in Europe of the first fully modern man – *Homo sapiens sapiens.*

Fortunately, we can date these "first Welshmen" with some confidence, for one discarded a piece of flint, from which he had been striking sharp cutting flakes, on to a fire where it became burnt, and this may be dated by a technique called Thermoluminescence. Other dates at Pontnewydd come from stalagmite, which formed on top of the sediments containing human finds. This dating is based on the ratio of the radioactive isotope Uranium-234, present when the floor is formed by a slow build-up of calcium carbonate precipitated from dripping roof-water, and Thorium-230, which is not present when the floor is first laid down, but which forms naturally from the decay of the uranium.

The present report, though comprehensive, is designed as an interim statement which necessarily treats some aspects of the work in more detail than others. It gives, however, an opportunity for the Museum to present the findings to a wide audience, and to thank the many experts and grant-giving bodies who have supported the project. Above all, we must thank the landowner, Major David Williams-Wynn, a member of an old and distinguished Welsh family, whose ready permission to excavate and generous donation of the finds to the National Museum of Wales have been matched by his help and many kindnesses in the field which have alone made possible the results here described. The cave is one of the few protected under the Ancient Monuments Acts, and it is therefore with some satisfaction that this important provisional account is rendered on work conducted by permission of the Secretary of State for Wales.

D. A. Bassett
Director

CONTENTS

LIST OF PLATES

LIST OF FIGURES

xiii

xiv

LIST OF TABLES

TECHNICAL TERMS AND ABBREVIATIONS

BP	Before present
ka	Thousands of years before present (e.g. 75 ka = 75,000 BP)
U-Th	Uranium-Thorium
TL	Thermoluminescence
Terminus ante quem	Literally "boundary before which". A minimum age.
Terminus post quem	Literally "boundary after which". A maximum age. Thus a date valid for the middle layer of a sequence gives a *terminus ante quem* for the underlying layers and a *terminus post quem* for the overlying layers.

It would be inappropriate to give an extended glossary in a report of this nature. The reader is referred to John Challinor *A Dictionary of Geology,* various editions, (University of Wales Press, Cardiff) and to comparable works for many of the terms used here.

ACKNOWLEDGEMENTS

It is both a duty and a pleasure to acknowledge the very generous help given by a number of grant-giving bodies, namely the Board of Celtic Studies of the University of Wales, the Cambrian Archaeological Association, the British Academy, the Society of Antiquaries of London, the LSB Leakey Foundation and the Foundation for Research into the Origin of Man.

The site is a scheduled Ancient Monument and I am indebted to the Welsh Office and its Principal Inspector of Ancient Monuments, Dr. M.W. Thompson, for authorisation to excavate there. The cave is owned by Major David Williams-Wynn, who has given his willing consent to the operations which are the subject of this present monograph. His unstinting help and kindness through all seasons of excavation have placed me for ever in his debt. Particular mention must be made also of Dennis Matheson, formerly farm manager, who sustained and supported our efforts in so many ways during the first few seasons.

The specialists who have taken an active part in the work at the site are my co-authors in this project and to them my debt is incalculable. I must thank also Philip Gibbard who has looked unsuccessfully for pollen in the deposits and Angela Fussell, our surveyor. Nicholas Taylor confirmed the identification of the hominid fossils in the field. The successive seasons of excavation have been site-supervised by Simon Collcutt, Stephen Hartgroves, Jill Cook and Sheila Coulson. The growing complexity of the excavation led to the appointment, in 1982, of Kenneth Brassil as Assistant Director and Susan Stallibrass as Site Supervisor. Of the individuals who have worked as volunteers on the excavation nd particular mention must be made here of Andy Buchan, Rod Harrison, Peter McDonald and Liz Neville.

Many people have been involved in the production of this report. The artefact drawings are the work of Pat O'Leary and the remainder of the illustrative work prepared in the National Museum of Wales has been expertly carried out by Paul Hughes and Paul White. My special thanks go to Eric Broadbent, Kevin Thomas and Dennis Donovan for their excellent photographic work. The composite bibliography is the work of Yolanda Stanton and considerable help has been given, in the preparation of the report, by Gareth Lewis, Kate Cockburn and Monica Cox. Dr. C. Forbes of the Sedwick Museum of Geology very kindly placed the McKenny Hughes finds on temporary loan at the National Museum of Wales in order to facilitate their study.

Finally, I must thank those archaeological colleagues who have taken such a personal interest in the excavation and who have read through and commented on Chapter V, namely Derek Roe, Mark Newcomer and Roger Jacobi. Above all, I must thank George Boon, my head of department, for his constant enthusiasm and practical help at all stages of this project.

H. Stephen Green
Cardiff. 31 October, 1983.

ABSTRACTS

CHAPTER I

INTRODUCTION

In 1978, the National Museum of Wales initiated a research programme, of which Pontnewydd Cave forms part, into the Palaeolithic Settlement of Wales. The site lies near Rhyl in N. Wales, in a region far beyond the main area of earlier Palaeolithic settlement in southern and eastern England. The first investigations of the site took place in the 1870s by Professor William Boyd Dawkins, who seems to have removed substantial deposits but who produced incomplete and untrustworthy results, and, shortly after, by Professor Thomas McKenny Hughes, who outlined the stratigraphy of the site and discovered artefacts and Pleistocene fauna together with a human tooth (now lost). In 1940, the site suffered some damage when it was converted for use as a war-time munitions store. The recording methods used in the modern excavations are outlined in some detail.

H. Stephen Green
Department of Archaeology & Numismatics,
National Museum of Wales, Cardiff

CHAPTER II

LOCATION, SETTING AND GEOMORPHOLOGY

A tentative model of the sequence of glacial events in North Wales is described, involving ice of both Northern (Irish Sea) and Welsh origin. It is argued that the lower Elwy Valley developed by glacial diversion of the river, the date of which is certainly pre-Ipswichian and possibly much older. The lower Elwy valley was then further deepened, receiving later deposits of glacial, glacifluvial and fluvial origin. During the Devensian, terraces of glacifluvial material were formed in the valley. The approximate accordance in level of the terraces near Pontnewydd with the height of the cave entrance suggests that formation or re-modelling of the terrace surface by the Elwy caused a break-through of water and debris flows into the cave system which had been partially choked by older deposits.

Clifford Embleton
Department of Geography,
Kings College, University of London,

CHAPTER III

THE SEDIMENT STRATIGRAPHY

A. THE SEDIMENTS

Detailed description of each deposit and exposure is presented, followed by lithologic correlation and justification of a composite stratigraphy. The greatest part of the sequence was accumulated by repeated mass movement events (debris flows), leading to the emplacement of allochthonous sediments and reworking of existing deposits. Glacially derived exotic material was progressively diluted by more local limestone debris up through the sequence. Mass movement events were separated by long periods of quiescence, with sporadic speleothem formation and minor subaqueous sedimentation. This site was subject to a deep cave (hypogean) environment and all mammalian and archaeological remains are in secondary context.

S.N. Collcutt
Donald Baden-Powell Quaternary
Research Centre,
University of Oxford,

B. SCANNING ELECTRON MICROSCOPE STUDIES OF SEDIMENTS

Investigation of sand grain surface textures undertaken on samples taken in Pontnewydd Cave suggests that the sediment (mostly externally derived) originated from many sources. Some sediments show evidence of long distance fluvial travel and subsequent mixing in the vicinity of the cave with angular material (glacial?) and with local sandstone-derived breakdown.

Whilst some samples contain a mixture of all sediment types, others present a uniform assemblage of angular rounded fluvial material. Together with other contributory evidence, these findings support the idea of a large timespan between some of the sedimentary units.

Peter Bull
Christ Church
Oxford

CHAPTER IV

ABSOLUTE AND RELATIVE DATING

A. URANIUM-SERIES DATING AND STABLE ISOTOPE ANALYSIS OF CALCITE DEPOSITS

Absolute ages of speleothems (stalagmites, stalactites, etc.) have been determined by radiometric analysis of the activity ratios of ^{230}Th/^{234}U and ^{234}U/^{238}U. Most of the samples were derived fragments embedded in breccia; a few were *in situ* stalagmites or flowstones. *In situ* deposits on the Lower Breccia range in age from 215±36 to 83 ka. The Upper Breccia and Red Cave Earth contain derived fragments ranging in age from 307 to 123 ka. An oxygen isotope profile of an *in situ* stalagmite on the Lower Breccia shows it to have formed in a cooling episode from 96 to 89 ka, while the cave was sealed.

Henry P. Schwarcz
Department of Geology
McMaster University
Hamilton, Ontario, Canada

B. BRIEF REPORT ON DATING THE *IN SITU* STALAGMITIC FLOOR FOUND IN THE EAST PASSAGE IN 1982

A sample (D1288C) of a stalagmitic floor discovered in the East Passage during the 1982 digging season was divided into three layers and several aliquots from each layer were used for the repeat uranium series disequilibrium analyses at Harwell. The average uranium content of the samples is 0.27 ± 0.01 p.p.m. and the associated average ^{234}U/^{238}U activity ratio is 1.34 ± 0.06. The spread in the nine reported ^{230}Th/^{234}U ages is within the two standard deviations quoted and, therefore, the ages obtained for each layer could not be distinguished statistically from each other. The average age for the whole sample is 224 +41/−31 ka. The archaeological implication is that the hominid remains found beneath this stalagmitic floor must pre-date the quoted age of 224,000 years before present.

Miro Ivanovich
Geophysical Tracer Studies
AERE Harwell, Oxon

C. THERMOLUMINESCENCE AND URANIUM SERIES DATING OF STALAGMITIC CALCITE

Twelve samples of stalagmitic calcite have been dated by the Thermoluminescence (TL) method. Details of sample preparation and the TL measurements are given, together with an account of the assumptions used in the date calculations and the possible effects of their non-validity. The ages of the stalagmites were independently measured by the Th-230/ U-234 disequilibrium technique, using alpha spectrometry. The main points of the chemical extractions of U and Th and of the age calculations are described. There is generally good agreement between the two sets of measured ages. These results therefore broadly support the basis of the TL method, and encourage a fuller assessment of its potentials.

Nicholas Debenham
Laboratory for Archaeology & the
History of Art,
University of Oxford

D. THERMOLUMINESCENCE (TL) STUDIES ON BURNT FLINT AND STONES FROM PONTNEWYDD CAVE

Thermoluminescence investigations of five burnt samples from three areas within the cave are reported. The samples were of mudstone, siltstone, vitric tuff and flint. It was possible to give a TL age only for the burnt flint and this was $200,000 \pm 25,000$ years.

Joan Huxtable
Laboratory for Archaeology & the
History of Art,
University of Oxford

E. RELATIVE DATING AND ASSESSMENT OF DEPOSITIONAL ENVIRONMENT FROM TRACE ELEMENT ANALYSIS OF FOSSIL BONES

The hominid fossils found during the recent excavations at Pontnewydd that are of doubtful provenance either because of the nature of their find-context (old excavation dumps) or the complexity of their depositional environment (reworked beds) have been shown to have similar levels of acquired elements (fluorine and uranium) as bones of known Pleistocene age. This application of relative dating methods cannot, however, distinguish bones of Middle from those of Upper Pleistocene age. Analysis of the distribution of fluorine in buried bones using PIXE techniques has proved a valuable adjunct in the interpretation of the depositional environments.

Theya I. Molleson
Department of Palaeontology
British Museum (Natural History)
London

CHAPTER V

THE ARCHAEOLOGICAL DISCOVERIES

A. THE ARCHAEOLOGICAL ARTEFACTS

Typological analysis has revealed an assemblage – made largely on siliceous volcanic pebbles – with important handaxe, Levallois and side-scraper components. The commonest handaxe type is the amygdaloid; the most typical Levallois products are flakes showing evidence of centripetal preparation, but present also are flake-blades and points; Levallois, discoidal and crude cores are all common. Other tool-types present include a chopper, chopping tools and a flake-cleaver. Arguments are adduced for regarding the artefacts – notwithstanding their derived context in debris flows – as products of a single industry perhaps in the range 250–225 ka. Comparison is made with Continental Upper Acheulian industries.

H. S. Green

B. FLAKING EXPERIMENTS WITH PONTNEWYDD RAW MATERIALS

Experiments in making replicas of the Pontnewydd Acheulian stone tools revealed that all the major artifact classes could be made by direct percussion with a hammerstone, and that the coarsest raw materials yielded high proportions of waste flakes which did not show the diagnostic features of intentionally struck flakes. Assessing the effect the hard-to-flake materials had on the archaeological assemblages was more difficult, but it seems probable that the intractable rocks made it difficult to produce refined-looking tools, but did not affect the types of tools made.

Marle H. Newcomer
Institute of Archaeology
London

CHAPTER VI

THE HOMINID FINDS

The first stratified hominid find from the present excavations (PN1) was excavated in 1980 from the Intermediate complex in the East Passage. It is an upper molar, probably a left M^2 of a young adult, and displays taurodontism. The 1982 excavations produced a fragment of right maxilla (PN4) from a close, but slightly higher, stratigraphic position near the base of the Lower Breccia. Two teeth are present, dM^2 and M^1 suggesting a dental age of $c.8$–9 years, but there appears to be an anomalous position for the P^4 crypt. The M^1 of this individual is also taurodont, and both PN1 and PN4 resemble early Neanderthal specimens from the Upper Pleistocene site of Krapina in Yugoslavia. Two unstratified specimens have also been found, a right posterior mandibular fragment containing an unerupted molar (PN2), and a fragment of an adult thoracic vertebra (PN3). PN2 probably represents an individual aged between 11–14 years and, from the preserved parts, neither it nor PN3 can be excluded from the range of anatomically modern specimens. The 1983 excavation produced two lower first premolars, one probably from an 8–12 year old and the second from a somewhat older individual. Between 3–6 individuals are thus already represented in the Pontnewydd hominid sample.

Christopher B. Stringer
Department of Palaeontology
British Museum (Natural History)
London

CHAPTER VII

THE MAMMALIAN REMAINS

Quaternary mammal remains from Pontnewydd Cave, North Wales, are divisible into three distinct assemblages, the earliest of which includes hominid remains. Biostratigraphic indicators show a depositional history spanning the later Middle Pleistocene and parts of the Late Pleistocene (Late Devensian).

Andrew P. Currant
Department of Palaeontology
British Museum (Natural History)
London

CHAPTER VIII

MINERALOGY AND PETROLOGY

A. SAND AND CLAY MINERALOGY

Sediment mineralogy has been studied with the aim of, firstly, identifying possible sources for five of the cave deposits and, secondly, obtaining information about environmental conditions during deposition. From their contribution of distinctive "heavy minerals" to the sand fraction, local North Welsh rocks (mudstones) apparently dominated sediment sources, although small differences are evident in contributions from dolerites, sandstones and, in the later deposits, of glacial drift of Northern (Irish Sea) origin. From the composition of the clay fractions, the "Intermediate" deposits would appear to have been deposited during periods of relatively intense/prolonged weathering.

David A. Jenkins
Dept. of Biochemistry & Soil Science
University College of N. Wales
Bangor, Gwynedd

B. THE FLINTS

Upper Cretaceous flints comprise about 10% of the lithic finds at Pontnewydd. Acid etching of the samples differentiates two broad structural types: a main set of coalesced (and more rarely "open") lepispheric flints and a smaller group of skeletal-rich forms, either of lephispheric or chalcedonic type. These two groups were derived originally from different Chalk outcrops. There is no clear differentiation of flint types recovered from the different stratigraphic units in the cave. Possible Palaeolithic sources for these materials were the Irish Sea Drift deposits of either the Shropshire-Cheshire Plain or the North Wales coast. The flints in the drift probably were derived originally from sources in Western Scotland.

Christopher Clayton
Department of Geology
University of London

C. PETROLOGICAL INVESTIGATIONS

Petrological investigations of material from Pontnewydd Cave have been undertaken on both artefacts and erratics. The majority of the artefacts were manufactured from a variety of altered, predominantly silicic igneous, pyroclastic and volcaniclastic rocks. The erratic lithologies are broadly similar to those of the artefacts and the conclusion is that the erratics contained within local glacial drift sequences were the source of raw material for artefact-manufacture. The erratics are not of local origin, some being from the Snowdonia area with others possibly derived from the English Lake District.

Richard E. Bevins
Department of Geology
National Museum of Wales, Cardiff

CHAPTER IX

SUMMARY AND DISCUSSION

The work of 1978–81 is summarised and updated with results from 1982–3. The stratigraphic sequence is described and assessed. Human settlement at the cave may belong within the time range 250–225 ka. Artefacts, where not reworked into younger deposits, are contained within the early debris flows of the Intermediate complex and the Lower Breccia. A review of the evidence for the source of these flows indicates an origin in the region of the original cave-mouth, with a higher river-level as the possible source of their water-content. The relevant dating evidence is brought together and presented in a single figure (Fig.IX.3) and demonstrates the generally successful application of the Uranium-Thorium and Thermoluminescence techniques at Pontnewydd, where some three dozen dates are now available. The faunal sequence of Intermediate-Lower Breccia shows a possible inter-glacial phase followed by a cool-temperate assemblage and it is tempting, taken with other evidence from the cave, to relate this to the successively warm and cool Oxygen Isotope substages 7c (c.250–230 ka) and 7b (c.230 ka), with the human occupation certainly initiated in 7c and ending before or during 7b. The hominid and archaeological finds are summarised. The human occupation of the site is seen as perhaps no more than brief and seasonal. Only a single industry, with important handaxe, Levallois and scraper components, appears to be present and this can best be compared with Continental Upper Acheulian industries. The strategy for future work is outlined.

H. S. Green

8

Plate I   View of Pontnewydd Cave taken, in 1979, from the S.E.

CHAPTER I

INTRODUCTION

by

H. Stephen Green

"The further back we research the past, the more the 'documents in the case' accumulate and the more reluctant we feel to open their pages, to disturb the dust."

Graham Greene

The results to be discussed below are based on work which began in 1978 with a decision by the National Museum of Wales to support a research programme into the Palaeolithic settlement of Wales. Pontnewydd Cave in Clwyd was the first site to be examined and the findings proved to be so exciting that it has become the core of the research programme. Other sites on which work is taking place include both the nearby Cefn Cave (Falconer, 1868; Valdemar, 1970) and a hitherto untouched local site which we have named Cae Gronw. In addition, publication, by myself and Kate Scott, of the work of the late Charles McBurney and of John Clegg (Clegg, 1970) at the now destroyed site of Coygan Cave, Dyfed, is well in hand.

This report covers the excavations which took place between 1978 and 1981 with some additional material from the 1982–3 seasons. The present report does not seek to be a definitive account of the whole excavation. Many matters must necessarily be reserved for the final report which will follow completion of the whole project.

THE NAME OF THE CAVE

Pontnewydd was the spelling used in the 1870's by Professor Thomas McKenny Hughes, the first investigator of the site to discover Palaeolithic artefacts. I have retained this form of the name as a mark of *pietas* to McKenny Hughes, himself a Welsh-speaking Welshman. Those familiar with the Welsh language will know that, under certain circumstances, "P" will mutate to "B" and it is for this reason that the modern village near the site is called Y Bont Newydd, meaning "the new bridge". The cave also appears in the literature as Bont Newydd (Valdemar, 1970) or Bontnewydd (Roe, 1981, 246).

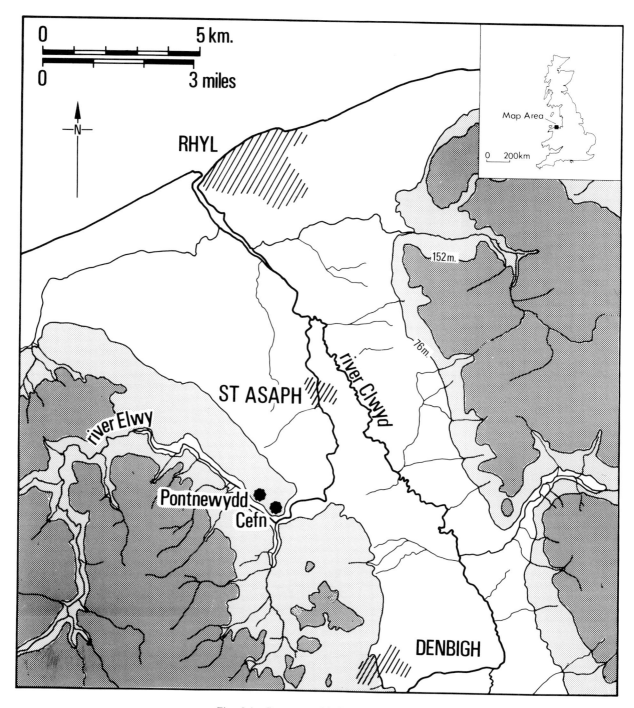

Fig. I.1 Pontnewydd Cave. Location.

LOCATION

The cave (Pl.I) lies ten kilometers due south of the modern coastal resort of Rhyl, about 90 metres above sea-level, in the Carboniferous Limestone of the Elwy Valley and several kilometers upstream of the point where the river enters the broad Vale of Clwyd (Fig.I.1). It is important to understand its geographical situation in the context of the geology and glacial history of the whole of the north-western British Isles. The site lies at the point of contact of the two great ice-sheets represented by the so-called Irish Sea (or Northern) and Welsh drifts; and some, and possibly all, of the raw materials used for the lithic artefacts found in the cave have been transported to the Elwy Valley by glacial action. The glacial history of the Elwy Valley was studied some years ago by Clifford Embleton and it is a great pleasure to me that the results from the cave excavation have encouraged Professor Embleton – and now his research student Helen Livingston – to return to the field to make a detailed study of its geomorphology.

The glacial history of Britain is one of the factors relevant to the vast areas in the north and west which are empty of Palaeolithic finds (Fig.I.2). Around 40,000 handaxes are known from England, but in Wales, besides the Pontnewydd Cave series, only five have been recorded: two are stray finds, from Penylan in Cardiff (Lacaille, 1954) and Rhosili in Gower (Green, 1981c) and three come from Coygan Cave near Laugharne in Dyfed (Grimes, 1935, fig.6, p.109; Clegg, 1970). However, destruction of sites and artefacts by glacial action is perhaps not the principal reason for the striking absence of finds from the Highland Zone of Britain, for they are scarce in the unglaciated south-western peninsula of England even though stone suitable for making them is plentiful there. Indeed, on an European scale, Desmond Collins (1976) has shown how the focus of distribution in south-east England is linked to another in north-west France. We may deduce, therefore, that whilst there must have been other earlier Palaeolithic sites in Wales, these are likely to have been few and would probably have represented no more than isolated periods of settlement. Hence the great interest of the work now reported.

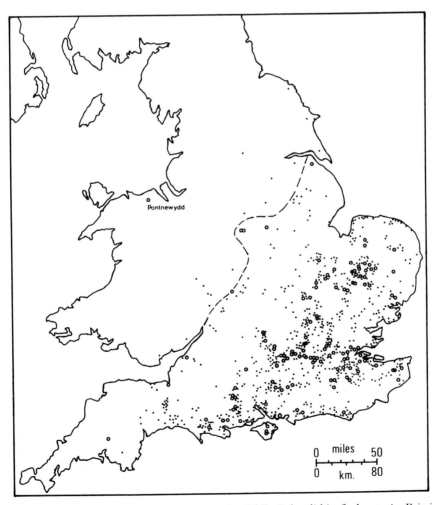

Fig. I.2 Pontnewydd Cave in relation to Lower and Middle Palaeolithic findspots in Britain. The circles represent more than 10 finds. The broken line indicates the N.W. limit of *in situ* flint in England and Wales. Based on work by Derek Roe.

THE MODERN HISTORY OF THE SITE

The cave is first recorded by the Reverend E. Stanley in 1832 who, following a description of his own excavation in the nearby Cefn Caves, both mapped and described Pontnewydd Cave (Stanley, 1832, 53 and Pl.I): "I found [it] to be entirely blocked up with soil, and has clearly never been open to human observation. But I have no doubt, from its appearance and character, that it will . . . exhibit as rich a prospect [as Cefn], whenever its recesses may be explored, in search of those organic remains now unknown in the temperate zones". Stanley records also how the modern road up the hill from Bont Newydd Village to Cefn was then being built "with great taste and judgement". The building of this road gave, and continues to give, easy access to the site.

The next references to the cave are those of Professor William Boyd Dawkins (1874, 286–7; 1880, 192) who records an investigation in 1870, by Mrs. Williams-Wynn, the Reverend D.R. Thomas and himself, which yielded only faunal remains. Dawkins published no plan or section and gives no clue of the extent of his work (discussed further by A.P. Currant (p.172)), but at the time of the examination of the site a few years later by Professor McKenny Hughes and the Rev. D.R. Thomas it is clear that substantial deposits had been removed (Hughes and Thomas, 1874, Pl. XXIII). Their section and elevation are reproduced here (Figs.I.3–4) together with our own elevation. The latter shows the McKenny Hughes and Thomas valley-profile to be no more than a sketch but their section is more valuable and shows the three main units detected by ourselves, viz.

McKenny Hughes and Thomas		New Classification
b.	Yellow Cave Earth	= Upper Clays and Sands
c.	Breccia	= Upper and Lower Breccia
d.	Gravel	= Upper Sands and Gravels

Boyd Dawkins claimed not to have found any artefacts but our excavation of what we believe to be his dump of spoil outside the cave entrance – which itself underlies the dump of Second World War age (Plate II) – has yielded artefacts in plenty besides Pleistocene fauna. McKenny Hughes' work was of an altogether better quality and yielded both fauna and artefacts. In addition, Hughes found a human molar tooth, since lost, described by Professor Busk (in Hughes and Thomas, 1874) as looking "quite as ancient as the rest" and as being of "very large size". The artefacts which McKenny Hughes found were described by him as made of "a compact grey felstone, sometimes porphyritic". He added that this raw material "does not occur in the drainage basin of the Elwy, but is common in the drift of the neighbourhood. Even in a highly-finished implement this rock does not show the care bestowed upon it in the same way that flint does". These artefacts were compared with finds from Le Moustier and St Acheul; and before the present excavations commenced the conventional wisdom was that the finds were a Mousterian of Acheulian Tradition Industry of last glaciation age. McKenny Hughes' finds are now in the Sedgwick Museum of Geology in the University of Cambridge where he was one-time Woodwardian Professor of Geology. The original labels on the artefacts in the Sedgwick collection are instructive and throw some light on the operations at the cave. It is a clear impression from reading McKenny Hughes' account (Hughes and Thomas, 1874) that these operations were confined to examination of visible sections and to scouring of Boyd Dawkins' excavation dumps. That finds were being made in just this way is evidenced by a letter from McKenny Hughes to Boyd Dawkins recording and illustrating (Fig.I.5) the find, by Professor Tiddeman, of a handaxe (now in the Sedgwick Collection ref. no. SMG-D2894) on what must have been Boyd Dawkins' dumps. Details on some labels are set out in Table I.1; these make it clear that the finds illustrated by McKenny Hughes (1887) had been picked up both at the time of his original investigations and over succeeding years. It is certain that some

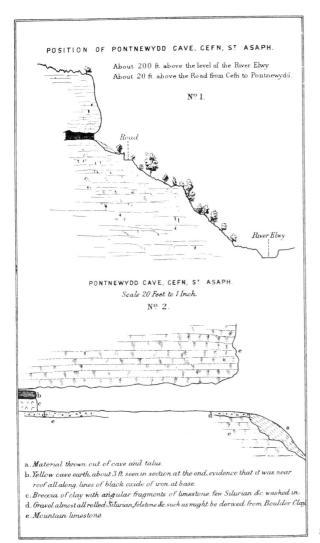

Fig. I.3 Pontnewydd Cave. Profile of hill-side and cave-section from Hughes and Thomas (1874).

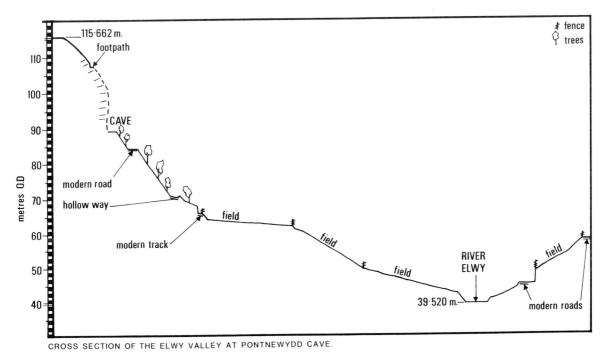

Fig. I.4 Pontnewydd Cave. Profile of modern valley by Angela Fussell. Horizontal scale is 50% of the vertical scale. Accurate to 1:500.

Plate II   Pontnewydd Cave. The Boyd Dawkins dump, overlain by the World War II dump and separated from it by a thin turf-line. 1979, from S.E.

Plate III   Pontnewydd Cave in the 1920's. View from a 3¼″ square lantern slide taken by J. Wilfrid Jackson. The view faces East from a position near the South Fissure. The South Passage (with drainpipe) may be seen to the right. Copyright: Buxton Museum.

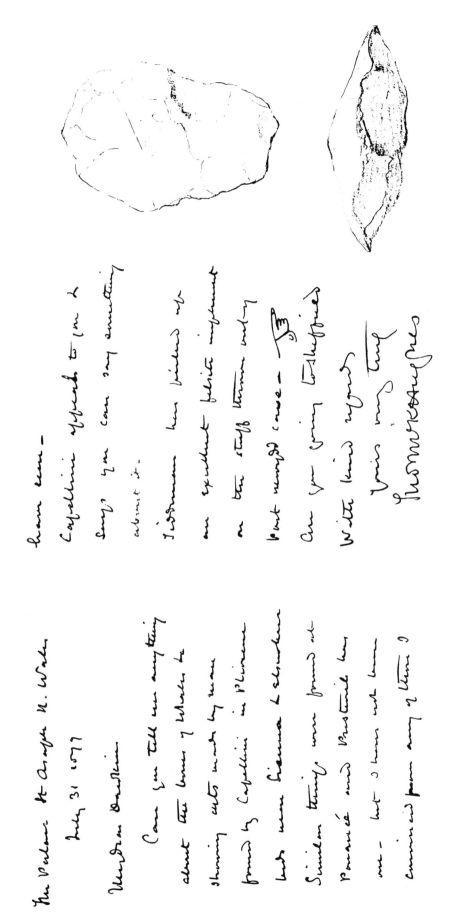

Fig. 1.5 Letter written in 1879 from McKenny Hughes to Boyd Dawkins describing the find of a handaxe (Sedgwick Museum of Geology Collection no. D2894) on Boyd Dawkins' dumps. Copyright Museum and Art Gallery, Buxton.

Ref. No	Details recorded on artefact	How recorded
D2894	"on earth thrown out of Pontnewydd Cave St Asaph 1879"	label
D2904	"Pontnewydd Cave, Jan. 3rd, 1876"	label
D2915	"Pontnewydd Cave, Jan. 3rd, 1876"	label
D2899	"Herbert Chamber, Pontnewydd Cave; W.S.S. 4 Sept. 1878"	label
D2896	"Pontnewydd Cave, St Asaph, Dec. 26th 1880"	label
D2895	"Pontnewydd Cave, July 24th, 1881"	label
D2892	"Pontnewydd Cave, Cefn, St Asaph, July 29/81"	in ink on artefact

TABLE I.1 Sedgwick Museum of Geology Collection. Labels recording date of discovery of artefacts.

at least were found by others besides Professor Tiddeman and, no doubt, by the Williams-Wynn family on Boxing Day and New Year walks. The description "Herbert Chamber" recorded on a number of finds in the Sedgwick collection presents an enigma. It is possible that some such area of the cave as the South Passage or South Fissure was given this name after the 7th baronet Colonel Sir Herbert Lloyd Williams-Wynn (born June 1860, died May 1944) who was a boy at the time of the investigations by Boyd Dawkins and McKenny Hughes.

That the extensive clearance of cave-deposit recorded by McKenny Hughes took place at the time of Boyd Dawkins' work is suggested both by the lack of allusion to any earlier work either by Dawkins or Hughes and by the fact that one artefact in the Sedgwick collection (SMG-D2900) is simply marked "New Cave".

Hughes' published section shows that excavation had advanced, by the early 1870's, to the point where we found the edge of the undisturbed deposits in 1979 (Fig.I.6) A $3\frac{1}{4}$ square lantern slide (Pl.III), taken by J. Wilfred Jackson in the 1920's, shows the cave much as we found it but with thicker wall sediments and without the extensive modern dump masking the East Passage sediments. (Fig.I.6).

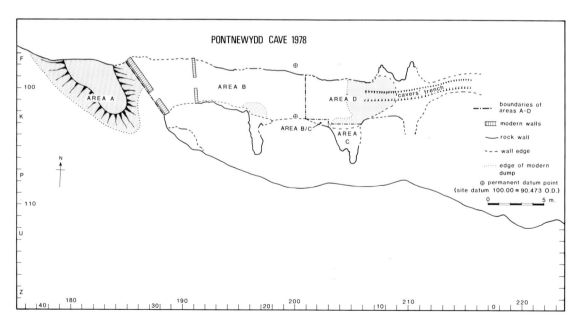

Fig. I.6 Pontnewydd Cave. Site plan before excavation in 1978.

Plate IV   Pontnewydd Cave. The interior of the cave in 1979 showing the floor levelled by the army. The Deep Sounding and South Fissure are to the left. View facing West.

Plate V   Pontnewydd Cave. The external wall of the guard chamber. View from S.W., 1979.

18

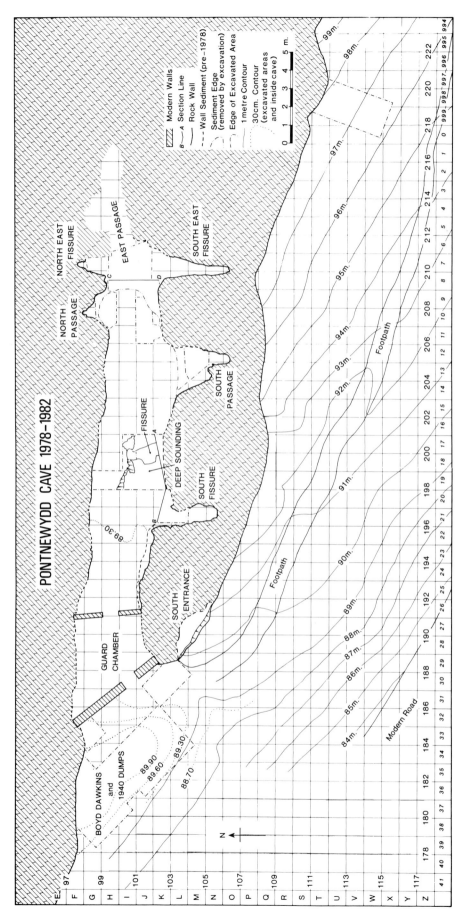

PONTNEWYDD CAVE 1978-1982

Modern Walls
B——A Section Line
Rock Wall
Wall Sediment (pre–1978)
Sediment Edge (removed by excavation)
Edge of Excavated Area
1 metre Contour
30cm. Contour (excavated areas and inside cave)

0 1 2 3 4 5 m.

NORTH EAST FISSURE
NORTH PASSAGE
EAST PASSAGE
SOUTH EAST FISSURE
FISSURE
SOUTH PASSAGE
DEEP SOUNDING
SOUTH FISSURE
GUARD CHAMBER
SOUTH ENTRANCE
BOYD DAWKINS and 1940 DUMPS
Footpath
Footpath
Modern Road

Fig. I.7 Pontnewydd Cave. Plan of excavations 1978–82.

Plate VI   Pontnewydd Cave. The South Fissure at an early stage of excavation in 1978. View from the North.

In 1940, the cave was converted as a store for land mines and depth charges and the guard chamber was constructed at this time. In conjunction with this work, the floor was levelled and covered with gravel (Pl.IV). On this were placed duck-boards on which the mines themselves were placed and covered with tarpaulins. At the entrance to the cave was built a concrete-floored guard chamber which was fitted with a coke stove, the outer wall being faced with limestone as camouflage against possible enemy bombers (Pl.V).* A dump of material associated with this levelling and clearance has been recognised overlying the nineteenth century dump and separated from it by a turf line. More recently in 1966 or 1967, members of the Birkenhead YMCA Spelaeological Club dug into the back of the cave with a view to extending knowledge of the cave system. This work was published, in the form of a letter to a now defunct magazine called *The Spelaeologist* (Kelly, 1967). Animal bones –

---

* I am indebted to Mr Hugh Jones of Cefn, who has known the cave since *c.* 1903, for valuable information on its modern history.

said to be those of a wolf and hare – were the only finds and the excavator, evidently interested in the now fashionable subject of taphonomy, concluded that the hare "had probably been captured and killed by the wolf". Regrettably, this operation was illegal, the cave having been protected by law as a Scheduled Ancient Monument since July 1933.

THE PRESENT EXCAVATION

I first visited Pontnewydd Cave in 1977. The doors of the guard chamber were missing; a hearth inside evidenced modern use as an overnight shelter and the cavers' trench and dumps of spoil were clearly visible. Our excavations began in 1978 and were concentrated on the old excavation dumps visible outside the cave and on three areas inside the cave, unfortunately isolated from each other by the removal of deposits which took place either last century or during World War II (Fig.I.7). These are the South Fissure (Pl.VI), the South Passage (Pl.VII) and the East Passage (Pl.VIII). These areas have also been denoted by capital letters, *viz*:

Area B(1978+) The South Fissure and contiguous wall sediments.
Area C(1978) the South Passage and (in 1978 only) the East Passage.
Area D (1979+) the East Passage and associated Fissures (N.E. and S.E. Fissures) and the North Passage.
In 1978 the designation 'C' was used to cover both the South Passage and the East Passage (which became Area 'D' in 1979) but only unstratified material was excavated from the latter in 1978. There are two other Area designations:
Area A (1978+) Boyd Dawkins and World War II dumps.
Area E (1980) A trench on the hillslope above the cave excavated to examine a resistivity anomaly detected by Arnold Aspinall of the University of Bradford. It yielded a cemented periglacial scree.
Finds are numbered within Areas of the site and accordingly carry A, B, C, D or E prefixes.

Two horizontal recording systems are in operation at the site (Fig.I.7). The first, used principally during excavation, is a single system of numbered one-metre squares (e.g.K2l, H9 etc.) which are more easily remembered by people digging than six (or more) figure co-ordinates. The second, used principally during surveying, is a metric co-ordinate system which locates squares by their *north-west* corners: for example H2O is also 197/99 and its N.W. corner, or to be precise the square centimetre in the N.W. corner, is 197.00/99.00. The horizontal co-ordinates are permanently marked on site by metal hooks set into the cave-roof.

There is also a vertical co-ordinate system. The centres of the holes in which two metal rawlbolts are located in the cave-wall (Fig.I.6) are at 100.00 exactly on the site datum (100.00 Site Datum = 90.473 O.D.).

The finds recording system has been progressively refined during the course of the excavation but, from the outset, all finds were recorded not only by layer but with three-dimensional co-ordinates also. The present system is:

(1) All artefacts, identifiable bones, stalagmite and flint (whether worked or not) are three-dimensionally recorded within metre squares (e.g. J13, K21 etc.) using x, y and z co-ordinates (Fig.I.8) where
   x   is the distance from north to south (i.e. from left side of cave across the cave when facing inwards)
   y   is the distance from west to east (i.e. from the entrance of the cave inwards)
   z   is the levelled height relative to site datum (+ 100.00m).

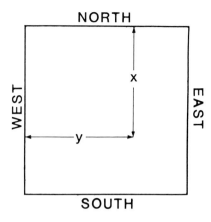

Fig. I.8 Pontnewydd Cave. The use of x and y co-ordinates to locate finds within one-metre squares.

(2) The following categories of find are recorded by 10 centimetre spits (e.g. z = 99.62-52) both *within* the stratigraphic layer and within a horizontal 50 cm. square (e.g. J10NW): (a) all non-sedimentary pebbles and rock fragments ("exotics"), (b) bone splinters. There may be a number of finds in one bag but different types of find (e.g. bone or exotic rocks) are separately bagged under different number.

(3) All stalagmite is marked with its orientation (i.e. the north point must be marked by an arrow on its upper surface, and each find is shown to the Director for recording whilst still *in situ*).

(4) All artefacts, identifiable bones, burnt flint and stalagmite are given a unique number, not repeated from year to year.

(5) All flint is shown to the Director (to determine whether burnt and therefore potentially suitable for thermoluminescence dating).

(6) On each finds bag is marked in black biro the site-code "PN + year + Find no. + layer code + nature of find: e.g. PN82 D1032 LB Bone (i.e. Pontnewydd 1982, Area D, Find 1032, Lower Breccia, Bone). All artefacts and identifiable bone are marked on site with the year and finds no. only (e.g. PN82 D1032).

STRATIGRAPHY

The stratigraphy revealed up to and including 1983 is outlined in Chapter IX and Simon Collcutt (Chapter III) has described *in extenso* the stratigraphy revealed by the end of the 1981 season. A system of generic layer names has been used, based on sedimentological correlation of the discontinuous sediments of the different Areas (B, C, D) within the cave. We recognize, however, that the correlation proposed (Chapter III) is a matter of probability, not fact, and so the layer names – except where distinguished by a unique adjective (such as "Buff" or "Orange" which are applied only to the Intermediate layer of the East Passage) – are generally qualified by a topographical statement ("Upper Breccia of the East Passage" etc.). It is not strictly necessary to add such a topographical phrase when describing the sediments of the South Fissure, since this is the type-section for the site, but we have generally done so in order to avoid any possible uncertainty.

Plate VII   Pontnewydd Cave. The South Passage from the North, 1979.

Plate VIII   Pontnewydd Cave. The East Passage, from the West, 1979, showing the face of the undisturbed deposits as found after clearance of modern spoil and showing our initial cutting into the centre of the face. The cavers' trench may be seen in the background.

CHAPTER II

LOCATION, SETTING AND GEOMORPHOLOGY

by
Clifford Embleton

INTRODUCTION

Pontnewydd cave is situated in an area of great geomorphological interest, one that presents many problems in terms of landform evolution and Quaternary history (Fig.II.1). The Cave entrance stands about half way up a steep escarpment of Carboniferous Limestone at the foot of which flows the River Elwy (Pl.IX; Fig.I.4). The difference in level between the cave and the present day river is 50 m, and the elevation of the cave entrance is 89.5m. The limestone escarpment here forms the north-eastern side of the Lower Elwy valley whose opposite side, consisting of Silurian rocks (Lower Ludlow according to Boswell, 1949), rises rather less steeply. The valley also contains Quaternary glacial deposits and recent alluvium, and one of the key points of geomorphological interest is to establish a link between the glacial stratigraphy of the surrounding area and the geochronological evidence provided by the cave deposits.

THE ELWY DRAINAGE SYSTEM

The Elwy drains some 200 km² of the Denbigh Uplands which rise to a height of nearly 500 m on Mynydd Hiraethog (Fig.II.2). Its main tributaries, such as the Cledwen, Aled and Deunant, rise at over 350 m on the surface termed the Middle Peneplain by Brown (1960), and flow generally northward before being collected one by one into the generally eastward flowing Elwy below Llangernyw. The evolution of the Elwy drainage has been examined by Embleton (1960) who has shown that, probably up to late Tertiary time, the drainage was essentially to the north, the rivers passing through what are now wind-gaps and heading for the coast between Colwyn Bay and Abergele, though at considerably higher levels (more than 200 m) compared with present sea-level. The eastward-flowing Elwy probably evolved by gradual exploitation of structural weaknesses in the Silurian rocks and successive capture of the original north-flowing drainage.

THE LOWER ELWY VALLEY

The lower Elwy now enters the Vale of Clwyd about 2 km downstream from Pontnewydd cave, turning suddenly by Cefn Rocks to break through the relatively narrow ridge of

a

Plate IX a   View looking across the River Elwy from just above Bont Newydd village. The bridge across the Elwy is located off-picture, left nearground. The cave, obscured by trees, lies beneath the rock face.

b

Plate IX b   The Elwy Valley at Cefn Rocks. Pontnewydd Cave lies 700 metres upstream (to the left of the photograph).

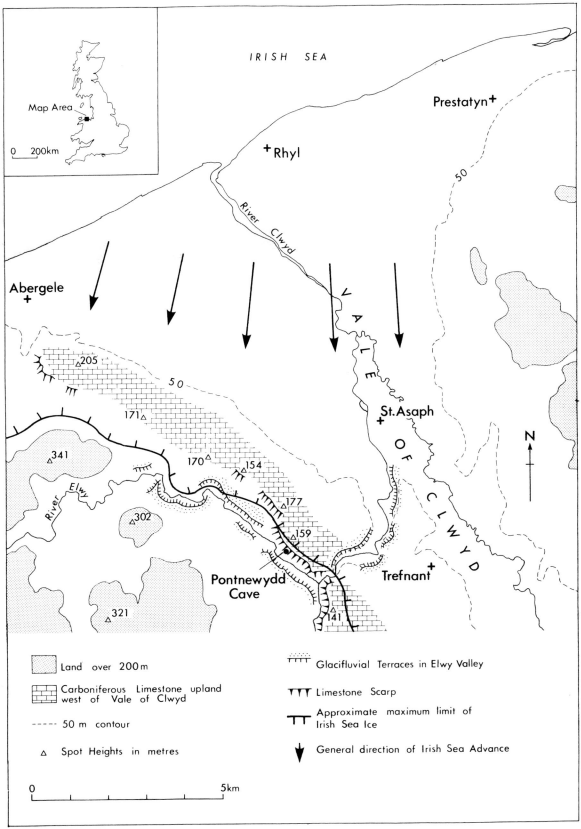

IRISH SEA

Prestatyn +

+ Rhyl

River Clwyd

Abergele
+

Map Area

0   200km

205

171

341

170

154

River Elwy

302

177

159

321

Pontnewydd
Cave

141

VALE OF CLWYD

St. Asaph
+

Trefnant +

N

Land over 200 m

Carboniferous Limestone upland
west of Vale of Clwyd

---- 50 m contour

△   Spot Heights in metres

Glacifluvial Terraces in Elwy Valley

Limestone Scarp

Approximate maximum limit of
Irish Sea Ice

General direction of Irish Sea Advance

0   5km

Fig. II.1   Pontnewydd Cave. Its location in the context of the local geomorphology. The Denbigh Moors lie to
the south-west.

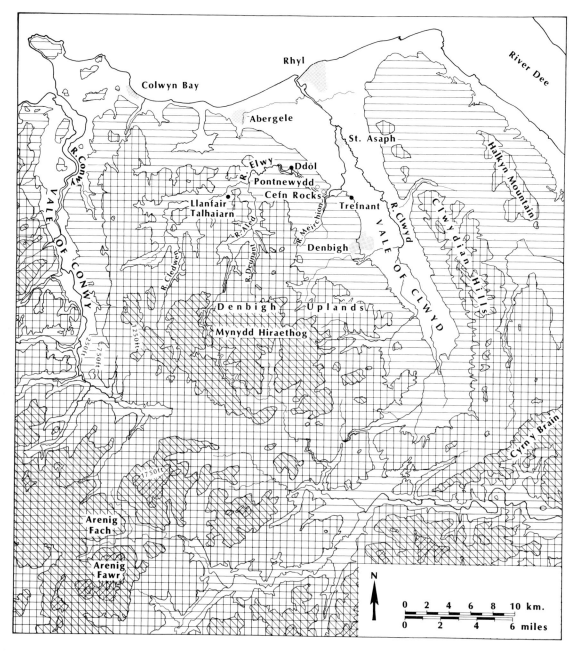

Fig. II.2 The Elwy drainage system in its regional context. Contours at 250 ft. (76 M.), 750 ft. (228 M.), 1250 ft. (381 M.) and 1750 ft. (533 M.).

Carboniferous Limestone (Pl.IX). The first encounter of the Elwy with the limestone is just below Pont-y-Ddol and from here, past Pontnewydd cave, the river flows south-east approximately along the strike of the Carboniferous Limestone, and at the foot of the Limestone escarpment already mentioned, to Cefn Rocks. There is some evidence that, preglacially or in the early Quaternary, the Elwy used to enter the Vale of Clwyd due east from Ddol, crossing the Limestone ridge at a height of about 160 m. The abandonment of this course, in favour of its present more circuitous one, has been attributed by Embleton (1960) to glacial diversion, though for reasons to be stated later, such an event must have occurred in an early glacial period and not in the latest one. An alternative view is that diversion was effected by capture; in this case the Elwy below Ddol developed as a strike stream along the weaker beds of the Lower Carboniferous Limestone outcrop, gradually extending its catchment north-westward until it intercepted the main river at Ddol. A similar strike-stream, though one that has not succeeded in capturing any other important drainage, may be seen to the south of Cefn Rocks, the Afon Meirchion. Diversion of the lower Elwy by capture, however, seems less likely than glacial diversion. First, the result of diversion in this case is to lengthen the river's course (by about 4 km) rather than to shorten it, which does not readily accord with a capture hypothesis; secondly, the lower Elwy, even allowing for the effects of drift deposits in its valley, does not exactly follow the strike of the Carboniferous Limestone nor any other known major weaknesses in its outcrop. On the other hand, the hypothesis of glacial diversion is consistent with several aspects of known glacial history in this area. As will be described below, the lower Elwy valley marks approximately the limit of penetration of Irish Sea Ice from the north. A broad lobe of ice spreading up the Vale of Clwyd roughly as far as Denbigh could have impeded the former course of the Elwy east of Ddol, turning it south-east along the ice margin until it was able to escape into the Vale by Cefn Rocks. Glacial diversion of this type cannot, however, be attributed to the last glaciation of the area, for two reasons: first, the lower Elwy valley at present contains drift of the last glaciation and must therefore be older, and secondly, the depth of incision of the valley, some 90 m below the crest of the limestone escarpment, means that the valley is unlikely to be Post-glacial in age. It is suggested, therefore, that the lower Elwy valley is a result of glacial diversion that occurred in the penultimate or a still older glaciation.

THE GLACIATIONS

The glacial deposits of the area have yet to be surveyed in detail, and this is one of the prime tasks for geomorphological research in the next few years. At present, separation of glaciations is tentatively based on a few sections where superimposition of tills has been described, on attempts to define the limits of different glaciations, and on broad considerations of the Elwy valley in the context of the glaciations of North Wales generally (Embleton, 1970). Ice from two different major source regions is known to have reached the lower Elwy valley: first, Welsh Ice, moving generally eastwards from Snowdonia, and secondly Irish Sea Ice, moving southwards from Scotland, the Lake District and other northern source regions. The tills left by these ice sheets can be distinguished lithologically since that of the Welsh Ice consists dominantly of crushed and broken Silurian material, often grey or blue-grey in colour, with some distinctive igneous clasts from Snowdonia or Arenig, whereas that of the Irish Sea Ice is often composed of a pale reddish matrix derived from Triassic sandstone forming the floor of much of the Vale of Clwyd and presumed to outcrop on the sea-floor to the north, together with erratics from northern England or Scotland.

The Irish Sea Ice is known to have invaded the coastlands of North Wales, riding up the flanks of the coastal hills to heights of 580 m on Moel Wnion (Gwynedd) and almost 300 m on Halkyn Mountain (Clwyd). It penetrated the Vale of Clwyd for 20 km, leaving northern erratics 1.6 km south of Denbigh. It is, however, uncertain whether all these limits were related to the same phase of glaciation. It is possible that the high-level deposits on Moel Wnion, for instance, date from an earlier more extensive phase of glaciation when Welsh Ice had already overrun North Wales, holding back the Irish Sea Ice and causing its surface level to rise. Clearly at such a time the Irish Sea Ice could never have pushed up the Vale of Clwyd; that event must have occurred later, as will be discussed below. There is also some meagre evidence that, either during a temporary halt in the recession of the last Irish Sea Ice, or during a separate readvance, the ice margin in the Vale of Clwyd for a time stood in the vicinity of Trefnant, for in this area a series of low hills, possibly of morainic origin, crosses the Vale.

The Welsh Ice, at least at one stage in the Pleistocene, probably covered the whole of Clwyd, moving E, ENE, or in places NE across the Vale of Clwyd and the Clwydian Range. Erratics from Arenig are found lodged in cols through the latter at heights up to 350 m and even, father south, on the summit of Cyrn-y-Brain at 560 m. Such elevations imply that, on the Denbigh Uplands, the ice surface must have reached heights of at least 600 m, possibly much more, so that one cannot escape the conclusion that even the highest point of the Uplands, Mynydd Hiraethog (497 m) was overrun by the ice.

The relationships between the Welsh and the Irish Sea Ice are far from clear. Because the source region of the former is much closer to Clwyd, it must be deduced that Welsh Ice would be able to spread over the area in the initial phase of a glaciation long before the Irish Sea Ice arrived. How, then, was it possible for the latter, on at least one occasion, to penetrate 20 km up the Vale of Clwyd? One possible answer is that this happened during a glacial stage of less severity when the thickness of the Snowdonian ice was insufficient to allow it to cross the western edge of the Denbigh Uplands (rising to 300 m or more). At the same time, the Denbigh Uplands themselves might not have been high enough or receiving enough precipitation to generate their own active ice-cap. Then the Vale of Clwyd and the northern coastlands would have been free of Welsh Ice and open to inundation by the Irish Sea Ice.

A possible chronological scheme is shown in Table II.I. The dating of the stages in the left-hand column is not yet based on any firm evidence, though work by Rowlands (1971) on radiocarbon dating of mammalian fauna in the Tremeirchion caves on the east side of the Vale of Clwyd points to stage 3 being the late Devensian. The Pontnewydd discoveries, however, yield the exciting prospect of being able to establish the earlier part of the chronological sequence.

THE DATE OF THE ELWY DIVERSION

It is quite certain that, if the river Elwy was glacially diverted, this cannot have happened in stage 3, when the level of the Irish Sea Ice in the Vale of Clwyd is unlikely to have exceeded 50 m at the Trefnant "moraine", or possibly 100-150 m at the north coast. Moreover, as has already been argued, the drift within the lower Elwy shows that this valley already existed during the last glaciation.

	Irish Sea Ice	*Welsh Ice*
Stage 3: Late Devensian	A tongue penetrating the Vale of Clwyd as far as the Trefnant "moraine".	Absent in Clwyd
Stage 2: Earlier Devensian or pre-Ipswichian	Vale of Clwyd penetrated for 20 km. Maximum height of ice on northern coast-lands approximately 200 m (Embleton, 1970)	Limited in Clwyd to highest parts of Denbigh Uplands, with ice tongues occupying parts of the Elwy Valley system.
Stage 1: Date unknown	Massive Irish Sea ice-sheet, attaining at least 600 m on north coast of Gwynedd, but unable to penetrate sig-nificantly inland because of presence of equally massive cover of Welsh Ice	Covering whole of Clwyd

TABLE II.1.   Glaciation in North Wales. A possible chronological scheme.

Diversion at stage 2 would require a level for the Irish Sea Ice east of Ddol of at least 160 m. This is not inconsistent with the limit of the Irish Sea Ice standing at its known maximum south of Denbigh, and with the maximum ice levels of about 200 m attained on the north coast of Clwyd. On the other hand, the existence of drift (of so far unknown derivation) within the lower Elwy valley implies that diversion, if due to ice blocking, had occurred prior to the emplacement of this drift. Thus it may be necessary to postulate further events, including glacial diversion of the Elwy, older than stage 2. At the same time, the type of glacierisation implied by stage 1 is not reconcilable with diversion of the Elwy, so that the latter is more likely to have occurred between stages 1 and 2.

THE TERRACES OF THE LOWER ELWY

Terraces built of or cut into drift are a striking feature of parts of the Elwy valley below Llanfair Talhaiarn. They appear here at heights of about 130 m, and at progressively lower levels downstream. Between Ddol and Bont Newydd, they are well-developed on the north-east side of the river, at heights of about 90 m, that is, the elevation of the cave entrance. Until the terraces have been precisely mapped and levelled, and until the materials of which they are composed have been analysed, it is only possible to speculate on their origins and age. One hypothesis is that they represent a stage in the re-excavation of the Elwy valley from a drift infill left by the preceding glaciation. If the approximate long profile that the terraces represent is extrapolated past Cefn Rocks, it would enter the Vale of Clwyd at about 75 m, which is within the levels (67–107 m) postulated by Rowlands (1955) for a proglacial lake impounded by Irish Sea Ice in the Vale of Clwyd during stage 3 (Table II.1). Such a temporary lake would provide a reason for the stabilisation of the Elwy's thalweg at the level of the terraces, followed by sudden down-cutting to its present floor in Post-glacial times when the lake drained. Since the terrace level near Pontnewydd is about the elevation of the cave entrance, it is possible that the drift-choked entrance of the cave was opened at the time that the Elwy was developing the terrace surface – maybe a chance meander of the river encountered the cave entrance and water then broke through it. This would agree with the sedimentological evidence of the Upper Breccia forming part of the cave deposits and is consistent with the Devensian age postulated.

CONCLUSION

It is evident that in this area many problems of geomorphology and geochronology remain to be solved. The principal questions are:

1) What is the age of the glaciation during which ice pushed up the Vale of Clwyd for some 20 km?
2) At this time, how much (if any) of the Denbigh Uplands was occupied by ice, and was the Elwy valley ice free?
3) Was the lower Elwy diverted by ice, and if so, during which glaciation?
4) What is the origin of the drift terraces in the Elwy Valley, and what is their relationship to (a) the glacial sequence and (b) the cave history?
5) Is the Trefnant "ridge" a moraine and if so, what stage of glaciation does it mark?

Until 1979 no absolute dates older than 18,000 BP were available anywhere in the area, and no firm answers to most of these questions were possible. Now, however, the Pontnewydd investigations and renewed study of the glacial drifts promise to improve immensely our knowledge of the Pleistocene in North Wales.

CHAPTER III

THE SEDIMENT STRATIGRAPHY

Simon Collcutt's detailed report on the sediments covers the period from 1978–81 inclusive. Collcutt was succeeded, in March 1982, as site-sedimentologist by Peter Bull. Detailed study in 1982–3 both of the fragmentary wall-sediment films surviving between the main Areas of the cave and of the sections already available in areas B, C, and D has produced more promising results than anticipated with supporting evidence being found for Simon Collcutt's sediment correlation between these Areas. This evidence will be presented, in detail, at a later stage. But the most important discovery, in view of its significance as a stratigraphic marker, has been that of the Silt beds in areas B and C – located at the junction of lithozones already recognized in the field as the Upper and Lower Breccia respectively. It is, however, now clear that the history of the sediments of the South Fissure is much more complex than had been supposed. In particular, between the face drawn in 1978 and that preserved now at the L/M grid line evidence has been found for the removal both of the Upper Breccia and, in part, of the underlying Intermediate followed by their replacement – though not necessarily as a causative agent – by Upper Breccia. The removal extends to a depth of 99.01 (site O.D.) and as close as 25 cm south of section line AB. The physical difficulties of digging these deposits in the cramped conditions of the South Fissure, combined with their poor differentiation (*cf.* Collcutt below, p.35), at a time when the very clear sequence of deposits now visible in the East Passage had not been exposed, has led with little doubt to some incorrect attribution of finds from the South Fissure to Lower Breccia or Intermediate. These must now be considered only as belonging somewhere in the Upper Breccia-Intermediate sequence. This has important implications for some apparently too-young dates obtained from the South Fissure (Tables IV.2A; IV.4). The result of the stratigraphic re-allocation of these samples in the light of this new work is to present a more internally consistent picture from the site as a whole.

The main addition to the stratigraphic sequence described by Collcutt is the revelation, in 1982–3, of the full sequence represented by the Lower Sands and Gravels. I have suggested (p.202) that three cycles of deposition may be involved here but the definitive description of the lithostratigraphy and lithogenesis of these deposits will be presented by Peter Bull in the final report on Pontnewydd.

H.S.G.

PART A
THE SEDIMENTS
by
S.N. Collcutt

SUMMARY

This section deals with the following major topics:
(1) Detailed description of each deposit in each exposure (pp.32–42);
(2) Correlation of the various exposures and justification of a composite stratigraphy for the site as a whole (pp.42–53);
(3) General considerations concerning the major sediment sources and processes which have resulted in the observed sequence of deposits (pp.53–67);
(4) Detailed examination of the development of the Pontnewydd sequence (pp.67–74);
(5) Discussion (pp.74–76).

The following is a summary of the sequence of sedimentary events which appear most likely to have given rise to the Pontnewydd deposits. It should be noted that periods of non-deposition and periods of sedimentation, the results of which have later been totally destroyed, probably represent by far the greater part of the total time span of this sequence.

The term 'debris flow' refers to the rapid, and often destructive, arrival of masses of water, mud and rocks (cf. p.54).

LOWER SANDS AND GRAVEL submember (LSGs) – A series of gravelly deposits, derived largely from glacial sediments, was brought into the cave by repeated debris flows and irregular stream action. Towards the top of LSGs, input of sediments slowed and probably stopped altogether for a time. Calcite cement began to form within existing deposits.

UPPER SANDS AND GRAVEL submember (USGs) – Debris flows brought further material, very like that of LSGs, into the cave.

INTERMEDIATE complex (Ic) – The history of the cave and its surroundings now becomes unclear. The surviving sediments have been violently dissected and disrupted, again apparently by debris flow. However, the period between the deposition of the last sediments of USGs and the final disruption(s) of the Ic sediments seems to have included a temperate stage, perhaps of interglacial status, when soils could provide organic matter and there could be significant growth of stalagmite. These patchy sediments also contain the first occurrence of limestone debris and animal bones, together with the remains and tools of man.

LOWER BRECCIA bed (LBb) – A major debris flow entered the cave, causing additional disruption of existing deposits and incorporating some older material into its own mass. Local limestone debris had become more important at the expense of glacially derived material from further afield.

STALAGMITE lithozone (Sl) – When sediment input ceased, stalagmites started to grow on the older deposits.

SILT beds (Sb) – Water began to reach the study area and a pool was formed in which silts collected. At first, stalagmite was still formed, interstratified with the pool deposits, but later the silts built up without interruption.

UPPER BRECCIA bed (UBb) – Another massive debris flow reached the area, chanelling into and incorporating older sediments. Local limestone debris had become dominant.

RED CAVE-EARTH bed (RCEb) – Traces of one final debris flow, by then almost exclusively composed of limestone debris, survive in one area of the cave.

UPPER CLAY AND SAND beds (UCSb) – A stream flowed westwards out of the cave depositing clays and sands. Water was probably running at this high level because the lower cave passages were still choked by masses of sediment.

LAMINATED TRAVERTINE lithozone (LTl) – As water found its way deeper, stalagmite began to grow, eventually building up a thick floor.

EARTHY lithozone (El) – Traces of organic-rich earthy material probably represent input during the Holocene.

1 – LITHOSTRATIGRAPHY

Those deposits rendered accessible by the end of the 1981 season, when the author last visited the cave, survive as extremely fragmented bodies of sediment. Intra-site correlation is often taken for granted in sites where sediments can be followed as more or less continuous units. This is not generally the case at Pontnewydd. Furthermore, no Area in which the whole stratigraphic sequence is present has yet been discovered, so that no master section is available. Consequently, correlation between the various Areas within the site must be clearly demonstrated. The validity of the suggested stratigraphic sequence, and of the geological, environmental and chronological interpretation put forward later in this chapter, will be largely dependent upon the accuracy of the correlation so far achieved.

To this end, the sequence in each Area will be described separately. This entails frequent repetition and a monotonous, dense presentation, resulting in a text which is, admittedly, totally indigestible. It is suggested that the following section be regarded as optional; the main argument may be resumed on p.42.

The following lithologic description of the Pontnewydd sediments, as observed up until October 1981, is based upon the framework set out in the *International Stratigraphic Guide* (Hedberg, 1976).

Each 'Area' within the site is denoted by a capitalised alphabetic label (*cf.* Fig.I.5). Areas may be subdivided if necessary by adding to the Area label the terms (N), (E), (S), (W) or (C), the last referring to 'central'. The Area label is terminated by a colon.

Each Area sequence is divided into lithostratigraphic units, informally referred to as 'lithozones', numbered continuously from 1 downwards.

Sediment samples collected by the author appear, with the prefix 'PN', in brackets after the unit label. Munsell colours are given throughout, except in the cases where the verbal description is not accompanied by a colour code; the colours apply to fresh, damp sediment on site. 'Pebble' is here used to denote a siliceous rock fragment, of more than 2 mm. diameter, that displays extreme rounding. When the word 'gravel' is preceded by the adjective 'siliceous', the deposit contains numerous pebbles. When the word 'gravel' appears without the adjective 'siliceous', it refers to particles of more than 2 mm. diameter, irrespective of lithology and shape characteristics; these may or may not be indicated by additional qualification. Information derived from laboratory analyses is included at a qualitative level only when it is felt

that such detail could be recognised on site with relatively little difficulty.

No claim is made that the following descriptions are in any way exhaustive.

Description of the Deposits (Figs.III.1–2)

CAVE EXTERIOR (Area A)

A:2 – Angular limestone rubble with fine sand matrix; grades smoothly from loose deposit, to well packed material with clasts aligned in continuation of bedrock jointing, to sound bedrock; matrix colour reddish brown (5YR 5/3); thickness variable but not usually over 20 cm.

A:1 – (PN 13) Pockets of cemented pebbles and sand; no limestone. These deposits occur as a thin veneer on the rock wall north of the entrance, as the fill of a shallow depression in A:2 just south of the outer door, and as the fill of a small fissure *c.*5 metres south-east of the main entrance (this fissure, the 'South Entrance', runs parallel with the main cave chamber); nowhere do these deposits survive beyond the modern drip-line. The small fissure, developed on a near-vertical joint, is

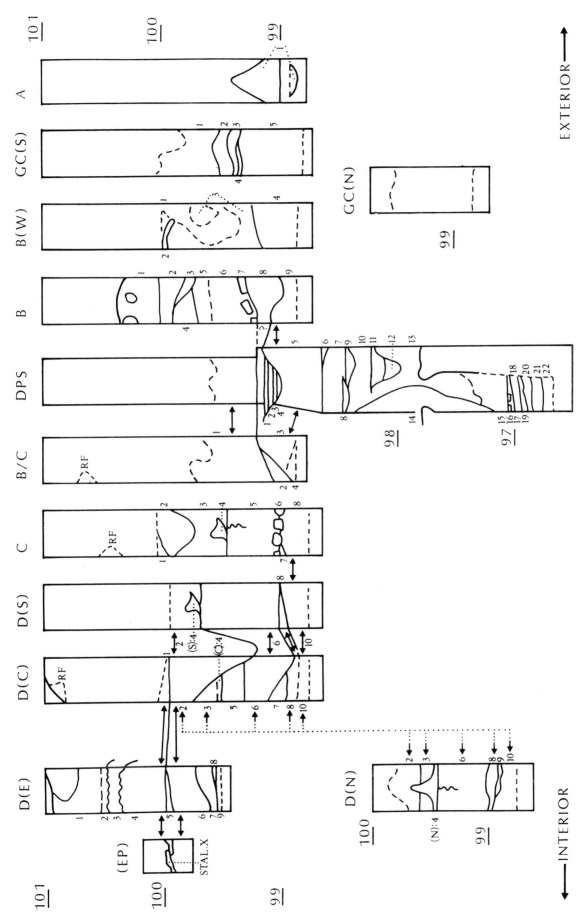

Fig. III.1 Pontnewydd. Schematic composite lithostratigraphy.

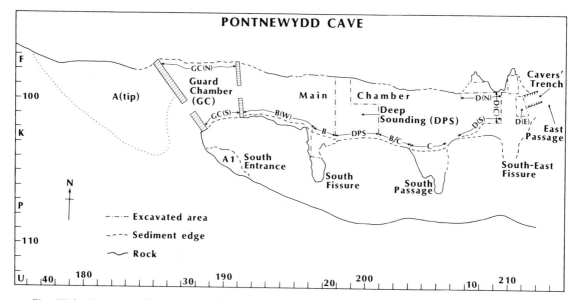

Fig. III.2 Pontnewydd. Site plan, showing location of deposits studied by sedimentological analysis.

triangular in section with a base of *c*.75 cm. The floor has a series of parallel flutes set a right angles to the fissure; there is a gentle dip inwards and a marked asymmetry of the flutes, with the steeper flank east of each ridge. The pebbles of the highly carbonate cemented deposit (sampled; matrix colour light brownish grey (10YR 6/2)) are randomly oriented and usually unfractured; the top 2–3 cm. consist of fine sand and silt completely filling the fissure; the whole deposit is vuggy and penetrated by modern roots; there is no apparent bedding. The texture of this deposit is discordant with the sculpting of the bedrock.

A(tip) – Compound tip (demonstrable) overlying A:1–2 right across the cave mouth but especially thick towards the north-west, where it is present as a mound. There are buried turf-lines but there is no extensive differentiation of deposits within the tip, although the lithologic range is identical with that of the undisturbed sediments within the cave. There is no turf-line at the base.

GUARD CHAMBER (Area GC)

The Guard Chamber, constructed during the last war, has an intact concrete floor. There are restricted deposits cemented to both the north and south rock walls.

GC(N) – Cemented pebbles in a coarse sandy matrix; matrix colour light brownish grey (10YR 6/2); extending from the concrete floor upwards for a maximum of *c*.65 cm., reaching Site Datum 99.50; unconformably overlain in places by dormant and active flowstone; rock wall highly fissured and dangerous.

GC(S):5 – Pebbles in a coarse sandy matrix with finer gravel and sand lenses; rich in colloids; well compacted but only slightly cemented; some imbrication visible at various levels, nose-up into cave; sets of graded bedding quite well developed; matrix colour brown (10YR 5/3); from concrete floor up to Site Datum 99.35.

GC(S):4 – Thin (*c*.1–2 cm.) band of yellow (10YR 8/6) colloids, mostly carbonates; not plastic; no structure; sharp lower boundary.

GC(S):3 – Thin lens of heavily cemented gravelly coarse sand; matrix colour brown (10YR 5/3); max. thickness *c*.5 cm.; sharp lower boundary.

GC(S):2 – Patches of heavily cemented sandy silt with limestone clasts and a few pebbles; some small (5–15 cm.) blocks of corroded stalagmite; matrix colour yellowish brown (10YR 5/4); max. thickness *c*.14 cm.; sharp lower boundary.

GC(S):1 – Cemented limestone clasts, with some fractured pebbles, in a matrix of sandy silt and clay; matrix colour brown (8.75YR 5/4); sharp lower boundary; highest point reaching Site Datum 100.05.

CAVE INTERIOR (Pl.X)

The floor of the main cave chamber was levelled by the army and a coarse limestone grit laid down, usually *c*.5–10 cm. thick. Wherever this grit has been removed during the present excavation, the deposits below have been found intact. The deposits remaining against the walls and in various side passages will be described generally from west to east (Fig.III.2)

AREA B (WEST)

From the inner brick wall of the GC to the South Fissure; shallow and discontinuous deposits adhering to the rock wall; in places overlain unconformably by quite extensive flowstone.

B(W):4 – Pebbles in a coarse sandy matrix; rich in colloids; apparently bedded but difficult to observe due to massive carbonate cementation; matrix colour brown (10YR 5/3); max. thickness *c*.55 cm. to grit floor.

B(W):3 – Highly cemented sandy silt with limestone clasts and a few, mostly fractured pebbles; bone present; matrix colour yellowish brown (10YR 5/4); extremely patchy survival but max. thickness *c*.80 cm.; sharp lower boundary.

B(W):2 – (PN 240) Laminated (with laminae less than 1 mm. thick) crystalline stalagmite, in places slightly corroded and friable, containing small blocks of more massive stalagmite and fragments of stalactite; cemented into its lower part, large limestone particles and artefacts; the lithozone lies unconformably on B(W):3 and dips down southwards behind the lower deposits to fill, partially, a cavity between them and the rock; max. thickness of purer speleothemic portion *c*.4 cm.; max. height Site Datum *c*.99.97.

Plate X Pontnewydd Cave, 1979. View looking out of cave. Bedrock lies immediately beneath the planks on the right of the cave but steps down, left, into the Deep Sounding on the South side of the cave. The South Fissure lies to the left beyond the Deep Sounding behind the hanging light cable. The wall sediments described as Site B(W) may be seen, in position, between the South Fissure and the brick inner wall of the Guard Chamber.

B(W):1 –   Clayey deposit partly filling small cavities between B(W):2 and rock wall.

The stratigraphic links between Areas B(W) and B are obscure; it may be possible in the future to demonstrate that some lithozones in one Area are co-extensive with lithozones, or parts of lithozones, in the other.

AREA B (South Fissure) (Fig.III.3)

Deposits largely intact and present in some quantity.

B:9 –   Sandy siliceous gravel; just showing above modern grit floor at Site Datum 98.90.

B:8 –   (PN 21, 202, 203) Informal name: "Intermediate". Cemented coarse deposit with over 90% of the gravel being pebbles, often fractured, and the remainder, highly corroded (granular) limestone particles and carbonate concretions; matrix of badly sorted sand and silt with a high carbonate content; non-carbonate sand fraction positively skewed; bone present; matrix colour brown (10YR 5/3); $c.35$ cm. thick; lower boundary quite sharp but becoming more diffuse into Fissure.

B:7 –   (PN 25) Blocks (5–25 cm.) of crystalline stalagmite, slightly altered and partially recemented into a discontinuous lithozone; individual pieces not more than $c.8$ cm. thick; defines a sharp boundary between the deposits above and below but disappears as a lithozone very quickly towards the east and deeper into the Fissure; no longer extant.

B:6 –   (PN 20, 204, 205, 206) Informal name: "Lower Breccia". Heavily cemented coarse deposit with fractured pebbles and superficially altered limestone particles in roughly equal proportions; mat-

rix of badly sorted sandy silt with a high carbonate content; non-carbonate sand fraction positively skewed; some small rounded stalagmite blocks especially near base; moderate organic content towards top; bone present; matrix colour yellowish brown (10YR 5/4); $c.25$ cm. thick, thinning to min. 8 cm. into Fissure; lower boundary with B:8, where B:7 is absent, rather diffuse.

BOUNDARY B:6/5 – Due to the masking effect of the carbonate cementation, this boundary cannot be seen within the metre band K. However, the sediments of the two deposits, once disaggregated in the laboratory, are perfectly distinct. Two sediment samples (PN 19, 207) were collected from as near the top of B:6 as possible but it is likely that they just overlap the true boundary. The B:6/B:5 distinction was proposed before excavation of Area D (*infra*) and before excavation had proceeded beyond line K/L into the South Fissure. The boundary becomes progressively clearer into the Fissure and is perfectly visible by the time line L/M is reached.

B:5 –   (PN 18, 208) Informal name: "Upper Breccia". Heavily cemented coarse deposit with nearly 75% of gravel being slightly altered limestone clasts and the remainder, fractured pebbles and carbonate concretions in roughly equal proportions; matrix of silt with badly sorted sand and a high carbonate content; non-carbonate sand fraction negatively skewed; some stalactite and stalagmite fragments, including a disturbed stalagmitic boss at the junction with B:4; bone present; matrix colour yellowish brown (10YR 5/4); $c.10$–15 cm. thick, thickening to max. 40 cm. into Fissure.

B:4 –   (PN 17, 209, 210) Informal name: "Red Cave

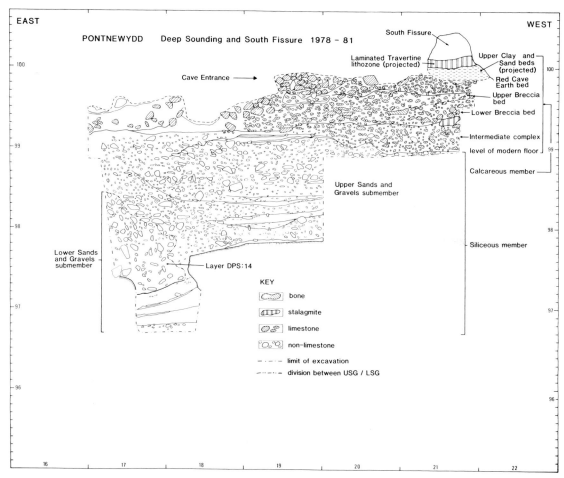

Fig. III.3 Pontnewydd. Section AB. South Fissure and Deep Sounding. 1978–81.

Earth". Coarse deposit containing angular limestone clasts and small amorphous concretions with extremely rare small pebbles; silty matrix with a high carbonate content but the deposit is not cemented; abundant crystalline dendritic concretions and a few stalagmite fragments; bone present; matrix colour reddish brown (5YR 5/4); c.30 cm. thick at greatest development but wedging out southwards into the Fissure and destroyed by earlier excavations eastwards; sharp lower boundary; no longer extant.

B:3 – Indurated lithozone; limestone badly corroded or present only as ghosts; matrix highly cemented by carbonates and FeMnAl oxides; variegated colour (informally – buffs, blacks, rusts, etc.); basin-shaped cross-section; developed above B:4 in the entrance to the Fissure but, as B:4 wedges out into the Fissure, developed above B:5; dipping and thickening southwards; max. thickness yet observed c.20 cm.; moderately distinct lower boundary.

B:2 – Clayey deposits not yet accessible for detailed study since they have been destroyed in the first 2 metres or so of the Fissure; probably susceptible to subdivision at a later stage; approx. colour reddish brown (5YR 4/4); greater than 20 cm. thick; penetrating down laterally for at least 50 cm. in a thin (1–3 cm.) fill between the cave walls and B:4–6; lower boundary not yet observed in detail away from the walls.

B:1 – Travertine overlying B:2 deep within the Fissure; so corroded that it can be penetrated with the hand; lower boundary not yet closely observed;

c.15 cm. thick at its surviving northern edge but becoming thicker towards the south where it is augmented by roof columns (after c.3–4 metres the South Fissure widens out to an unknown extent); highest point yet observed Site Datum 100.15.

AREA DPS (Deep Sounding) (Fig.III.3)

The deposits of the Deep Sounding lie in two channels cut into the rock floor of the cave. The lower channel appears to run approx. north-south; its floor has not yet been reached at Site Datum c.96.65. The tops of its west and east walls have been exposed and form lips, c.80 cm. apart, which are both deeply undercut. The upper channel, with its floor at Site Datum 97.80, appears to run approx. east–west. Its south wall has not yet been exposed and must therefore lie south of the visible south wall of the (higher) main chamber (i.e. this channel undercuts the south wall of the main chamber). Part of the north wall of this channel has been exposed approximately two thirds of the way across the main chamber (cf. Fig.III.2). This wall displays large (on average c.15 cm. long) scallops which are not markedly asymmetrical. The floor of this channel, where it is not interrupted by the lower channel, is approx. horizontal and has solutional boxwork (Pl.XI). The deposits in the lower channel remain well organised right up to the rock wall, whilst those in the upper channel lose all signs of bedding before reaching the north wall. None of these deposits contain recognisable bone or limestone particles, save for two instances of large heavily corroded limestone blocks in the upper deposits near the north wall. The deposits will be described primarily as seen in the south section of the Sounding.

DPS:22 – (PN 229) Medium siliceous gravel and badly classed sand; rich in colloids; only exposed to a thickness of *c*.10 cm.; matrix colour yellowish brown (10YR 5/4).

DPS:21 – (PN 228) Fine siliceous gravel and moderately well classed fine sand; rich in colloids; bedding apparent; matrix colour yellowish brown (10YR 5/4); *c*.8 cm. thick; sharp lower boundary.

DPS:20 – (PN 216, 227, 215) Moderately well classed medium to fine sand, fining upwards, but with some small pebbles near the top; rich in colloids; matrix colour brown (10YR 5/3); *c*.12 cm. thick, thinning eastwards to *c*.7 cm.; lower boundary sharp.

DPS:19 – (PN 226) Strong carbonate and FeMnAl concretion developed on sands identical to DPS:20; rather vuggy; matrix colour dark brown (10YR 3-4/3); *c*.2-5 cm. thick, disappearing towards west wall; lower boundary moderately sharp.

DPS:18 – (PN 225, 214) Laminated (less than 1mm.) silty fine sand and clay; matrix colour dark yellowish brown (10YR 4/4); *c*.17 cm. thick, thinning to *c*.7 cm. eastwards; lower boundary sharp.

DPS:17 – Coarse sand; rich in colloids; matrix colour dark brown (10YR 4/3); *c*.2-3 cm. thick, wedging out towards west wall; lower boundary moderately sharp.

DPS:16 – (PN 224) Strong carbonate and FeMnAl concretion developed mostly on sands identical to DPS:17; rather vuggy; matrix colour dark brown (10YR 3-4/3); discontinuous, present in patches not thicker than 3 cm. and absent towards west wall; rather diffuse lower boundary.

DPS:15 – (PN 223) Fine siliceous gravel and badly classed sand; rich in colloids; bedding apparent; matrix colour dark brown (10YR 4/3); *c*.18 cm. thick; lower boundary sharp.

The boundaries and bedding of DPS:22–15 are not horizontal but in section dip gently to the east, with the greatest dip at the top of this sequence (*cf*. Fig.III.3). These surfaces are not planar but are slightly concave-up.

DPS:14 – (PN 222) Massive carbonate and FeMnAl concretion in which fine particles are almost totally absorbed into the ground mass and large (up to 5 mm.) pure calcite crystals (dog-tooth spar) are common; rather vuggy; some coarse and medium siliceous gravel with long axes often almost vertical; the base of this mass lies within the lower channel but its summit stands (at about site Datum 98.40) well above the floor of the upper channel; matrix colour yellowish brown (10YR 5/4) with blotches of brownish yellow (10YR 6/6); max. vertical extent *c*.120 cm.; sharp boundaries on all sides.

The deposits DPS:22–14 have been informally named: "Lower Sands and Gravels".

The deposits in the upper channel will be described, from the channel floor upwards, in the area immediately to the west of the lower channel. The coarser units of these deposits swing over the protruding summit of DPS:14, losing thickness and stratigraphic definition; the finer units wedge out before reaching DPS:14. The mass of DPS:14 does not reach the western lip of the lower channel and there is a gap of 15–20 cm. (*cf*. Fig.III.3). This gap is filled with a chaotic deposit which, at its upper end, seems to be co-extensive with the lowest unit of the upper fill (DPS:13) but, at its lower end, seems to disturb DPS:15. The floor of the upper channel has a variable thickness (0–2 cm.) of black sticky sand, especially within solutional features.

DPS:13 – (PN 1) Very coarse siliceous gravel and cobbles with badly classed sand; rich in colloids; no apparent bedding; matrix colour light yellowish brown (10YR 6/4); 10–35 cm. thick.

DPS:12 – (PN 220, 2, 221) Fine siliceous gravel, present in the west section of the Sounding, but not in the south section; fines upwards into laminated (less than 1 mm.) sand, present in both sections; laminations undulate whilst retaining their relative thickness; matrix colour various olive browns (2.5Y var.); *c*.12 cm. thick, wedging out towards east and north (i.e. the lithozone occupies a trough oblique to the excavation grid); lower boundary sharp.

Plate XI   Pontnewydd Cave, 1981. Deep Sounding showing solutional boxwork on bedrock beyond the deep Fissure (running left to right, foreground). View taken from East.

DPS:11 – (PN 3, 213) Moderately well classed medium sand with some fine siliceous gravel; rich in colloids; no obvious bedding; matrix colour greyish brown (2.5Y 5/2); c.10 cm. thick, thinning to the west and wedging out to the east; lower boundary sharp.

DPS:10 – (PN 4) Medium siliceous gravel with badly classed coarse sand; rich in colloids; graded bedding; matrix colour yellowish brown (10YR 5/4); c.5–10 cm. thick, thickening to c.25 cm. eastwards before thinning out over DPS:14; lower boundary sharp.

DPS:9 – (PN 5) Badly classed medium sand with some siliceous gravel; rich in colloids; weak bedding; matrix colour greyish brown (2.5Y 5/2); c.8 cm. thick, thinning westwards and wedging out eastwards; lower boundary sharp.

DPS:8 – (PN 218) Fine sand lens; matrix colour light grey (2.5Y 7/2); c.4 cm. thick, wedging out rapidly east and west; sharp boundary with DPS:9 and DPS:7 (infra).

DPS:7 – (PN 219) Fine siliceous gravel and badly classed sand; rich in colloids; no apparent bedding; matrix colour yellowish brown (10YR 5/4); c.17cm. thick; lower boundary sharp.
(Having cleaned this section back some 15 cm. further south, it was noted that in reality DPS:8 lies stratigraphically within DPS:7. However, the boundary which would separate DPS:7 into two units cannot be followed beyond the restricted occurrence of DPS:8 and the nomenclature was therefore left unchanged.)

DPS:6 – Fine sand lens; matrix colour light grey (2.5Y 7/2); c.2 cm. thick, wedging out rapidly eastwards; lower boundary sharp.

DPS:5 – (PN 6, 201, 7) Coarse siliceous gravel and cobbles, becoming finer from approximately midway up the unit, with badly classed sand; rich in colloids; bedding apparent; matrix colour greyish brown (10YR 5/2); c.50 cm. thick, thinning slightly eastwards; boundary with DPS:7 rather diffuse.

DPS:4 – (PN 8) Laminated (less than 1 mm.) silt and fine sand with a little fine siliceous gravel; very small colloidal carbonate content; matrix colour pale red (2.5YR 6/2); c.2 cm. thick, wedging out rapidly east and west; lower boundary sharp.

DPS:3 – (PN 9) Medium and coarse sand with a little fine siliceous gravel; no apparent bedding; tiny red (2.5YR high chroma) flecks (oxides) giving a matrix colour of yellowish red (5YR 4/6); c.2 cm. thick, wedging out rapidly east and west; lower boundary sharp.

DPS:2 – (PN 10, 212) Silt with some colloidal carbonate; no apparent bedding; matrix colour pale red (2.5YR 6/2); c.8 cm. thick, wedging out rapidly east and west; lower boundary sharp.

DPS:1 – Laminated (c.1 mm.) sand; matrix colour various pale reds (2.5YR var.); 2–3 cm. thick, wedging out rapidly east and west; lower boundary sharp.

The deposits DPS:13–1 have been informally named: "Upper Sands and Gravels".

The relationships of the higher DPS deposits with those of Area B to the west and Area B/C to the east are not always clear. DPS:5 is almost certainly co-extensive with B:9. DPS:5 also appears to be co-extensive with parts of B/C:4–3, but other parts of these latter deposits must lie stratigraphically above DPS:1; the single boundary theoretically formed when the lithozones DPS:4–1 have finally all wedged out to the east cannot be followed into the much coarser sediments of DPS:5 and/or B/C:4–3. Furthermore, there is a band, c.5 cm. thick, of fine gravel and sand (PN 11) which lies directly above DPS:1 and below traces of a deposit with limestone particles; the band appears to be co-extensive with both B:8 and B/C:3. Since the sediment of this band is quite coarse, shows no bedding and is masked by carbonates, any internal boundary would be very difficult to observe; a stratigraphic link

between B:8 and B/C:3 makes very little lithologic sense. Further work on this problem is obviously required.

AREA B/C (Fig. III.4)

From the east side of the Deep Sounding to the South Passage.

B/C:4 – Coarse siliceous gravel and badly classed sand; matrix colour dark brown (7.5YR 4/4); max. thickness to grit floor c.8 cm.

B/C:3 – (PN 14) Medium siliceous gravel and badly classed sand; rich in colloids; imbrication in places, nose-up into cave; matrix colour dark brown (7.5YR 4/4); maximum thickness to grit floor c.35 cm.; very diffuse lower boundary with B/C:4; distinction between B/C:4 and B/C:3 fading rapidly westwards.

B/C:2 – (PN 26) Fine siliceous gravel and badly classed sand; rich in colloids; moderate carbonate content including some coarse sand sized particles (corroded); no apparent bedding; traces of bone; flecks of FeMnAl and high organic content giving matrix colour of yellowish brown (10YR 5/6); max. thickness c.18 cm., but present in two separate lithologically identical lenses (cf.Fig.III.4); lower boundaries quite sharp.

B/C:1 – (PN 211, 217) Weakly cemented veneer of sandy silt and clay, with some large limestone fragments and some traces of corroded stalagmite of uncertain status; large mottles, reddish yellow (7.5YR 6/6) and red (2.5YR 5/6); bone present; thickness extremely variable; reaches Site Datum 99.70 in places; lower boundary usually sharp but more diffuse where the veneer is very thin.

Between Areas B/C and C there is clean rock down to the grit floor, separating the deposits in the two Areas by a minimum of 40 cm.

AREA C (South Passage)

This 'passage' was named in the belief that a larger cavity than the South Fissure lay behind the sediments. In fact, this embayment in the rock, which is developed on a major joint, narrows down rapidly to little more than a crevice, blocked by flowstone. It is possible that the cavity may be larger at a lower level.

C:8 – Coarse and medium siliceous gravel with badly classed sand; rich in colloids; organic matter present at top; matrix colour yellowish brown (10YR 5/6); exposed above grit floor for 10 cm.

C:7 – Small lens of sandy silt towards eastern side of embayment; matrix colour pale brown (10YR 6/3); max. thickness c.7 cm.; sharp boundaries.

C:6 – Irregular band of large limestone fragments (up to 30 cm. but mostly nearer 15 cm. in length); highly altered and stained red (2.5YR high chroma) in their lower parts (organic matter present), quite sound on top; variable thickness; irregular lower boundary, some fragments penetrating up to 10 cm. down into C:8.

C:5 – (PN 23, 232) Cemented coarse deposit with highly altered limestone particles and fractured pebbles in roughly equal proportions, though the pebbles are mostly small and the limestone larger; cemented matrix of sandy silt with a high carbonate content; non-carbonate sand fraction markedly polymodal; moderate organic content; matrix colour yellowish brown (10YR 5/4); bone present; c.35cm. thick; sharp boundary between finer elements of C:5 and C:8 in between the blocks of C:6.

C:4 – (PN 24) Badly corroded stalagmitic boss; the apron and root are still crystalline; the boss was found lying at a slight angle from the vertical (leaning eastwards); the material cemented into the root is identical to C:5; there is a prominent rock pendant almost immediately above the boss;

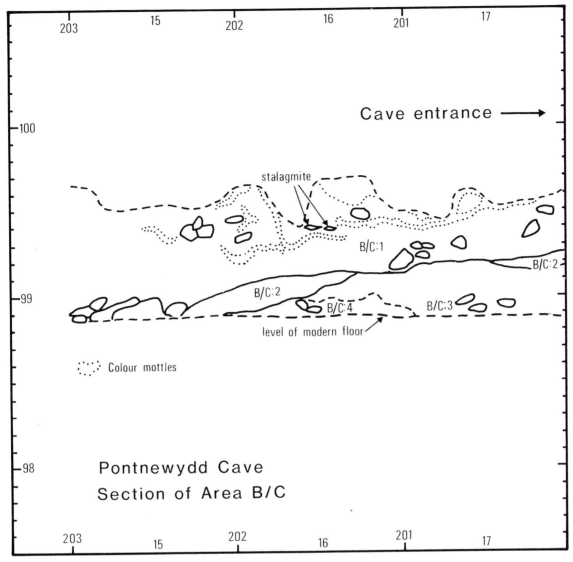

Fig. III.4 Pontnewydd. Wall sediment between areas B and C.

crystalline calcite, similar to that forming the root of the boss penetrates C:5 immediately below the rock pendant; width of the vertical component near its base greater than 10 cm.; no longer extant.

C:3 – (PN 22) Coarse deposit with over 60% moderately altered limestone, *c*.10% large carbonate concretions, and the remainder, fractured pebbles; cemented matrix of silt with some fine sand; non-carbonate sand fraction extremely negatively skewed; small fragments of stalactite and stalagmite; matrix colour yellowish brown (10YR 5/4); bone present; *c*.50 cm. thick; lower boundary rather diffuse but nevertheless visible on site.

C:2 – (PN 15) Informal name: "Pan". Indurated lithozone; limestone present only as ghosts; matrix highly cemented by carbonates and FeMnAl oxides; variegated colour (informally – buffs, blacks, rusts, etc.); traces of bone; basin-shaped cross-section; maximum thickness in centre of section *c*.35 cm.; moderately sharp lower boundary.

C:1 – (PN 16) Small pocket of silty clay with a few small pebbles; fissile in the horizontal plane but bedding not obvious; matrix colour reddish brown (5YR 4/4); the pocket, which has a maximum thickness of 10 cm., lies between C:2 and the eastern wall of the embayment; lower boundary sharp.

These deposits have been truncated by recent disturbance; their highest point (C:2–1) lies at about Site Datum 100.00. Between Areas C and D(S) there is clean rock down to the gravels, separating the majority of the deposits in the two Areas by a minimum of 150 cm.

AREA D (Threshold of East Passage)

This Area may be considered to have three subdivisions. D(S) consists of deposits, running E–W, adhering to the south wall of the main chamber. D(C) consists of deposits, running N–S across the main chamber at the threshold to the East Passage; its southern extremity is contiguous with the eastern extremity of D(S). D(N) consists of deposits, running E–W, adhering to the north wall of the main chamber; its eastern extremity is contiguous with the northern extremity of D(C). The form of these exposures is therefore approximately a right square bracket (*cf.* Fig.III.2). The stratigraphy is clear in this Area; the subdivisions will only be used to give more precise locational information and, with one exception, lithozones will be defined that are valid for the whole of Area

D. Although separated from Area D by sediments rather than by a hiatus, the deposits of Area D(E) must be described independently until they are linked to the main Area by excavation.

Towards the eastern end of D(N) there is another embayment, similar to but apparently smaller than the South Passage. As this embayment is also developed upon the same structural feature as the South Passage, for consistency it may be referred to as the North Passage. (*cf.* Fig.III.2).

D:10 – Coarse to medium siliceous gravel and badly classed sand; rich in colloids; organic matter and FeMnAl oxides near top; matrix colour yellowish brown (10YR 5/6–8). This sediment has only been exposed for a few tens of centimetres all along the base of the exposures. If the bedding of these gravels is oblique to the unconformity at their upper boundary, the material subsumed under 'D:10' may in fact be referable to more than one similar lithozone. With this caveat, co-extensive with C:8.

D:9 – Small discontinuous lenses of sandy silt and sandy clay in D(N) and northern end of D(C) only; matrix colour olive brown (2.5Y 4/4) with 'ginger' specks (high chroma); maximum thickness *c*.3 cm.; sharp but slightly convoluted upper and lower boundaries.

D:8 – (PN 12, 244, 309) Informal name: "Orange Intermediate" – junior homonym which must not pre-empt the demonstration of the correlation of the various "intermediate" deposits (*cf.* section 2, below, p.42). Medium to fine pebbles, fining upwards, with badly classed clayey sand; in general, low to moderate carbonate content, more carbonate in D(S) where it is localised in tiny calcite growths, the size and shape of fish scales, lying horizontally within the sediment; flecks of FeMnAl oxides and rich organics, within the fine matrix and associated with the calcite growths, give a varied matrix colour of red (2.5YR 4/8) to brown (7.5YR 4/4) with flecks of higher chroma; no obvious bedding; a few corroded particles that are cold dilute HCl-soluble and which are not speleothems; thickening eastwards from 4 to 15 cm. in D(N), maximum 20 cm. in D(C) and thinning again (lower boundary rising) in D(S) to nothing more than a stain at the western extremity; lower boundary variable, from sharp to diffuse, extremely diffuse in the centre of D(C).

D:7 – (PN 308) Informal name: "Buff Intermediate" – junior homonym which must not pre-empt the demonstration of the correlation of the various "intermediate" deposits (*cf.* section 2, p.42). Medium coarse deposit containing mostly medium to fine pebbles, often fractured, with a few extremely corroded (granular) limestone particles; matrix of very weakly cemented, badly classed silt and sand with a moderately low carbonate content; non-carbonate sand fraction positively skewed; rich in colloids; FeMnAl aggregates in sands; much organic matter in aggregates and as coatings to sand grains; bone present; matrix colour dark brown (10YR 4/3), drying very rapidly to a lighter 'buff' colour; present in D(C) only; wedging out before reaching northern and southern extremities of D(C); thickening eastwards, maximum observed thickness 15 cm.; sharp lower boundary.

D:6 – (PN 242, 241, 307) Medium coarse deposit with medium and fine pebbles, often fractured, and some altered limestone, so altered in D(C) as to be 'granular'; more and larger limestone clasts as the main chamber walls are approached, especially limestone rich in the mouth of the North Passage; matrix of sandy silt; non-carbonate sand fraction positively skewed; carbonates, moderate and giving weak cementation in D(C), become much

richer towards the walls of the main chamber where the deposit is strongly cemented, especially near the North Passage; moderate organic matter and some FeMnAl aggregates, the latter more common in D(C) and more localised in quite discrete pockets (*c*.1–10 cm., redder colour); small corroded stalagmite fragments; bone present; matrix colour yellowish brown (10YR 5/4); channels through D:7 and slightly into D:8 in the centre of D(C); *c*.30–40 cm. thick; lower boundary progressively sharper eastwards.

D:5 – (PN 306) Medium coarse deposit containing mostly medium and fine fractured pebbles with some carbonate concretions but very little (corroded) limestone; in all other parameters, almost identical to D:6 in D(C); present only in D(C); *c*.15–20 cm. thick, with a distinct lower boundary in the present exposure in D(C), but the whole deposit becoming indistinguishable from D:6 by *c*.100 cm. further west.

D:4 – Discontinuous stalagmite occurrences which must be separately referenced with the Area sub-division code:

D(S):4 – Stalagmitic boss lying on D:6 and below a rock pendant; may be approximately *in situ* but not convincingly cemented into D:6; removed by excavation.

D(C):4 – Very thin spreads of calcite with a biscuity texture associated with the base of D:3 (*infra*) and interstratified with the lower part of D:3.

D(N):4 – A stalagmite (dated sample D534 – Chapter IX); its apron, which is only *c*.2–3 cm. thick and is finely laminated, extends all around its base for *c*.50 cm.; its root penetrates and further cements D:6; it is vertical and lies directly below a rock pendant; it is *c*.25 cm. high, its undamaged apex being in D:2 (see below); quite constant width reduction upwards, culminating in a close approximation to the minimum diameter given by Curl's Theory; no longer extant, although parts of the apron remain.

D:3 – (PN 302', 302″) Informal name: "Pond" – not accceptable as a lithostratigraphic designation. Laminated (less than 1 mm.) silts with some clay partings and very little coarse material; a few very fine pebbles, small corroded limestone particles and FeMnAl aggregates; very low organic content present only as coatings to larger sand grains; dendritic concretions and bone present; intimately associated with D(C):4 and also containing at least one floating limestone block with dripstone on its upper surface; matrix colour brownish yellow (10YR 6/6); present only on north side of D:2 channel (*infra*) in D(C), and in D(N); *c*.8 cm. thick, thickening eastwards to *c*.15 cm. in D(C); in general terms, the base of D:3 approximates to a horizontal plane, with only about a 6 cm. range in absolute height over its entire exposure, but in detail the lower boundary is either gradational with D(C):4 or sharp but irregular, with infiltration between larger elements of D:6 in D(N).

D:2 – (PN 239, 238, 237, 305, 304, 303) Medium coarse deposit containing mostly slightly altered limestone particles but with some medium and fine fractured pebbles; limestone particles are smaller and more compact (equidimensional) away from cave walls, larger and more elongate or platy near the walls and especially in the North Passage; limestone has a blocky fracture near the top of the deposit in D(C); matrix of silt with some sand, weakly cemented by carbonates away from the cave walls but very strongly cemented near walls, especially in the North Passage; non-carbonate sand fraction negatively skewed; small fragments of stalagmite and stalactite, the latter quite common; bone present; only traces of organic matter, associated with larger sand grains; modern roots in places; matrix colour light yellowish to yellowish brown (10YR 5–6/4); in places in D(N) only 5–8 cm. thick before disturbance, in D(S) *c.*25 cm. thick before disturbance; in D(C) undisturbed, *c.*30 cm. thick but up to 80 cm. thick in an east–west trending channel in the centre of the chamber which cuts through the underlying D:3, D:5 and D:6; lower boundary sharp and often marked by larger particles aligned flat along the boundary.

D:1 – Clayey deposit which may be slightly disturbed; matrix colour reddish brown (5YR 4/4); up to 15 cm. thick before certain disturbance; present only in D(C); lower boundary patchy, rather diffuse to quite sharp, with some minor infiltration between particles of D:2.

AREA D(E)

A cavers' trench (p.20, *c.*50 cm. wide) has been dug into the upper deposits of Area D(C) and on, *c.*15 metres, into the East Passage. A small section has been cleaned on the north side of this trench. Another section has been cut north-south across the trench, slightly into a small side passage (the South-East Fissure), also partly disturbed by cavers (*cf.* Fig.III.2), This is Area D(E), starting 2 metres east of the section described above in D(C).

D(E):9 – Coarse deposit with limestone and pebbles; only upper surface as yet exposed, at about Site Datum 99.40–50.

D(E):8 – Thin band of silty clay; very high carbonate content including calcite 'wafers'; matrix colour various pinks (5YR var. high value); *c.*1–2 cm. thick; lower boundary sharp.

D(E):7 – Laminated (less than 1 mm.) silts with some clay laminations; very little coarse material; bone present; matrix colour brownish yellow (10YR 6/6); *c.*10–20 cm. thick, but up to 35 cm. thick (upper boundary rising) in the mouth of the South-East Fissure; lower boundary sharp.

D(E):6 – Medium coarse deposit, the upper half of which can be traced west along the cavers' trench and is co-extensive with D:2; up to 50 cm. thick towards the north of this Area, but only *c.*15 cm. thick in the mouth of the South-East Fissure.

D(E):5 – (PN 236) Badly consolidated lithozone; limestone altered with a blocky fracture; FeMnAl oxides and carbon (no structure) present giving a black colour to the matrix; not cemented; developed to a thickness of *c.*5 cm. in D(E) but thinning westwards along the cavers' trench and wedging out or disturbed before D(C); diffuse lower boundary.

D(E):4 – (PN 235, 243) Laminated (less than 1 mm.) clays and silts with very little coarse material; irregular silt lenses at or near base in places; some clay pellets (aggregates of fine to medium sand size); moderate carbonate content mostly localised in dendritic concretions; modern roots; traces of bone; matrix colour reddish brown (5YR 4/4); *c.*30 cm. thick; becoming disturbed westwards towards D(C) but may possibly be intact at base and co-extensive with D:1; lower boundary sharp and gently undulating.

D(E):3 – (PN 234) Laminated (*c.*1 mm. and less) sand with some clay; very little coarse material; a few small only superficially altered limestone particles, pebbles and FeMnAl aggregates; some clay pellets up to coarse sand size; very few modern roots; moderate carbonate content, mostly particulate; bone, mollusca and other faunal remains present; matrix colour dark brown (10YR 4/3); *c.*25 cm. thick; lower boundary sharp and irregular with minor convolutions; in addition to the main body of sediment which occupies the total width of the East Passage (if correlation across the cavers'

trench is allowed), there is an east–west channel, at least 25 cm. wide and reaching D(E):5, filled with this deposit and also with some pockets of sediment resembling D(E):2 (*infra*), against the south wall; the bedding within this channel is highly convoluted.

D(E):2 – (PN 233) Clayey sand with very few coarse particles; some modern roots; no apparent bedding in lower part, upper part *vide infra;* moderate organic and carbonate contents; bone, mollusca and other faunal remains present; matrix colour brown to dark brown (7.5YR 4–5/4); *c.*10 cm. thick; rather diffuse lower boundary with minor convolutions.

The deposits D(E):4–2 have been informally named: "Upper Clay(s) and Sands". D(E):4 has also been called: "Red Clay".

D(E):1 – Informal name: "Laminated Stalagmitic Floor". Laminated (*c.*1 mm. and less) crystalline to biscuity travertine; *c.*30 cm. thick; gradational lower boundary with D(E):2, with alternating clay and calcite laminations, the former thinning and the latter thickening up into the true travetine; co-extensive with flowstone on the walls.

EAST PASSAGE

Still further into the East Passage (at about grid reference 214.00 and beyond), between deposits that are co-extensive with D(E):6 and D(E):4, disturbed slabs of crystalline travertine begin to appear in some quantity. These slabs include minor bosses and are generally the right way up. In places there are two or more conjoinable slabs. Until this area can be examined in detail, this travertine will be referred to as STAL.X(EP).

RF (DEPOSITS ADHERING TO THE ROOF OF THE CAVE)

Nearly all the way around the cave, on the roof or high on the walls, there is a dark stain, which is sharpest at its top surface but which fades gradually downwards and is lost after *c.*15 cm. The top of this stain has been surveyed for ten metres on the north wall of the main chamber and nine metres on the south wall, starting at approx. the line of the section in D(C) and working westwards. Variations in height amount to no more than 60 cm., the gently undulating line always falling between Site Datum 100.35 and 100.95. If the cave were to be filled with deposits to this level, there would only be an air gap of at most 50 cm. between the sediment and the highest point of the roof in any area. In several places around the cave, in crevices and irregularities in the rock, there are small pockets of sediment (coded RF), which never lie above the top of the stain and which often end abruptly exactly against the top of the stain. The sediment has a plastic, earthy texture; rich in organics; bone present; matrix colour dark reddish brown (5YR 3/2–3); the pockets are not usually cemented or even well consolidated.

MAIN CHAMBER (NORTH)

There are various small patches of highly cemented sediment along the north wall of the main chamber, between the inner wall of the GC and Area D(N). There are no obvious major fissures or passages. These patches of sediment have not yet been studied and will be described at a later date.

NOTE: Reference Sediment Samples from the Pontnewydd Area

Five samples (marked CGR 1–5) from the sequence of deposits at Cae Gronw Cave (above and to the north of Pontnewydd Cave); to be described elsewhere.

PN 230 – modern soil *c.*30 metres south of the cave, on the hill slope (quite steep), well away from any possible disturbance associated with digging at the cave.

PN 231 – modern gravel from a spit (just above high water – summer) in the Elwy, approx. below the cave.

PN 301 – decomposed limestone (hardly any coherence) from a block of bedrock lying in a backwater (west bank) of the Elwy, c.5 metres north of the eponymous bridge at Bont Newydd.

NOTE: Local Bedrock

No detailed geological survey of this area is yet available. The rock was mapped (Geological Map 79SW, 1850) as undifferentiated "(Lower) Carboniferous Limestone", and the dip was shown as c.20° N.E. The 1973 edition (IGS sheet 107, Denbigh, solid 1:50,000) contains no significant revision or subdivision of the Carboniferous; the limestone as a whole is now referred to as "(Dinantian) Dyserth Limestone Group". The cliff exposures in the vicinity of the cave are heavily weathered and difficult to approach. There are major bedding planes at about 40 cm. intervals and only minor, widely spaced joints. Locally, the dip would seem to be a little less than suggested above and there is a greater northerly component.

Clasts, contained in the cave sediments, and bedrock, where it could be examined closely, seem to be of a very similar nature. The rock is a calcite mudstone with some patchy coarse recrystallisation, giving a slightly massive texture and only poor conchoidal fracture. On a fresh break, it is grey in colour (c.10YR 5/1 with tints of a higher chroma). Brachiopods have been noted. Porosity of the unaltered rock is estimated to be very low.

A sample of the rock from the cave wall contained 96.4% carbonates. The dark residue contained euhedral quartz crystals (often set in radial clusters), fossil hydrocarbons and complex sesquioxides. The residue was composed of only c.10% quartzitic sand (fine), the yet finer grades being too rich in non-particulate matter to give a meaningful size distribution.

From observation on site, chemical weathering of the limestone can be seen to proceed by intense alteration of the surface, with periodic exfoliation of the 'chalky' weathering crust, thus revealing a more or less fresh surface. Under the microscope, a series of distinct bands like onion skins can be recognised, each less altered than its outer neighbour. Only if weathering is extremely severe does the effect penetrate macroscopically more deeply than c.1 mm. The limestone may then become unsound with a highly blocky fracture (common in proximity to running water), reduced to a 'chalky' ghost (common in proximity to standing water) or extremely porous and granular (common in deposits not dominated by carbonate material). Drips that are not releasing carbonate attack the limestone, leaving a black clayey deposit, very similar to the residue under analysis noted above. Minor but apparently distinct variants have been noted amongst the limestone clasts in the cave sediments themselves; it is not yet clear whether these are separate facies or merely the result of alteration governed by different processes.

2 – CORRELATION

It can be seen from the deposit description that very similar lithologic trends are evidenced in each Area sequence. The lowest deposits comprise siliceous sands, often rather coarse, and gravels, the pebbles of which are only moderately fractured. At progressively higher levels in each sequence, there is generally an increasing limestone component, the non-carbonate sands become finer and pebbles become rarer and more severely fractured. The presence of such trends in each Area suggests that the deposits may be to some extent correlative.

However, before any attempt at correlation is made, it should be recognised that the mode of emplacement of many of the deposits could render purely lithologic correlaion either difficult or, conversely, spuriously easy. The bulk of the deposits throughout the cave are demonstrably the result of mass movement at various velocities but always significantly faster than creep. In the context of Pontnewydd, such movement will be referred to as 'debris flow'. This term is now preferred in place of "solifluction" (Green 1981) and "mud-flow" or "mudflow" (Green et.al. 1981; Green 1981) since the characteristics of these sediments are thus accurately and unequivocally described. It must be demonstrated that, for any proposed correlation involving such material, the processes involved in debris flow (cf. p.54) are not likely to have resulted in the creation of lithologically very similar, yet non-correlative sediment bodies.

Analysis for certain major characteristics has been carried out on sediment samples from the better exposed sequences in the cave: Areas B, DPS, B/C, C, D and D(E). These samples are not random for many of the characteristics, since spatial trends within the sediments are obvious. Such trends should make correlation more difficult, but if achieved, more reliable, as inter-unit variability will thus be shown to outweigh intra-unit variability. However, the spatial trends and the sampling plan, necessitated by the configuration of the extant deposits, disallow the calculation of the statistical significance of any observed association. Statistical methods will be used to suggest clustering but the resulting coefficients of similarity/correlation are best considered as being on an ordinal rather than a ratio scale, except in the case of more extreme values. The methods chosen are non-parametric, with grouping achieved by agglomerative hierarchical procedures or by total linkage to selected levels of association (see below, p.45). It should be noted that the choice of sediment characteristics to be used in the statistical analysis will inevitably affect the outcome of that analysis. An effort has been made not to allow preconceived opinions concerning correlation to influence the initial choice of sediment characteristics. Once a characteristic has been included, it has never been removed whatever its observed effect upon the calculations.

Data, reflecting ten major sediment characteristics, were first organised into a matrix using either a three or four state code (Table III.1). Some of the information was derived from observation (e.g. bedding) but most was extracted from numerical results on continuous scales (*cf.* Figs. III.5–18). Continuous variables were subdivided to give the discrete coding either at roughly equal intervals or at obvious discontinuities, depending upon the distribution of a variable over all samples analysed. Note that, in five cases, only a three state code could be justified; these variables are thus weighted so that they *potentially* contribute more to the overall association than do four state coded variables. The coefficient of similarity of Sokal and Sneath (1963) was then calculated for every pair of samples. This coefficient was used to construct the dendrogram in Fig.III.5 by means of unrestricted single linkage. The tighter groupings (S_{ss} greater than 0.900 – arbitrary) are shaded for ease of reference.

It was felt that the particle size distribution of non-carbonate material in the range 0.09 to 2.00 mm. might also afford information on correlation if considered in more detail. This material is fine enough not to produce difficulties over sample size, yet, owing to its relative coarseness and stability (both mechanical and chemical), it represents the sediment component that is most likely to resist major diagenetic modification or dislocation. The perentage results of this size analysis (*cf.* Fig.III.15), with nine half *phi* classes, were converted to ranks (Table III.2). It was argued that similar sediments should display statistical correlation between ranks for a given size class. In essence, the location and relative importance of size modes in one sample are compared with the same characteristics of modes in another sample. The rank correlation coefficient of Kendall (1948) was calculated for every pair of samples, using the correction for tied ranks. However, the correction had no effect upon the resulting clustering and was therefore abandoned. Fig. III.6 is a dendrogram produced using unrestricted single linkage of S-values, derivatives (without correction for tied ranks) of Kendall's *tau* which are easier to plot and tabulate (*cf.* Fig.III.6 for the relationship between S and *tau*). The tighter groupings (S greater than +24 – arbitrary) are shaded for ease of reference.

Certain major groupings appear to be reasonably constant under the procedures reported above. In Fig.III.5, the grouping on the left contains all the samples derived from the siliceous sands and gravels which always occupy the lowest position in every Area sequence. These sediments will be considered to be correlative at a high level in the heirarchy. In Fig.III.6, based upon non-carbonate sand data alone, this grouping is not so clear. Most of the coarser siliceous deposits still cluster on the left, but better classed medium sands (eg. PN3-DPS:11 and PN5-DPS:9) have dissociated from the main group. In that these sands are all stratified within the main siliceous grouping, it may be safely assumed that their location in Fig.III.6 represents facies similarlity rather than stratigraphic affiliation of any kind.

Two other groupings are constant in both Figs.III.5–6:
    (i)   PN19–?B:6 + PN20–B:6 + PN306, 307, 242–D:5–6
    (ii) PN18–B:5 + PN303, 304, 305–D:2
The correct stratigraphic order is maintained in these groupings, each of which comprise lithozones from both Areas B and D.

Further linkages in Figs.III.5–6 are more obscure, but they are in many cases informative and the reader is invited to return to them at the end of this section, when a full correlation scheme has been suggested.

	(1)	(2)	(3)	(4)	(5)	(6)	(7)	(8)	(9)	(10)
PN1–DPS:13	111	111	111	111	111	222	111	211	XXX	111
PN2–DPS:12	111	211	111	111	111	221	XXX	111	XXX	221
PN3–DPS:11	111	211	111	111	111	221	XXX	111	XXX	111
PN4–DPS:10	111	111	111	111	111	222	111	211	XXX	221
PN5–DPS:9	111	211	111	111	111	221	XXX	111	XXX	211
PN6–DPS:5	111	111	111	111	111	222	111	221	XXX	211
PN7–DPS:5	111	111	111	111	111	222	111	221	XXX	211
PN11	111	211	111	111	111	221	111	211	XXX	111
PN12–D:8	211	111	211	222	222	211	211	211	XXX	111
PN14–B/C:3	111	221	111	111	111	221	111	211	XXX	211
PN15–C:2	211	221	211	211	XXX	XXX	XXX	XXX	221	111
PN17–B:4	211	221	222	211	222	211	XXX	222	111	111
PN18–B:5	221	221	221	211	222	221	221	222	111	111
PN19–?B:6	221	111	221	221	221	221	221	221	XXX	111
PN20–B:6	221	111	221	211	221	221	221	221	211	111
PN21–B:8	211	111	211	211	211	221	211	221	221	111
PN22–C:3	221	221	211	211	222	111	221	222	211	111
PN23–C:5	221	211	211	221	221	211	221	222	221	111
PN26–B/C:2	211	211	211	222	211	221	111	221	221	111
PN222–DPS:14	111	111	XXX	111	111	222	111	XXX	XXX	111
PN226–DPS:19	111	111	XXX	111	111	221	XXX	XXX	XXX	221
PN229–DPS:22	111	111	111	111	111	222	111	211	XXX	111
PN234–D(E):3	221	221	211	211	221	111	XXX	221	111	221
PN235–D(E):4	211	221	211	211	221	111	XXX	222	XXX	221
PN242–D:6	221	111	221	221	211	221	XXX	221	211	111
PN244–D:8	211	111	XXX	222	111	221	111	221	XXX	111
PN302″–D:3	221	222	211	211	221	111	XXX	222	211	221
PN303–D:2	221	221	221	211	222	221	221	222	111	111
PN304–D:2	221	221	221	211	222	221	221	222	111	111
PN305–D:2	221	221	221	211	222	221	221	222	111	111
PN306–D:5	221	111	221	221	211	211	221	221	211	111
PN307–D:6	221	111	221	221	211	221	221	221	211	111
PN308–D:7	221	111	221	222	211	221	211	211	221	111

		(111)	(211)	(221)	(222)
(1)	Bone	absent	trace	common	–
(2)	Skewness, non-carb. 2–0.09 mm.	+ve	neutral	–ve	–
(3)	% Carb., 1–0.063 mm.	0	1–40	41–60	61–100
(4)	% Organics, <1 mm.	<0.2	0.2–0.75	0.76–1.5	>1.5
(5)	% Carb., 22.6–1 mm.	0	1–10	11–60	61–100
(6)	% 22.6–1 mm. in <22.6 mm.	<25	25–50	51–70	71–100
(7)	% Pebble fracturing	<50	50–80	81–100	–
(8)	% 0.063 mm. in <1 mm.	<25	25–50	51–75	76–100
(9)	Limestone alteration	weak	moderate	extreme	–
(10)	Bedding (macroscopic)	none	weak	strong	–

XXX not available/not applicable

Table III.1 Coded sediment characteristics (*cf*. Figures III.5–18 and Section 1 of text)

	(+3.5)	(+3.0)	(+2.5)	(+2.0)	(+1.5)	(+1.0)	(+0.5)	(0)	(−0.5)
PN1–DPS:13	9	8	7	6	5	4	1	2	3
PN2–DPS:12	6	4	2	1	3	5	7	8	9
PN3–DPS:11	9	8	6	3	1	2	4	5	7
PN4–DPS:10	9	8	6.5	4	5	6.5	3	2	1
PN5–DPS:9	9	8	7	4	2	1	3	5	6
PN6–DPS:5	9	8	7	4	5	6	3	2	1
PN7–DPS:5	9	8	7	5	3	6	2	4	1
PN11	9	8	5	1	2	4	6	7	3
PN12–D:8	9	7.5	2.5	2.5	6	5	7.5	4	1
PN14–B/C:3	6	3	2	1	4	9	7	8	5
PN15–C:2	3	1	2	4	5	6	7	8	9
PN17–B:4	3	2	1	4	5	6	7	8.5	8.5
PN18–B:5	3	2	1	4	5	7	6	9	8
PN19–?B:6	6	7	4	5	9	8	2	3	1
PN20–B:6	6	5	4	7	9	8	2	3	1
PN21–B:8	9	8	7	6	5	4	2	3	1
PN22–C:3	1	2	3	4	9	7	5	8	6
PN23–C:5	4	3	5	6	8	9	2	7	1
PN26–B/C:2	9	7	4	3	5	4	3	1	2
PN222–DPS:14	9	8	7	6	5	1	3	8	9
PN226–DPS:19	7	6	4	2	1	3	5	8	9
PN229–DPS:22	9	8	7	6	5	4	1	2	3
PN234–D(E):3	2	1	3	4	6	5	7.5	7.5	9
PN235–D(E):4	1.5	1.5	3	4	5	6	7.5	7.5	9
PN242–D:6	8.5	4	6	3	8.5	7	5	2	1
PN244–D:8	9	8	7	2	5.5	5.5	4	3	1
PN302″–D:3	1	2	3	4	5.5	7.5	9	7.5	5.5
PN303–D:2	1	2	3	4	6	7.5	9	7.5	5
PN304–D:2	1	2	3.5	3.5	7	8	9	6	5
PN305–D:2	1	2	3	4	6	7.5	9	7.5	5
PN306–D:5	5	3	6	4	9	8	7	2	1
PN307–D:6	6	5	7	4	9	8	3	2	1
PN308–D:7	8	5	7	3	9	6	4	2	1
I.L.R. (insoluble lime- stone residue)	3	1	2	4	5	6	7	8.5	8.5

TABLE III.2   Ranked non-carbonate sand grade proportions (*cf.* Fig. III.15) The lower limit of each half Φ grade heads each column.

Using the same coefficents and sediment characteristics as above, it will be interesting to observe how linkages are located between different Areas, with the deposits of each Area in stratigraphic sequence. This will avoid the chaining that may obscure relationships in the dendrograms. However, in order that the diagrams be readable, some choice must be made as to the range of values of the coefficients to be plotted. Therefore, the *assumption (supra)* is made that values of S_{ss} greater than 0.899 and of S greater than +24 are significantly higher than S_{ss} = 0.899 to 0.800 and S = +24 to +18 respectively, and that values of S_{ss} greater than 0.799 and of S greater than +16 are significantly higher than S_{ss} less than 0.800 and S less than +18 respectively. Should any reader find the assumption unwarranted, the exact values of the coefficients are also tabulated alongside each diagram.

Figs.III.7 (S_{ss}) and III.8 (S) represent the relationships between Areas B and D+D(E) (the stratigraphic order is demonstrable since D:2 is co-extensive with D(E):6). PN19, which probably slightly overlaps the B:5/6 boundary, has here been eliminated, but on both diagrams it plots exactly as PN20. In Fig.III.7, note that the similarity between B:6 and D:2 is no greater than that between B:6 and B:5. If one goes to Level A inter-sequence links, exactly the same groupings as in the dendrograms can be seen, namely B:5+D:2 and B:6+D:5–6. In Fig.III.8, no Level A or B links cross the 'boundary' B:5/6–D:3/5, again

46

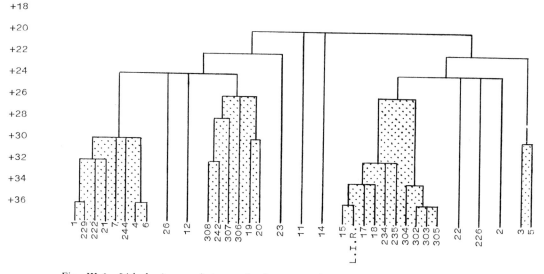

Sokal & Sneath Coefficient of Similarity S$_{ss}$

Data: cf. Table III.1
Agglomerative hierarchical
Unrestricted single linkage
Mixed 4 and 3 state code
Constituents = 10
Sample = 33

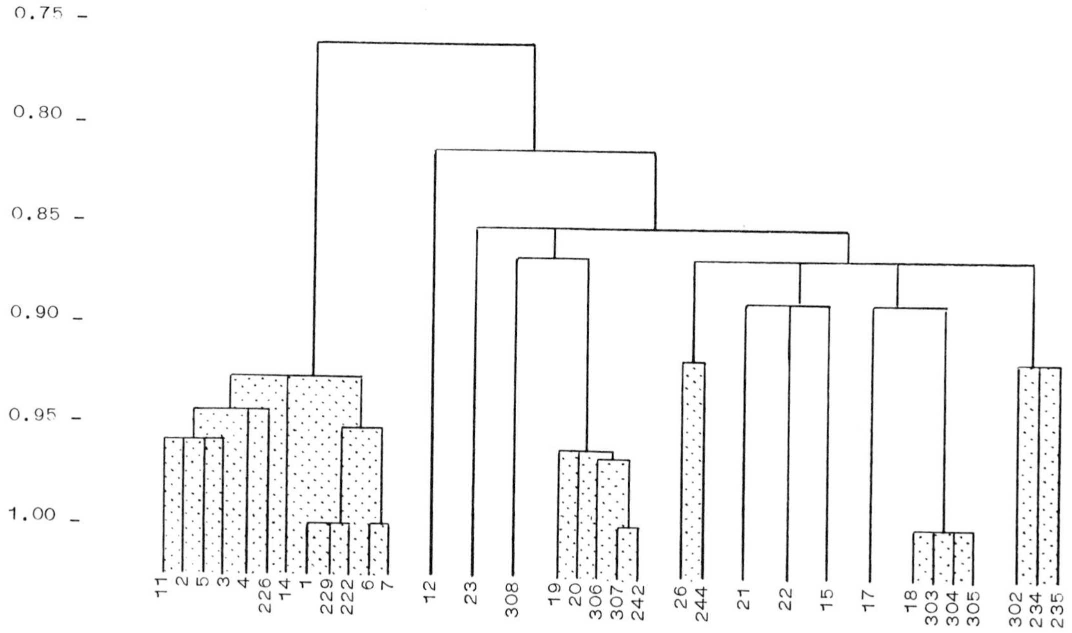

0.75
0.80
0.85
0.90
0.95
1.00

Fig. III.5 Lithologic correlation – dendrogram of similarity coefficients.

S-Derivative of Kendall's Rank Correlation Coefficient $\underline{tau} = \dfrac{2S}{m(m-1)}$

Non-carbonate sands 2.00-0.09 mm. (cf. Table III.2)
Agglomerative hierarchical
Unrestricted single linkage
Constituents m = 9
Sample n = 34

+18
+20
+22
+24
+26
+28
+30
+32
+34
+36

Fig. III.6 Lithologic correlation – dendrogram of rank correlation coefficients.

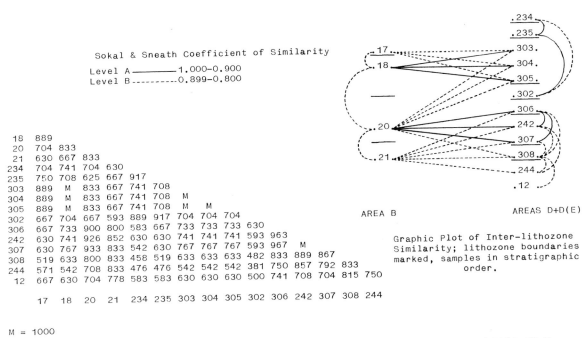

Sokal & Sneath Coefficient of Similarity

Level A ——————1.000-0.900
Level B ---------0.899-0.800

	17	18	20	21	234	235	303	304	305	302	306	242	307	308	244
18	889														
20	704	833													
21	630	667	833												
234	704	741	704	630											
235	750	708	625	667	917										
303	889	M	833	667	741	708									
304	889	M	833	667	741	708	M								
305	889	M	833	667	741	708	M	M							
302	667	704	667	593	889	917	704	704	704						
306	667	733	900	800	583	667	733	733	733	630					
242	630	741	926	852	630	630	741	741	741	593	963				
307	630	767	933	833	542	630	767	767	767	593	967	M			
308	519	633	800	833	458	519	633	633	633	482	833	889	867		
244	571	542	708	833	476	476	542	542	542	381	750	857	792	833	
12	667	630	704	778	583	583	630	630	630	500	741	708	704	815	750

AREA B   AREAS D+D(E)

Graphic Plot of Inter-lithozone
Similarity; lithozone boundaries
marked, samples in stratigraphic
order.

M = 1000

Fig. III.7 Lithologic correlation – Areas B, D and D(E) – coefficient of similarity. (*cf.* Table III.1).

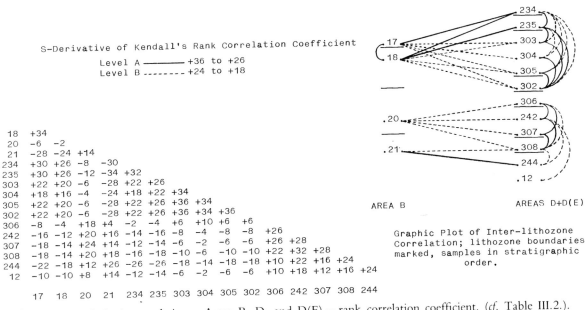

S-Derivative of Kendall's Rank Correlation Coefficient

Level A ——————+36 to +26
Level B --------+24 to +18

	17	18	20	21	234	235	303	304	305	302	306	242	307	308	244
18	+34														
20	-6	-2													
21	-28	-24	+14												
234	+30	+26	-8	-30											
235	+30	+26	-12	-34	+32										
303	+22	+20	-6	-28	+22	+26									
304	+18	+16	-4	-24	+18	+22	+34								
305	+22	+20	-6	-28	+22	+26	+36	+34							
302	+22	+20	-6	-28	+22	+26	+36	+34	+34						
306	-8	-4	+18	+4	-2	-4	+6	+10	+6	+6					
242	-16	-12	+20	+16	-14	-16	-8	-4	-8	-8	+26				
307	-18	-14	+24	+14	-12	-14	-6	-2	-6	-6	+26	+28			
308	-18	-14	+20	+18	-16	-18	-10	-6	-10	-10	+22	+32	+28		
244	-22	-18	+12	+26	-26	-26	-18	-14	-18	-18	+10	+22	+16	+24	
12	-10	-10	+8	+14	-12	-14	-6	-2	-6	-6	+10	+18	+12	+16	+24

AREA B   AREAS D+D(E)

Graphic Plot of Inter-lithozone
Correlation; lithozone boundaries
marked, samples in stratigraphic
order.

Fig. III.8 Lithologic correlation – Areas B, D, and D(E) – rank correlation coefficient. (*cf.* Table III.2.).

confirming the groupings. Note that, in Fig.III.8, inter-sequence Level A links with Area D(E) are not markedly greater than intra-sequence links, even if overall lithology allowed such a correlation.

Figs.III.9 (S$_{ss}$) and III.10 (S) show the relationships between the Areas already examined and Areas B/C and C. Note that PN26–B/C:2 has been allowed to find its own position since there is no stratigraphic contact with Area C. This position was subsequently found to be concordant with all other available evidence. From the dendrograms, it was to be expected that Areas B/C and C would not group very closely with other Areas. However, the dichotomy already observed is clearly maintained at the 'boundary' B:5/6–C:3/5–D:3/5. Fortuitous links in Fig.III.9, such as B:8–C:2 and B/C:2–C:2, are the result of vaguely similar sediments being assessed on only six characteristics, including four three state codings (*cf.* Table III.1).

Sokal & Sneath Coefficient of Similarity

Level A ——————— 1.000-0.900
Level B ─ ─ ─ ─ ─ ─ 0.899-0.800

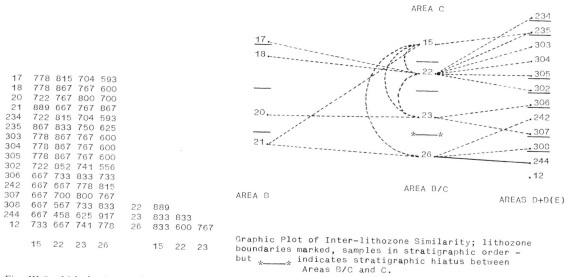

17	778	815	704	593				
18	778	867	767	600				
20	722	767	800	700				
21	889	667	767	867				
234	722	815	704	593				
235	867	833	750	625				
303	778	867	767	600				
304	778	867	767	600				
305	778	867	767	600				
302	722	852	741	556				
306	667	733	833	733				
242	667	667	778	815				
307	667	700	800	767				
308	667	567	733	833	22	889		
244	667	458	625	917	23	833	833	
12	733	667	741	778	26	833	600	767
	15	22	23	26		15	22	23

Graphic Plot of Inter-lithozone Similarity; lithozone boundaries marked, samples in stratigraphic order – but *———* indicates stratigraphic hiatus between Areas B/C and C.

Fig. III.9 Lithologic correlation – Areas B, B/C, C, D and D(E) – coefficient of similarity. (*cf.* Table III.1).

S-Derivative Of Kendall's Rank Correlation Coefficient

Level A ——————— +36 to +26
Level B ─ ─ ─ ─ ─ ─ +24 to +18

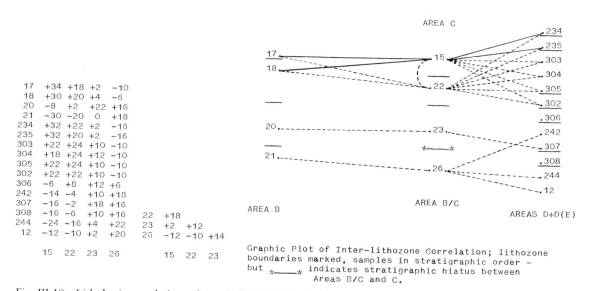

17	+34	+18	+2	-10				
18	+30	+20	+4	-6				
20	-8	+2	+22	+16				
21	-30	-20	0	+18				
234	+32	+22	+2	-16				
235	+32	+20	+2	-16				
303	+22	+24	+10	-10				
304	+18	+24	+12	-10				
305	+22	+24	+10	-10				
302	+22	+22	+10	-10				
306	-6	+8	+12	+6				
242	-14	-4	+10	+18				
307	-16	-2	+18	+16				
308	-16	-6	+10	+16	22	+18		
244	-24	-16	+4	+22	23	+2	+12	
12	-12	-10	+2	+20	26	-12	-10	+14
	15	22	23	26		15	22	23

Graphic Plot of Inter-lithozone Correlation; lithozone boundaries marked, samples in stratigraphic order – but *———* indicates stratigraphic hiatus between Areas B/C and C.

Fig. III.10 Lithologic correlation – Areas B, B/C, C, D and D(E) – rank correlation coefficient. (*cf.* Table III.2).

It must now be decided whether the observed similarities between B:5, C:3 and D:2 on the one hand, and between B:6, C:5 and D:5–6 on the other, all of which represent debris flows, are *likely* to reflect some reality other than that they are parts of the same two, formerly continuous sediment units. Note that these groupings have long been recognised on site; the present numerical treatment only serves to formalise the pattern. It is my firm opinion that the chances of erroneous correlation are minimal with respect to these deposits. Sediment geometry and lithogenetic considerations support this view *(infra)*. This is the only reasonable conclusion – a conclusion that does not involve special pleading and untestable hypotheses – that can be reached from the present lithologic data. If this correlation is indeed proven, beyond doubt, to be incorrect by some means other than sedimentological, the only course available is to abandon any attempt at lithologic correlation within the debris flows, on the grounds that their *gross* composition is subject to aleatory variation. Note that the weakest component in the suggested correlation is Area C; the relevant deposits in Areas B and D are remarkably similar. If the correlation between Areas B and D is disproved, there is no way the correlation between Areas C and D can be salvaged using lithologic data.

Using the B:5–C:3–D:2 and B:6–C:5–D:5–6 links as markers, the following overall correlation may be suggested. At the same time, the opportunity will be taken to organise the deposits into an *informal* lithostratigraphic framework, following as closely as possible the guidelines set out in Hedberg (1976). Since Pontnewydd Cave is likely to be of some importance to quaternary geology in North Wales, it is hoped that this framework, with any necessary modification, will be raised to formal status at some point in the future. The matter of unit-stratotypes is not discussed here; the lithozones from which some units derive their names are indicated in the preceding section. The term 'breccia' is retained from Hughes and Thomas (1874). The framework is summarised in Fig.III.11 and the resulting deposit geometry is schematically represented in Fig.III.12. This same correlation was used as the basis for the Stratigraphy in Green (1981) and Green *et al.* (1981).

The *Pontnewydd Cave formation* may be divided into two members:
   Siliceous member (Sm), with a dominant siliceous component;
   Calcareous member (Cm), with common matrix carbonate, speleothems, limestone clasts and bone.
Sm may be divided into two submembers:
   Lower Sands and Gravel submember (LSGs). This unit, exposed only in the Deep Sounding, contains lithozones DPS:22–14. It comprises a series of generally well stratified sands and siliceous gravel, some lithozones being heavily cemented, mostly by carbonates. Note that the massively indurated lithozone DPS:14 may be in the right (youngest) stratigraphic position or it may be considerably older than some or all of the other deposits of this unit.
   Upper Sands and Gravel submember (USGs). This unit is best exposed in the Deep Sounding where it contains lithozones DPS:13–1. Elsewhere, deposits of similar lithology underly lithozones clearly belonging to higher units; these include GC(N), GC(S):5, B(W):4, B:9, (PN11), B/C:4–3, C:8–7 and D:10–9. Lithozone A:1, although isolated, is also probably part of this unit. The deposits comprise moderately well to badly stratified siliceous gravels with occasional beds of finer material. These gravels may be cemented near the cave walls but there are no discrete horizontal zones of carbonate cementation as in *LSGs*.

Cm may be divided into three subunits:
   Intermediate complex (Ic). This unit is termed 'intermediate' since its deposits have lithologic characters in common with both the units below *(USGs)* and above *(CSs; infra)*. It is a 'complex' as its component lithozones, each rather different, are often present only as lenses or pockets, and even when more continuous, show rapid lateral facies changes. In some cases, it is not yet possible to identify the relative stratigraphic order of the lithozones. The complex is polythetic in the sense that not all the component lithozones show all the identifying charateristics: coarse sand and siliceous gravel (usually quite fine); high organic and sesquioxide contents; small quantities of highly corroded limestone; moderate to high matrix carbonate, sometimes crystalline; traces of bone. The lithozones involved are B:8, B/C:2 and D:8–7. The disturbed speleothem fragments of B:7 are probably best included in this complex, as is the colloidal carbonate of GC(S):4. The status of the cemented sands GC(S):3 is uncertain since this very restricted deposit is of unique lithology at this depth in the sequence; it will be included here until its affinities can be clarified. Note that the complex is as

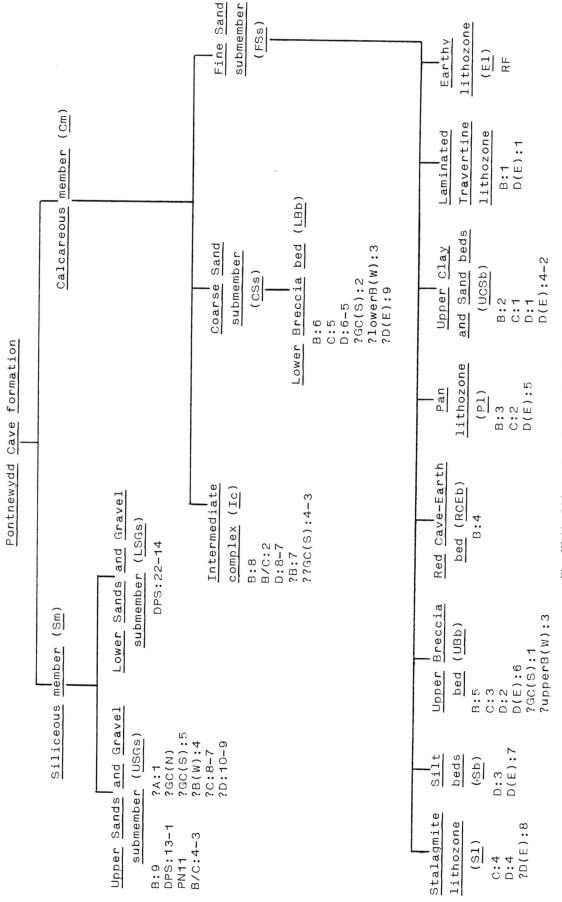

Fig. III.11 Lithostratigraphic classification.

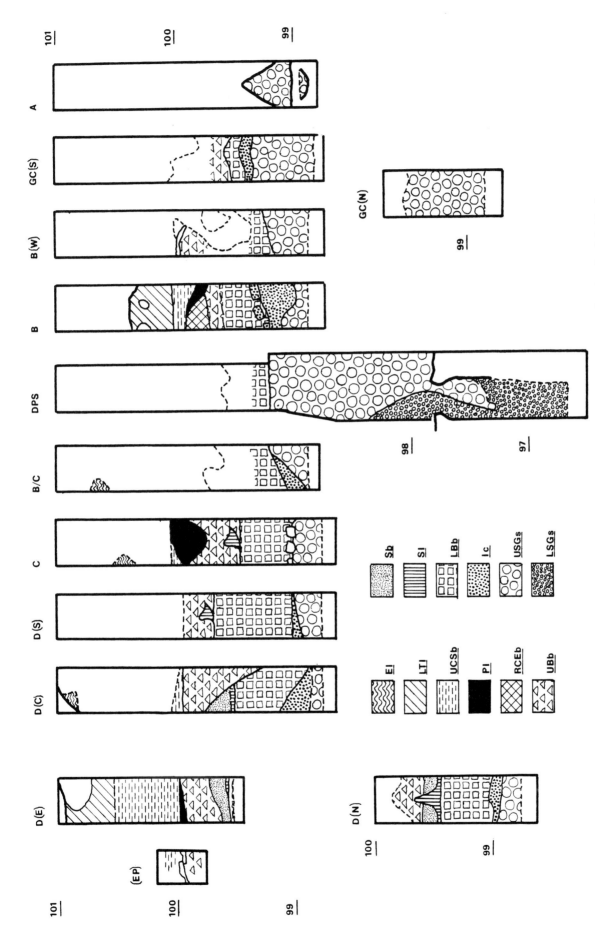

Fig. III.12 Schematic geometry of lithostratigraphic units. (cf. Fig. III.1). Uncorrelated units left blank.

51

much defined by the more easily recognisable units which lie above and below it as it is by internal homogeneity.

Coarse Sand submember (CSs), which at present contains only the *Lower Breccia bed (LBb).* This unit includes B:6, C:5 and D:6–5. D(E):9, although not yet penetrated to any great depth, almost certainly belongs to this unit. Remnants of the unit are probably represented in GC(S):2 and in the lower parts of B(W):3; a polluted remnant may even be present near the base of B/C:1. The deposits comprise coarse, badly classed siliceous sand, with common fractured pebbles and a little corroded limestone. There is some matrix carbonate and the deposits are usually cemented, becoming strongly cemented towards the cave walls. Bone and organic matter are quite common. Lithozones included in this unit are considered to be the result of a single 'event'.

Fine Sand submember (FSs). This unit is differentiated from other units by the fact that its component deposits contain non-carbonate sand that is predominantly fine; major speleothems and limestone clasts are also common. It is possible that it may prove useful in the future to abandon this unit and replace it with three new submembers which would contain *Sl + Sb, UBb + RCEb + Pl* and *UCSb + LTl + El* respectively, as defined below.

At present, *FSs* may be divided into the following eight subunits:

Stalagmite lithozone (Sl). The unit contains C:4, the various occurrences of D:4 and possibly D(E):8. The unit comprises several isolated stalagmites and bosses, together with thin, more or less corroded spreads of speleothem, intimately associated or interstratified with *Sb (infra).* Correlation, apart from the recognition of the lithologic similarity of speleothems in general, depends upon the grouping of units which lie above and below.

Silt beds (Sb). The unit includes D:3 and most probably D(E):7. These deposits are laminated silts, with very little coarse material. Their relationship with *Sl* has been noted above.

Upper Breccia bed (UBb). The unit includes B:5, C:3, D:2 and D(E):6. Remnants of the unit are probably represented in GC(S):1 and in the upper part of B(W):3. The deposit includes abundant, slightly altered limestone clasts with a few fractured pebbles. The matrix contains high proportions of silt and fine sand, much of which is carbonate. The deposit is usually cemented, highly cemented near the cave walls. Bone is quite common but organic matter is rather rare. Lithozones included in this unit are considered to be the result of a single 'event'. In addition to confusing similarities in overall texture, this deposit is often of a very similar colour (wet or dry) to *LBb.* However, if a sample of material less than 1 mm. is ignited, the resulting colour is almost always at least one point of hue redder than similarly treated material of *LBb.* Typical figures in Area D(C) are *UBb* 5–6YR, *LBb* 7YR.

Red Cave Earth bed (RCEb). This unit is only represented by lithozone B:4. It contains many, quite angular limestone clasts, set in a carbonate-rich silt. It is not cemented. There is a little bone present.

Pan lithozone (Pl). This unit is represented by B:3, C:2 and D(E):5. Although the unit is easily defined on lithologic grounds alone, it will be more informative to point out here that it is a zone of alteration rather than a depositional unit. It has always been observed associated with the base of *UCSb (infra);* it may be developed on the material of *RCEb* or *UBb* which it radically modifies, producing a dark, often indurated lithozone.

Upper Clay and Sand beds (UCSb). This unit includes B:2, C:1, D:1 and D(E):4–2. The deposits comprise laminated silty clays, passing upwards into well bedded clayey sands, and finally becoming increasingly clayey again near the top. There is much small bone present, and some organics, especially in the upper part of the unit. Near the cave walls, material from this unit has usually penetrated down between the walls and the lower units, so that young bones and fines have been mixed with older coarse elements.

This situation is particularly well evidenced in the thin veneers of GC(S):1 and B/C:1.

Laminated Travertine lithozone (LTl). This unit includes B:1 and D(E):1. There are small corroded remnants of travertine adhering to the cave walls at similar heights in various parts of the cave. Given the survival potential of such material, further study will be required before they are assumed to be correlative. Lithozone B(W):2 appears to be in the right stratigraphic position for inclusion in this unit but, unlike undoubted components of *LTl*, it contains extremely varied speleothem fragments and cement; its geometric expression is also atypical. *LTl* forms thick, horizontally bedded shelves which probably were once part of a more or less continuous 'floor'. It has a gradational boundary with *UCSb* below (*cf.* p.41).

Earthy lithozone (El). Isolated remnants of this unit adhere to the roof and walls (RF) in many areas of the cave (*cf.* p.41). No stratigraphic contact with any other unit has yet been observed. It is a dark, plastic deposit, rich in organics and small bone.

Four remaining lithozones cannot as yet be allocated their proper place in the above framework. B(W):1 may be only an extremely localised deposit of no great significance. It has already been noted above that B(W):2 is anomalous with respect to other defined units. C:6, composed entirely of limestone blocks, probably represents localised collapse of wall or roof. However, it is not entirely impossible that this is a sorting phenomenon associated with *LBb*, which is a debris flow. STAL.X(EP) has not yet been observed closely. If it does in fact represent approximately *in situ* travertine, it must be allocated separate unit status and be placed in the stratigraphy between *UBb* and *UCSb*. Whether is could be proven to lie stratigraphically above or below *RCEb* depends upon the recognition of the latter deposit in the East Passage.

The suggested framework represents a lithologic correlation. Further information, bearing upon general correlation of the deposits, may be found in the following sections and in other chapters in which geological, biostratigraphic and chronostratigraphic data are presented.

3 – LITHOGENESIS: GENERAL CONSIDERATIONS

Sediment Sources

The areas of the cave now under investigation must have formed a relatively passive recipient for coarse sediments derived from nearer the contemporary entrance(s) or from outside the cave. Similarly, the fine sediments are mostly allochthonous and some of them have demonstrably arrived from deeper within the system as well as from areas of the cave to the west of the excavations.

It is not necessarily valid to assume that a sediment was formed only shortly before its emplacement in the study areas. Both surface terrain and cave systems are capable of storing large quantities of sediment and of releasing them, millennia later, under very different environmental conditions from those during which the sediment was formed. Since so little is known about the geomorphological system of which Pontnewydd was a part, it is not even apparent to what extent sediments from originally discrete sources may have been mixed, perhaps long before they reached the study areas and by processes which had long since ceased to operate.

Consequently, there is as yet poor resolution, only allowing the recognition of very generalised sources, such as 'till' or 'cave entrance facies'. In the following sections, it should not be assumed that the term 'source' refers to temporally, or even geographically, discrete material. Furthermore, all 'sources' are at present hypothetical in that they have been inferred from mixed cave sediments. Although in the future it may be possible to identify actual sources *in situ*, it seems likely that much of this material would have been destroyed long ago. Hopefully, regional sediment bodies will prove an exception (*cf.* Embleton, Chapter II).

Speleothems

Major speleothems in growth position are comparitively rare at Pontnewydd and most of these have been dated by radiometric methods (Chapter IV). D(E):1 was clearly in place (dates D188:226al). The heterogeneous speleothem B(W):2 (date B274) was in place and contained material referred to *UBb* cemented into its base. The stalagmite D(N):4 (dates D534) was also convincingly *in situ* (*cf.* p.40). The stalagmitic boss C:4 (dates C0:78852 and C133) was disturbed but appeared to be approximately *in situ* (*cf.* p.38). The boss D(S):4 (date D604) was at a sediment boundary but was not cemented into the underlying *LBb* (*cf.* p.40). Thin spreads of stalagmite and an occurrence of dripstone, D(C):4, were *in situ* but have not been dated. Other dated speleothems recorded as having been *in situ*, or possibly *in situ*, were not observed by the author.

Most authorities are agreed upon the environmental implications of major speleothems in the British context:

"In general, stalagmite deposits are indicators of warm events in the paleoclimate record. However, present-day growth of speleothems in caves in a glacial environment serves as a warning that paleotemperature data may not directly reflect the true surface conditions." (Gascoyne, 1977, 209; *cf.* also Gascoyne, 1981). Again ". . . there are good reasons for supposing that speleothem deposition ceased, or was at least drastically reduced, during past periods of periglacial and glaciated conditions." (Atkinson *et al.*, 1978, 26).

Debris Flow

The deposits resulting from debris flow have rarely been examined in detail in the cave situation. For obvious reasons, exact reports of such flows observed in caves during the phase of faster movement are lacking. The subject has, however, been studied in open sites, especially in connection with the formation of alluvial fans. Statham gives a general description of this process: "One style of flowslide which has been noted in widely different climatic regimes and sediment types is the *debris flow*. Debris flows consist of a fluidized lobe of poorly-sorted coarse and fine sediments which originate on debris-mantled hillslopes. The lobe moves at a few kilometres an hour, leaving low ridges of debris or levées . . . on either side of its track as it goes. . . . The track itself may or may not be eroded by the passage of a debris flow; . . ." (1977, 93). Theoretical consideration of the various forces involved has been undertaken by many investigators (*cf.* Johnson, 1970; Fisher, 1971; Rodine and Johnson, 1976; Pierson, 1981).

Examination of the literature shows that debris flow is a complex process, with several different styles depending upon local geomorphology. In order to obtain information as closely applicable to caves as possible, we will concentrate on flows that, during some part of their descent, are restricted to channels.

Three zones of activity may be defined: (a) higher, steep slopes covered with debris, from which much of the sediment is derived by slippage or very rapid flow when the finite yield strength of the sediment is exceeded, usually after massive and sudden intake of water; (b) a middle zone of moderate slopes where flow is often confined to rock- or sediment-cut channels; and (c) a zone of low gradients where flow may be concentrated in ephemeral channels but, more often, is relatively unconcentrated and present as lobes and sheets (eg. outer margins of an alluvial fan).

The angle of slope required for initiation of debris flow depends largely upon the sediment type; reported angles vary from near vertical to a minimum of about 20° (*cf.* Statham, 1977).

The slope angle at which debris will continue to flow may be as little as 2° (Johnson, 1970; Pierson, 1980). Initiation of flows is always linked with the sudden availability of large quantities of water. The trigger mechanism may be high, but not necessarily exceptional, local rainfall (*cf.* Rapp, 1960; Prior *et al.*, 1970) or rapid melt, or partial melt (as in slush avalanches), of snow and ice (*cf.* Rapp, 1960; Jahn, 1967; Johnson, 1970). Climate is only important inasmuch as it may be considered that the trigger mechanisms are more or less likely to occur, or occur frequently, under given climatic conditions. Soil formation including a vegetation mat should reduce the frequency of debris flow events but might also ensure that they are more catastrophic when they do occur. Debris flow has often been observed in areas with a frozen substratum and, in this case, the distinction between debris flow and gelifluction is to some extent arbitrary. Debris flow is considered to be faster, often by several orders of magnitude, with initiation involving failure; continuation of the flow is not necessarily dependent upon the lateral persistence of the pergelisol.

At least in zones (b) and (c), observers report two distinct phases in the development of debris flows: (i) the true debris flow phase when comparatively viscous material with a high solid content is moving downslope, often as discrete pulses; (ii) a liquid phase, during which very muddy water is flowing (*cf.* Pierson, 1980). Temporary dams of debris often block channels, ponding water behind them; when the dams eventually rupture, the muddy water runs on ahead of the more slowly moving debris. Debris flow ceases when the combined effects of decreasing gradient and decreasing water content arrest the flow as internal frictional strength overcomes the kinetic forces. For a given sediment and a given gradient, this limiting point may be expressed as a critical thickness of deposit, below which it will not flow.

The amount of sediment transported in debris flows is obviously strictly a function of local conditions. Dry environments seem to produce most of the larger flows: R.H.Jahns (cited in Johnson, 1970) observed a flow in motion with a snout 35 feet high, whilst J.S.Shelton (cited in Johnson, 1970) recorded a frozen lobe, 2000 feet wide and 50 feet high. The upper velocity limit is similarly a function of slope, water content, sediment type, etc. Pierson (1980) records a peak velocity in channelled debris flow of 18 km./hour, corresponding to a debris discharge of 20 m³/sec. Much higher, but short lived velocities may develop near the source of the system if slippage as well as flow is involved. In some materials, much slower flows may occur, with velocities only slightly higher than in average gelifluction flows, if water content can be maintained for long periods.

Observations concerning the deposits and deposit geometry which result from debris flow are extremely varied and causative factors are sometimes obscure. All observers agree that the deposits are nearly always poorly or very poorly sorted; Pierson (1980) points out that this is necessary to prevent particle interlocking. Coarse elements may often float in the fine matrix. Reineck and Singh (1980) report poor graded bedding in more fluid flows but lack of such structure in viscous flows, whilst Fisher (1971) reports inverse grading. From the plates in Fisher's article, this feature would seem to be a zonation between coarser and finer particles rather than continuous grading. It seems probable that the reports of grading reflect a more general phenomenon which leads to sorting out of coarser particles towards all the boundaries of the flow; authors who record grading are either definitely referring to unchannelled flow or are making general statements with no reference to sediment geometry. Sharp (1942) named lateral ridges of coarser material "levées" and considered that they formed due to a 'snow-plough' effect at the snout; such a process has been confirmed by Statham (1976). However, Johnson (1970) and Pierson (1980, 1981) are convinced that a sorting process is also active within the flows (below p.56). Johnson (1970) reports coarser debris, carried near the middle upper surface of flows, which is moving faster than the flow mass; this debris therefore tips over the snout and is reabsorbed at the base, in the manner of 'caterpillar tracks'. Fisher (1971) records strong pebble orientation parallel to the base of the flow; Reineck and Singh (1980) confirm this in more fluid flows but report random and even vertical orientation in more viscous flows. Blatt, Middleton and Murray state: "Particles of non-spherical shape freely suspended in viscous shear flows tend to rotate continuously. The rate of rotation varies according to the orientation with respect to mean flow so that particles have a relatively high 'residence time' in orientations close to the flow direction." (1980, 122). Although it is not clear under what exact conditions the above observation was made, the present author has noted this behaviour in experimental debris flows. As the density of coarse particles increases, the tendancy towards horizontal bedding is accentuated due to interference between particles. Pseudo-vesicular structure, caused by entrapment of air, has been noted (Reineck and Singh, 1980).

Blatt, Middleton and Murray (1980) are the only authors amongst those cited above who have recognised the presence of imbricate structures in the coarse debris. They use this observation to question the generally accepted opinion that such structures indicate moderate to strong current (i.e. non-viscous flow) conditions in marine or fluviatile environments (cf. Pettijohn, 1975). These two points of view are not necessarily irreconcilable. It is suggested here that imbricate structures, developed in obvious debris flow sequences, might be due to the 'muddy water' phase noted by many observers.

Despite many general statements that debris flows may be entirely non-erosive, it is clear from the primary literature that, when confined within channels, the reverse may be true to a moderate or even radical degree (cf. Statham, 1976). Pierson (1980) reports up to ten metres of entrenchment in only a few days; he notes that it is the true debris flow phase, not the associated 'muddy water' phase, that is primarily responsible and cites corrasion as the process involved. Johnson (1970) considers the channels eroded by debris flows to be typically U-shaped. The 'snow-plough' effect at the snout, noted above, must also be erosive.

Given the diversity of observations on debris flows, it will be instructive to consider the main points of theoretical rheology that have been suggested to account for them. Sharpe (1938) considered these flows (included under the heading of "mudflows") to be due to continuous plastic deformation. Johnson (1970) has proposed a more complex Bingham viscosity model, combining aspects of Newtonian viscosity and plastic deformation, which seems to fit his experimental data quite well. Note that both the above models predict that velocity would be zero at the flow boundaries, a condition which cannot hold in reality. Such a flow could not be erosive by definition and observations recording the passage of debris flows with neither erosion nor deposition (cf. Statham, 1977) must reflect basal shear. Nevertheless, such models may be useful away from the boundary conditions. One of the results of the Bingham model is that velocity should increase away from channel sides until a stable velocity is achieved; a central "plug" of material, moving at maximum velocity but with little or no internal relative velocity, should result. Johnson uses this concept to explain how fragile objects can be transported within debris flows without damage. This might also help to account for the maintenance of discrete pockets of different sediments, although laminar flow at low shear rate gradients should accomplish the same end. Johnson's model requires that flow be laminar; Fisher (1971) supports this conclusion based upon his observation of parallel bedding of coarse elements. However, it is difficult to envisage truly laminar flow near irregular channel walls or where corrasion is actively eroding underlying sediments. Pierson (1980) has observed turbulent flow, indicated by downstream surface V-waves, at the height of each debris flow pulse; he states that lateral sorting of coarse debris is most effective at the transition from laminar to turbulent conditions. Just why V-waves should develop is not clear; turbulent flow should develop a velocity profile rather like the Bingham model. If the concept of Reynold's Number is applicable to such heterogeneous flows, with a given velocity and kinetic viscosity, turbulent flow will develop in a U-shaped channel more easily than in any other shaped channel of the same cross-sectional area.

Pierson (1981) also accepts Johnson's (1970) proposal that sorting may be achieved during laminar flow by dispersive pressure, involving migration of larger particles towards zones of lower shear rate. Johnson has also suggested that such a process should also produce a central core of coarse debris, which he likens to medial moraines in glaciers; it is difficult to accept Johnson's mathematical analysis on this point. Blatt, Middleton and Murray (1980) have pointed out that chaotic fabric should be characteristic of any central "plug" but this is only acceptable if the "plug" suffered practically no deformation.

One other form of debris flow may be mentioned briefly. The geologic record contains comparatively rare occurrences of tilloids that have been deposited as subaqueous flows (cf. Pettijohn, 1975). Individual beds may be tens of metres in thickness. Sliding and plastic deformation are usually involved and may even be dominant over true viscous flow. Erosion may be extreme, especially where slope suddenly increases. Because of constant total saturation reducing internal friction to a minimum, such flows are unstable and will easily be transformed into very high velocity turbidity currents. Most tilloids of this type contain some zones of good graded bedding, indicative of minor current events involving lift by turbulence.

As was noted at the beginning of this section, very little is known about debris flows in caves. Two factors, particularly characteristic of caves, should be of importance. First, few caves show simple slope profiles. Commonly caves are made up of alternating near horizontal passages and near vertical pitches; passages may even rise locally creating sumps. In plan, caves are also generally very much more tortuous than average surface channels. Boulder chokes and collapse blocks may effectively render a cave even more irregular. Consequently, the relatively simple pattern of erosion and deposition seen in open sites will have little chance to develop within a cave. The second factor of importance concerns the extremely slow draining of debris flows to be expected in most caves. With long term maintenance of the fluid state, local cave topography should be the main controlling factor in the development of flows.

Savage (1969) has described the events at G.B. Cave on Mendip, which led to the formation of a major debris flow. The sediments have still not been examined in detail, but several observations are strikingly reminiscent of features discussed above from open sites. The site lies only slightly above normally active streamways, so that flooding was also involved. The event was triggered by intense local rainfall. Lacustrine deposits in a small closed depression collapsed into the underlying cave. Further collapse was noted during the winter after the main event and it seems likely that this will continue for some years to come. When the present author visited the site in 1981, one side of the deep conical collapse cavity showed slumping with plastic deformation, but most of the perimeter was bounded by near vertical shear surfaces on which totally undisturbed lacustrine bedding was clear. Within the cave, the resulting debris flow (or flows) occupies one main topographic unit, extending up to c.100 metres from the point of entry. Savage's paper was published in March, 1969, some eight months after the initial collapse; events of December, 1968, are mentioned. He reports that at the time of writing large boulders were still moving in the "thick thixotropic mudflow" (op. cit., p.124), indicating that the deposit had not been able to drain and also illustrating the concept of critical thickness. Massive erosion of pre-existing deposits has taken place, at least beyond the observed debris flow. Much of this erosion was probably due to the large amounts of water which penetrated the system, both through the collapse cavity and through other surface links in the vicinity. It is tempting to visualise the possible destructive power that 'turbidity currents' might develop under these circumstances. The possibility of subaqueous flow or slide has also been suggested by Drew and Cohen (1980) for a fossil deposit in an Irish cave. It is to be hoped that data on the fabric and geometry of the G.B. Cave debris may become available in the near future.

Debris flows have sometimes been recognised more or less explicitly in caves in the past.

Till-derived material in unsorted deposits well within a cave may often indicate debris flow (eg. Cefn Cave, Dawkins, 1874; Cae Gwyn Cave, Hicks, 1886; Elder Bush Cave, Bramwell, 1964). Exotic material derived from alluvial gravels may be included in debris flows, as in the lower deposits of Joint Mitnor Cave★ and Pixie's Hole★, both in Devon. It is more difficult to recognise a debris flow if the source is purely local; Banwell Bone Cave★, Mendip, probably contains several such flows. A minor flow, this time in the upper levels at Pixie's Hole, reached a point within the cave where the slope changed from 5–10° to about 35°; it then channelled the underlying Late Pleistocene deposits to a depth of almost a metre, and with over five metres of headward erosion, redistributing fauna and Later Upper Palaeolithic artefacts up to 50 metres into the system. At Three Holes Cave★, Devon, a debris flow is exposed at the back of the cave, and contains masses of fauna, mostly carnivores, traces of a Lower Palaeolithic industry, and large numbers of truly spherical limestone cobbles. At La Belle-Roche, near Liège (Belgium), a debris flow has penetrated a low horizontal passage, carrying fauna and artefacts of Early Middle Pleistocene age (Cordy, 1980). It seems highly likely that debris flow was, and still is, a major agent in the development of cave sediments, at least in Europe. Such deposits must often have gone unnoticed; examination of the archaeological and palaeontological literature shows that, even when advanced wear or rolling of bones, limestone clasts and artefacts has been recorded well within a cave, excavators are still too ready to blame such processes as 'cryoturbation'.

The implications of the above survey for the study of the Pontnewydd sediments are many. First, it is clear that nowhere in the deposits are slopes sufficiently high to initiate debris flow. Although it is difficult to assess overall slope in these fragmented exposures, most bedding angles seem to lie between 2° and 5°, dipping into the cave. It is therefore necessary to suggest source areas for all the flows that lay at relatively high altitudes, most probably equal to or greater than the height of the cave roof at the present entrance. Source areas might have been provided by steep surface slopes, by some near vertical cavity in the cave system itself which has since been destroyed, or by some sort of piping or failure of major valley fill (eg. till) which had previously buried the cave mouth.

Once a flow had penetrated the extant areas of the cave, it is difficult to see why it should stop until it was forced to do so by cave topography. Note that debris flow possesses not only momentum but also limited cohesive strength, allowing it to override minor obstacles (cf. the effect of DPS:14 on later flows). In that a flow would tend to lose water to well below the critical level only when it had already reached stability within the local topography, it follows that it could never later be remobilised as a flow without massive erosion to re-establish high gradients. We might therefore expect flows to be represented as generally tabular bodies of sediment. Making due allowance for any later removal, this is exactly what is observed in *LBb* and *UBb* as they are defined above. Any other correlation scheme requires flows to change thickness radically with no apparent external influence; the physics of such a situation are difficult to visualise. Furthermore, had a flow in fact been arrested for any reason within the excavated areas, we would expect to find a well characterised armoured snout; such features would appear to be absent.

It has been noted that channelled debris flow is often erosive. That this is also true of the Pontnewydd material is indicated by several different observations. First, debris flow deposits, though generally tabular, may also be seen to occupy localised channels in underlying sediments; this is particularly clear in Area D(C). That these channels are not wholly the result of earlier erosion by running water is suggested by the lack of sediments characteristic of this process within the *Cm* sequence, and also by the survival of 'vulnerable' deposits, such as *Sb,* perched on top of the channel banks. Several units interpreted as debris

★ Unpublished research by S.N. Collcutt.

flows, such as some of the components of *Ic,* are only 10–20 cm. thick. Although precise quantification would be necessary to prove the point, it would seem highly likely that such thicknesses are well below the critical thickness for flow in such coarse deposits at these low angles of slope. Much sediment must therefore have been eroded even when channelling is not obvious. There is a series of quite continuous lithologic gradients, starting with the highest lithozones of *Sm* and passing upwards through the *Cm* sequence: (a) limestone particles become increasingly common upwards; (b) siliceous pebbles become decreasingly common upwards; (c) siltstone and mudstone pebbles become increasingly fractured upwards; (d) non-carbonate sand becomes increasingly finer upwards; (e) silt and carbonate fine sand become increasingly common upwards; (f) organic matter, usually very rich in *Ic,* becomes increasingly rarer in the deposits above (*cf.* Figs.III.13–18 and Pl.XII). Although these trends are undoubtedly reinforced by changes in primary sediment source through time, operating to the west of the excavated areas, the smooth persistence of the trends is most efficiently explained by reworking of old debris flows by each new one. Indeed, *LBb* in Area D(C) contains small discrete pockets of the underlying *Ic* sediments. The fact that flame structures, plications or push features have not been recorded in the present exposures may indicate that sediments underlying each new flow did not themselves become fluidised, thus underlining the importance of an initial steep slope. Note that it would seem unlikely that much coarse debris was contributed from the walls and roof of the cave in the immediate vicinity of the excavations. There are no major rubble cones or large blocks of limestone and no obvious feeder chimneys. The placement of ancient stalagmites under extant prominent rock pendants argues for long term stability of the roof.

Apart from the observation that debris flows *may* transport fragile objects without damage, there has been little consideration of how included coarser particles could be modified. Pebble fracturing (*cf.* Fig.III.18) is here considered to be the result of point loading, torsion or even impact, situations which might be expected to arise quite regularly in debris flows (*cf.* Currant, p.177, where the conditions of larger bones is discussed). Mechanical rounding has been noted in gelifluction flows and rockslides only after transport over considerable distances. There would appear to be even less reason to expect better lubricated debris flows to round coarse material to any great extent. Rounding may only be attributed to this transport process with any certainty when it is minor (i.e. edge-rounding) and is present on chemically unaltered clasts. At Pontnewydd, highly rounded and spherical stalagmite fragments and limestone particles are primarily the result of postdepositional alteration (*infra*). Transport of already altered material by debris flow should result in differential preservation, with most smaller particles being crushed to fine sediment and only larger spherical cobbles surviving (*cf.* p.58). No trace of any such deposit has been observed at Pontnewydd.

There has been little opportunity as yet to study the internal organisation of each debris flow. However, sorting of the type recognised in open sites has obviously been in operation. It is most probable that future quantification of spatial trends in shape, size, orientation and damage of sediment particles, bones (*cf.* p.174) and artefacts (*cf.* Chapter V) could be related to local details of flow regime and cave morphology. The general sorting trend already explains why the apparently unpromising remnants of sediment, left by earlier excavators against the walls and in small side passages, have proved to be so rich in large artefacts. The scope for an integrated taphonomic approach is substantial.

Plate XIII represents experimental debris flow produced in the laboratory with material of *UBb* from Area D(C). Particles of over 15 mm. diameter have been removed in order to scale down the flow. The velocity profile and lateral sorting are already apparent in (a). The velocity profile is more clearly shown in (b). The tendancy towards bedding parallel to the basal surface is seen in the long sections of (c). The cross-sections of (d) show sorting of coarser particles towards the flow boundaries and particularly towards the outer edges.

60

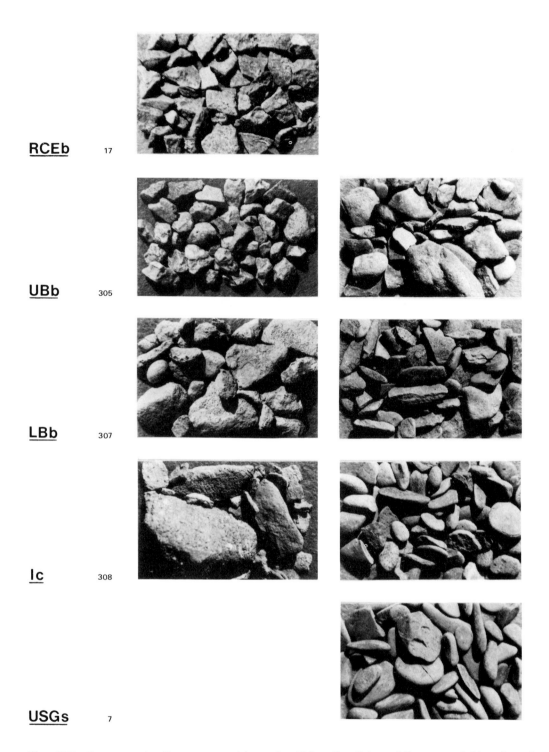

RCEb 17

UBb 305

LBb 307

Ic 308

USGs 7

Plate XII   Representative limestone particles and pebbles. Condition of limestone (left) and mudstone and siltstone (right) in PN sediment samples from major stratigraphic units. Particle sizes shown centre upon the fine gravel class.

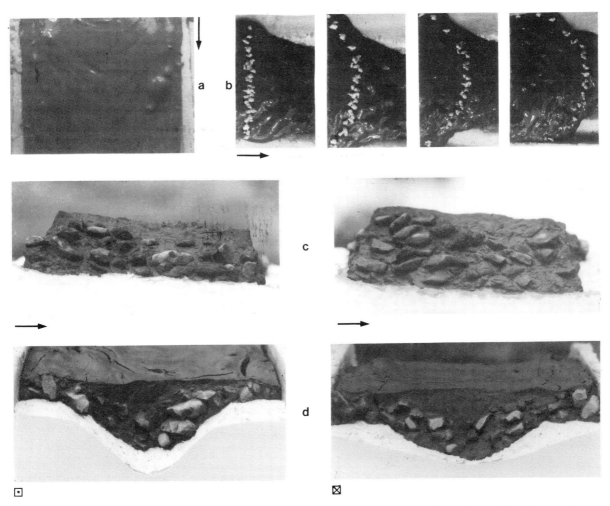

Plate XIII Experimental debris flow. (*cf.* p. 60). (a) Flow in motion seen from above. (b) Progressive distortion of a line of polystyrene chips floating on the surface of the flow. (c) Long sections of arrested flow. (d) Cross-sections of arrested flow. Arrow indicates direction of flow; flow towards observer in d (left) and away from observer in d (right).

Diagenesis and Carbonate Mobility

The presence in caves of deposits cemented by carbonates is commonplace; traditionally, though often rather inaccurately, such deposits have been called 'cave breccias'. They are usually interpreted as being due to postdepositional changes under warm, damp climatic conditions (*cf.* Schmid, 1969; Miskovsky, 1974), a proposition which is readily defensible if a vertical gradient has developed, suggesting strong leaching and/or input of carbonate-rich water. However, some cave deposits show lateral gradients in cementation, or no significant gradient at all, and may be well beyond the reach of large quantities of aggressive water, as at Pontnewydd. Furthermore, there is a marked tendency in Europe for older deposits to be more highly cemented than younger ones under similar topographic conditions. This would suggest that more complex processes may sometimes be involved rather than a single phase of postdepositional cementation under climatic control.

First, it should be noted that the Pontnewydd sediments do in fact show one type of sub-surface carbonate deposition which is definitely under direct climatic control. The deposits of both *UCSb* and *RCEb* contain quite abundant crystalline dendritic concretions that are obviously root casts. Indeed, roots, sometimes still alive, have been observed in association with these concretions even in the East Passage. Modern roots were common in the disturbed material and tip which covered the sections of *in situ* deposits before the present excavations. However, root casts have never led to even partial consolidation of the deposits.

When considering cemented sediments within a limestone cave, it is always necessary to consider the possibility of both external and internal sources for the carbonate cement. The former involves the penetration of carbonate-rich water, whilst the latter involves the penetration, or development within the deposit, of aggressive water which will mobilise existing carbonates. In practice, the same water may fluctuate between an aggressive and a non-aggressive state very rapidly and over very short distances. Since it may be argued that DPS:14 is unlikely to have had a significant original limestone content (*cf.* p.69), it will be best to start the discussion with that deposit, although the accuracy of this assumption makes little difference to the argument presented here.

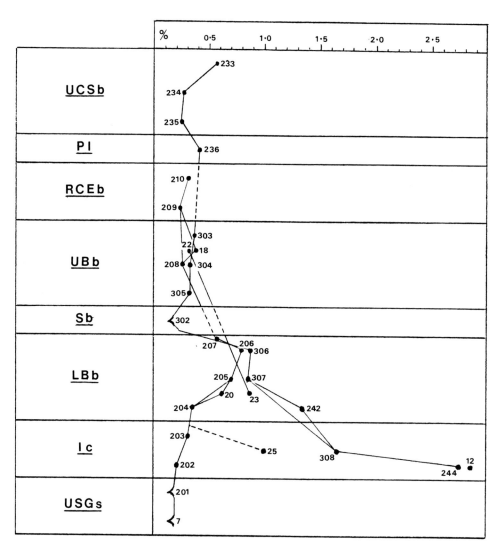

Fig. III.13 Percentage organic matter in the fraction under 1 mm. Points are PN sediment samples linked in stratigraphic sequences. NaOH extraction; colorimetric results; calibration by ignition of peat extract.

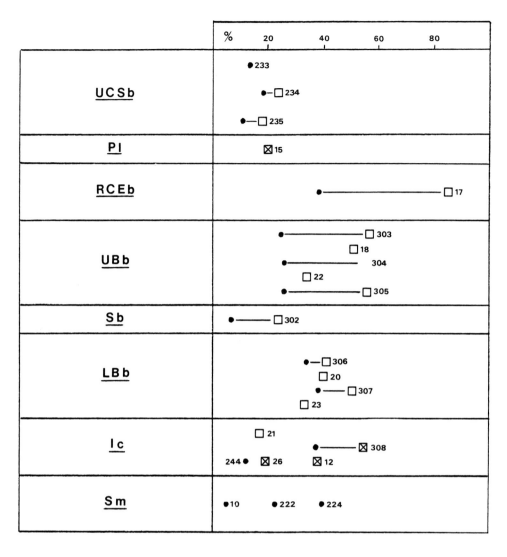

●% less than 1 mm.   □ % 1.000-0.063 mm.
☒ approximate value due to masking by organics + FeMnAl

Fig. III.14 Carbonate content. Points are PN sediment samples. Weight loss after cold 20% HCl treatment.

DPS:14 consists of pebbles that are supported in a matrix of coarse siliceous sand and clay, the whole being massively cemented, mostly by carbonates. Such a deposit would not be expected to have contained large primary voids, yet DPS:14 now has irregular and abundant vugs up to 5 mm. across, indicating that fines have been removed. The vugs are lined with drusy calcite crystals that may either show good euhedral development of the free faces or, in other areas, smooth hummocky surfaces. Sand grains, small pebbles and etched calcite crystals often float in younger clear calcite. Some vugs are partially filled with uncemented fine sand and silt. There are even tortuous vugs developed along the contacts between large calcite crystals. In some areas there are scalenohedral crystals up to 5 mm. long, whilst elsewhere there are patches of white, friable calcite. No hypothesis that does not involve major and recurrent remobilisation of carbonates can account for all these features.

Carbonate particles in *Ic* are heavily altered, whilst those in overlying units are progressively less so. Limestone clasts may be reduced to a fragile cryptocrystalline skeleton with very high porosity. Fragments of stalagmite may be vuggy, but more commonly regular porosity, at right angles to the bedding, has been developed along the contacts between the

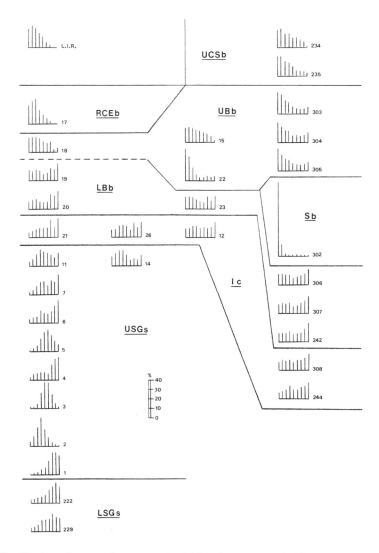

Fig. III.15 Size distribution of non-carbonate sands. 0.09 to 2.00 mm. at half Φ intervals, coarsest to the right. Bar-charts represent PN sediment samples. Dry sieving.

original prismatic crystals. Voids are usually still open but there are varying amounts of more or less crystalline cement with common impurities. There are also frequent patches of coarse crystalline mosaic, which could be truly neomorphic but which are beyond doubt primarily authigenic. Some fragments of speleothem have been completely reduced to a fragile, biscuity consistency.

Mass cementation at Pontnewydd is usually most highly developed near the cave walls, reflecting the control over drainage exercised by the bedrock morphology. Note especially the smoothly vaulted roof which favours sheet flow rather than drip. Much external carbonate could be introduced into the deposits with this water. However, even ignoring the alteration of carbonate particles noted above, the fact that most units of *Ic*, with very low carbonate content, are much more weakly cemented than *LBb*, with a higher but often only slightly less altered limestone content, indicates that internal carbonates have contributed significantly to the cement. Note that the unusually high level of corrosion seen in all the Area C deposits is probably due to the fact that they are blocking what may be an important drainage channel.

The question now arises as to how water may become aggressive in such an environment. Only when water penetrates very rapidly from the land surface in the form of stream flow might some major corrosive potential be maintained (*cf. Pan lithozone*). Otherwise it is necessary to invoke such processes as *Mischungskorrosion,* variations in agitation and flow rate of water, or fluctuation in the availability of chemical inhibitors and catalysts, all operating on the scale of individual pores and over very considerable lengths of time. The presence of nitrogenous organic matter will raise the local pH, at least until the most soluble humic and fulvic acids have been leached out. Organic phosphates will also react with carbonates.

This is diagenesis rather than 'weathering'. The process may accelerate, slow or change emphasis according to prevailing climate, but it is essentially a continuous modification of the geochemistry of the cave deposits. As a general statement, it may be said that only the silicates approximate to closed systems under such conditions.

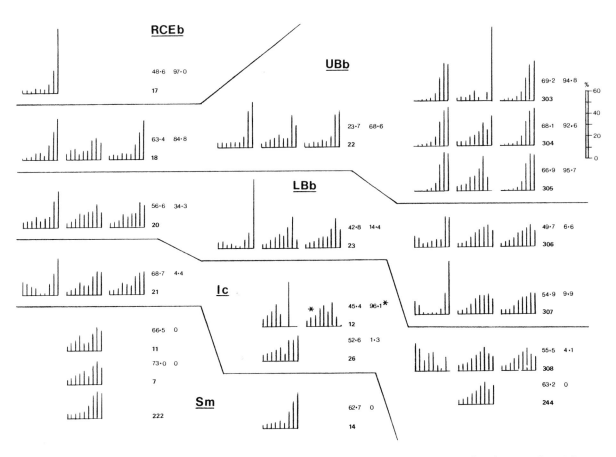

Fig. III.16 Coarse particles. Bar-charts, representing PN sediment samples, show size distribution of particles 1.0 to 22.6 mm. at half Φ intervals, coarsest to the right. For a given sample, the charts show carbonate particles (left), pebbles (middle) and the combined distribution (right). Material over 2.0 mm. was classed by hand using square-cut templates. Two percentages are marked for each sample: 1.0 to 22.6 as a percentage of total less than 22.6 (left) and percentage carbonate in the 1.0 to 22.6 fraction. ★ carbonate-rich aggregates only.

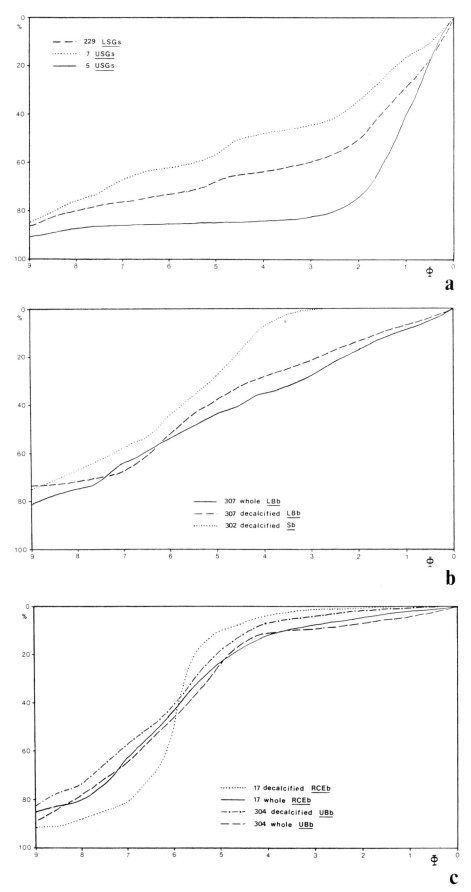

Fig. III.17   Representative particle size distributions of material under 2 mm. (a, b and c). PN sediment samples plotted. Wet separation at 0.063 mm.; dry sieving of sands; hydrometer method for silts and colloids. Size scales in Φ units (range shown 0.002 to 2.000 mm.)

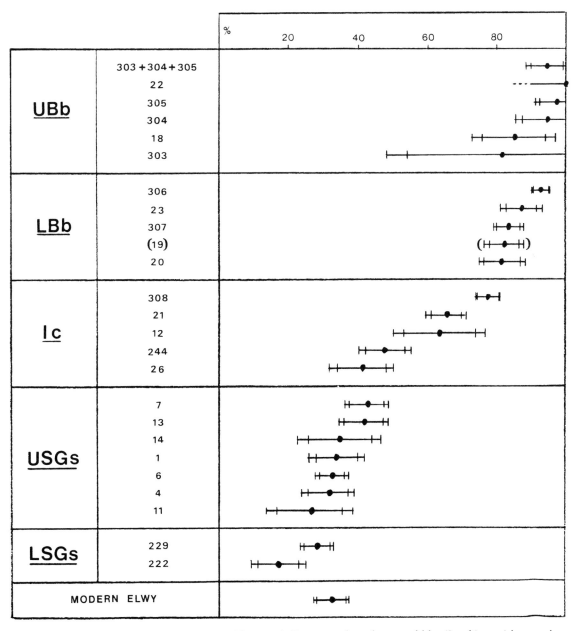

Fig. III.18 Pebble fracturing. Percentages of fractured siltstone and mudstone pebbles (8 to 16 mm.) by number
counts. Points are PN sediment samples. Bars represent confidence intervals:
$$p \pm (z\sqrt{(pq/n)} + 50/n), \quad z(95\%) = 1.96, \quad z(99\%) = 2.576.$$

4 – DEVELOPMENT OF THE PONTNEWYDD SEQUENCE

The Siliceous member

The gravels and coarser sands of these deposits consist of various siliceous rocks which are
foreign to the hard-rock basement of the Pontnewydd area. Texturally, the majority of the
larger particles are siltstones and mudstones with similar mechanical properties, but other
types, including some crystalline rocks, also occur. Rocks of this general character are still
common in the modern Elwy and are also present in the sediments of the valley slopes.
Their petrology and source is discussed elsewhere (Ch. VIIIC) but it is clear that a powerful
transport medium would have been necessary to bring them to the vicinity of the cave. It
seems most likely that glacial transport was involved (cf. Bull, Embleton and Bevins (this

volume)), though it is uncertain how much fluvial modification occurred before emplacement in the cave. These are quite soft rocks but none of the stigmata usually associated with glacial action have been observed on material from the cave. Overall pebble shape is wholly controlled by the bedding planes in the siltstone and mudstone; in these deposits, and also higher in the sequence, discoidal and ellipsoidal forms, with their main development parallel to the bedding, are always dominant. That some fluvial modification has taken place is indicated by the relatively common wear cupules which are probably the result of trapped, but not totally immobilised pebbles rubbing against each other in a fluid medium.

The mode of emplacement of these deposits appears quite variable. Many of the finer beds are indicative of flowing water, although they are never as well sorted as the deposits of average surface streams. The relatively high colloid content of these beds is of interest (cf. Fig. III.17 a) since the colloids are not present as discrete laminae but are distributed throughout the sediment. The finest beds, such as DPS:2, are silty and very badly sorted, suggesting settling in still water.

The coarse gravel beds, which make up the bulk of this member, are obviously not the product of an efficient stream. Sorting in these beds is extremely poor and irregular. However, they are not purely dry collapse deposits, since they are often bedded and may show imbrication. There is again a high colloid content, with colloids most apparent on the undersides of pebbles. Bull (pers. comm.) has pointed out that this feature is referable to clay rafting often seen in debris flows. However, there are also lesser amounts of colloids all over the pebbles, sometimes forming a very thin but continuous 'skin'. Given the probable antiquity of the deposits and the texture of the component rocks, liberation of fines from the rocks themselves cannot be ruled out as a source for at least part of the colloid content, both of the gravels and, indeed, of the finer beds. On the other hand, many beds show a degree of matrix support for the coarser elements that cannot be accounted for by such alteration products.

Whatever the exact mechanisms responsible for the emplacement of this material, they do not appear to have been particularly violent or disruptive. Samples of siltstone and mudstone pebbles (8–16 mm.) have been extracted from several beds in this member and compared with similar material from the modern Elwy. Particular attention was paid to pebbles fractured across bedding planes. These were counted, care being taken to eliminate the rare fresh breaks which may have occurred during sampling. Figures for *LSGs* and *USGs* are not significantly higher than those for the Elwy (cf. Fig.III.18), suggesting that emplacement was still a fluid process with little confined rotation and crushing. Note that fracturing due to alteration and compaction, observed in some pebbles at the base of DPS:13 against the bedrock, is quite different, producing splitting along bedding planes, crazing and very blocky break surfaces.

From the above discussion, it would appear that inefficient stream flow and ponding played some part in the development of *Sm*. However, the bulk of the deposits are referable to debris flows of relatively low viscosity. It was suggested above that imbricate structures might reflect the 'muddy water' phase often associated with such flows; the structures also indicate that flow was towards the east into the cave. It is even possible that sediments showing good graded bedding may indicate subaqueous debris flows that have briefly attained sufficient velocity to act as miniature 'turbidity currents'. The restricted exposures of these sediments exclude discussion of deposit geometry and the erosive power of the flows.

When comparing *LSGs* and *USGs,* it can be seen that the beds of the former are slightly more organised, although the extremely small exposure calls for caution. It is possible that *LSGs* represents more efficient stream action with fewer debris flow events. The character which served to establish the unit differentiation is the presence of several horizons of strong carbonate deposition in *LSGs,* whilst carbonates are usually totally absent in *USGs* away from the cave walls. It is clear that sedimentation in *LSGs* was interrupted by at least two periods of quiescence, during which carbonates and associated sesquioxides could be precipitated. If DPS:14 is indeed in stratigraphic order, and is not a much older deposit (there are no obvious lithologic characters which set it apart from the other beds of *LSGs*) then the last event evidenced in this unit is another, more massive cementation phase which would probably have taken a relatively long time. Note, in passing, that this deposit shows strong near vertical orientation of pebbles, probably indicating extremely viscous flow or even wet collapse. The total lack of limestone particles or ghosts, coupled with the coarseness of the sands (the limestone insoluble residue contains mostly fine sand and silt; *cf.* Fig.III.15), indicate that this cementation is unlikely to have been merely an authigenic effect. In any case, DPS:14 must have been already cemented in order to resist the influx of *USGs.* Finer beds of *USGs* fill channels around the mass of DPS:14 and several of the coarser beds override it. It is interesting that the only bed in *USGs* which contains carbonates, not apparently derived from the deposits above or from the walls, is DPS:2. This is a deposit that formed by settling under quiet conditions when some carbonate could be trapped. The obvious inference is that *USGs* represents a more continuous and probably a more rapid accumulation than *LSGs.*

The available evidence is not sufficient to determine whether there is any climatic significance in this change of sedimentation pattern. The difference between *LSGs* and *USGs* could be due to very localised topographic mechanisms. However, the low organic content of *Sm* as a whole (less than 0.2% in the fraction below 1 mm.) would indicate that a closed vegetation cover was not present in the vicinity of the cave at any time during the deposition of these beds.

One further point is worthy of discussion. The absence of limestone particles in these deposits as a whole is rather puzzling. Not only are clasts absent but so too are the dark, sticky ghosts that usually survive in ancient gravelly deposits in caves (eg. the lower levels at Joint Mitnor Cave, Devon★). Total removal of all traces of limestone would seem highly unlikely, especially since those units which show good bedding have never been observed to display the sort of disruption one would expect to see after patchy loss of volume. Note that one or two limestone blocks, *c.*15 cm. thick, were in fact found well into *Sm* towards the north side of the Deep Sounding. They appeared to have fallen from the nearby channel walls. They were corroded but by no means totally unsound, requiring a lump hammer to break them. It would seem that this member never contained limestone. Yet there is a major rockface above the cave. The sediments of *Sm* cannot therefore have been derived from any surface deposit (till, terrace material, etc.) that lay exposed for long with its upper surface near the level of the cave entrance. There would seem to be three possible explanations: (a) more or less pure exotic sediment was introduced into some part of the cave system west of the study areas very shortly after it arrived in the vicinity and before it could be polluted with limestone from the cliffs and slopes above; (b) exotic sediment was introduced via vertical cavities directly from the plateau above, where there were no cliffs in a position to supply limestone; (c) the sediments were derived from within a thick exotic sediment body that choked the valley to well above the level of the cave. These suggestions are similar to those put forward during the discussion of initial slope requirements for debris flows (p.58). If major fluvial deposits are envisaged as the immediate source of the *Sm* sediments under (a) above, it should be remembered that even the modern Elwy, in the present period of comparatively low scree production, contains significant quantities of limestone. Therefore, for this hypothesis to be tenable, it must be supported by an explanation for the lack of limestone in the cave deposits. The author is unable to suggest any such explanation.

★ Unpublished research by S.N. Collcutt

The Intermediate complex

It has already been stated that the sediments grouped into this complex are extremely heterogeneous and fragmented. If the information base improves in the future, it is possible that some units may be reallocated. Nevertheless, the complex is justifiable on lithogenetic grounds, both because the components contain the first traces of sediment derived from a strictly local source and because it is desirable to maintain the integrity of the overlying *LBb* as a single sedimentary event.

B/C:2 and D:8 represent modified sediments which, at least in their pebble and sand components, generally resemble some beds of *USGs* (such as B/C:3), beds from which they were probably in part derived. Sorting is even worse than in *USGs,* large pebbles (over 32 mm.) are rare or absent and there is a general increase in pebble fracturing. The major difference between these deposits and *USGs* lies in the important organic and carbonate contents of the former. The organic matter is present as dark amorphous coatings on mineral particles, often associated with considerable quantities of sesquioxides. The term 'sesquioxide' is used here, as elsewhere, to refer to material in which at least iron and manganese have been detected; the exact structure of the minerals has not yet been studied and it is likely that complicated oxides and hydrates are in fact involved. In B/C:2, the high carbonate content is distributed throughout the sediment with little structure; there are some highly altered carbonate sand grains which may be particulate in nature rather than precipitational. In D:8, much of the carbonate is highly organised into 'fish scales' lying horizontally in the sediments; these forms grade into some larger plaques of carbonate, up to 10 mm. long and 2 mm. thick. All these carbonates are heavily corroded. Organic matter and sesquioxides are associated with the carbonates, but they are always richest at the top surface and decrease down into the body of the carbonate particle, suggesting that the association is at least partly due to infiltration. Just how these 'fish scales' formed is not yet clear. They are generally too bulky to represent calcite rafts originating on a still water surface. They could possibly be the reworked remains of thin rimstone, but their good horizontal development, within a deposit that almost certainly represents minor debris flow and which is not itself particularly well bedded, favours a postdepositional origin. It is possible that they were precipitated from fluctuating carbonate-rich waters, which periodically saturated the sediments but never actually overlaid them as a free body (*cf.* absence of cap sediments deposited in water, but note possible erosive power of overlying debris flows). In these Areas, organic matter and carbonates have often penetrated the top of the underlying *USGs* deposits, so that it may be difficult to define an exact boundary (*cf.* D(C) in particular).

In Area D(C), the deposits of D:7 directly overlie the sediments described above. Much material has been reworked from D:8 but there is also a small, though significant content of highly corroded limestone particles, some of them quite large (*c.* 5 cm.). Note also the important bone component. The unit occupies a wide and very shallow trough which is probably erosional, but there is no true channelling of the underlying sediments. Again, this is a minor debris flow which is, in its own right, lithologically intermediate between D:8 and *LBb* in this Area.

In Area B, the situation is rather different. B:8 contains a few altered limestone particles, moderate quantities of finer carbonates and some bone material. The sand and gravel contents resemble those of *USGs* in this Area, although the pebbles are significantly more fractured. However, for some reason, either locational or temporal, there was no input of organic matter or sesquioxides. From what little can be seen of its geometry, it is possible that this bed represents a lateral debris flow, associated with the South Fissure and channelling the underlying *USGs*. Fabric studies will be necessary to confirm this suggestion. The blocks of stalagmite, which constitute B:7, were almost certainly derived from a major travertine floor, but all that can be deduced from their present stratigraphic position is that they must have been formed prior to the emplacement of *LBb*. It is interesting that this stalagmite contains significant quantities of organic matter, on average *c.*1.0%. Although the stalagmite is badly corroded, showing orthogonal development of porosity with respect to the bedding, the organics are not located in the pores but are stratified in very thin spreads between laminae of calcite. This organic matter is certainly syndepositional with the calcite. The organic content of other major speleothems in the cave has not yet been measured. Note that, in all other Areas, *LBb* contains small fragments of stalagmite but never anything like the concentration seen in B:7.

Lithozones 4 and 3 of Area GC(S) have not yet been studied in detail. GC(S):4 probably represents a decomposed speleothem. It is not clear how these two dpeosits may relate to the other units of *Ic*.

Attempting to interpret this complex may be somewhat premature. However, merely as a working hypothesis, it is suggested that the influence of an interglacial, or at least a major interstadial, is present. The inference is drawn solely on the association of organic matter and carbonate precipitation, an association which implies the presence of soils and vegetation in the vicinity of the cave. Such high levels of organics in non-fluvial sediments have only been observed by this author in certainly, or most probably, interglacial cave sites in this country, for instance, in the Hyaena Stratum at Tornewton Cave (Devon)★, in the talus cone (Layer 3) at Joint Mitnor Cave (Devon)★ and in Unit III at Sun Hole (Mendip; Collcutt, Currant and Hawkes, 1981). As at Pontnewydd, the organics are always present as amorphous coatings on sand grains or in association with calcite. The absolute levels of organics at Pontnewydd are similar to the maxima reported by Jefferson (1976) from modern cave sediments in South Wales. Jenkins (p.185) has indicated the presence of weathered minerals in the *Intermediate complex*, although Bull (p.79) has not recognised any strong pedogenic features on the quartz grains.

Beyond this hypothesis, it may be said that the sediments of *Ic* show signs of a complicated series of events, including debris flows. Unfortunately, the present restricted and frag-mented exposures are not sufficient to clarify the matter further.

The Lower Breccia bed

That some local material was already reaching the study areas from the direction of the cave entrance during some part of the deposition of *Ic* is evidenced by the inclusion of small quantities of limestone. The major debris flow of *LBb* continues this trend, the deposit having a higher and more evenly distributed limestone content. Other trends are also continued, such as increased pebble fracturing. A particularly pebbly facies of this unit, D:5, could possibly represent a separate (younger) flow, but it would appear more likely that it is the result of a collapse of a coarse remnant of *Ic* or *USGs* onto the surface of the main flow while the latter was still in motion. Partial integrity would be maintained by differential shear as long as flow remained more or less laminar (*cf.* p.56). The fine matrix of D:5 is almost identical to that of D:6. In Area D(C), *LBb* occupies a wide trough, as does *Ic* below it, but the trough is deeper, showing a tendency towards true channelling. Although not particularly marked, there is also a suggestion that some large particles have been displaced towards the cave walls.

The environmental implications of *LBb* are obscure. The scale of the debris flow is quite impressive. The portion removed by the various excavations alone totals some 55 cubic

---

★Unpublished research by S.N. Collcutt.

metres at a conservative estimate, and the whole flow may originally have been an order of magnitude larger. The drop in the organic content of this unit compared with *Ic* is quite marked. There is no evidence for a fresh influx of organic matter and the moderately rich organics that do exist could easily have been derived from sediments reworked from *Ic* or from the main source of *Ic*. These two factors might imply conditions cooler than full interglacial but, without exact knowledge concerning the morphology of the cave entrance and of the source sediment bodies, such factors could be misleading.

The Stalagmite lithozone and Silt beds

At some time after the emplacement of *LBb*, stalagmites began to grow on its surface wherever the roof morphology was favourable. Radiometric dating of speleothems (*cf.* Chapter IV) suggests that this process took place over tens of thousands of years, though not necessarily continuously. The shape of the stalagmite D(N):4 suggests that speleothem formation was waning at that point, although this may have happened at some time within this lengthy chronozone rather than at its end. That so little sedimentation occurred over such a long period can only be explained by assuming that this part of the cave was almost totally sealed off from more active areas, and especially from the land surface. Indeed, the stalagmites themselves suggest a relatively isolated cave environment.

Certainly towards the back of the cave, but probably rather further west than the extant exposures, a large pool formed in which badly sorted fine sand and silt settled. These sediments are rhythmites but further study will be necessary to ascertain whether there is likely to be any regular periodicity. Carbonate precipitation continued, at least during the earlier stages of pool sedimentation, and is represented by thin stalagmite laminae interstratified with *Sb*.

The sediments of *Sb* need have no climatic implications. From the point of view of overall particle size, the material could easily have been derived from existing deposits by elutriation. However, Currant (p.177) has recorded a new fauna, Bull (p.84) a new quartz grain suite and Jenkins (p.183) a degree of mineral alteration from these beds, all of which would indicate 'cold' conditions. If these authors are satisfied that the new material represents a direct link with the contemporary surface environment, and not just reworking of older sediments stored somewhere in the system, the fact that *Sb* has a low organic content may be significant. It will obviously be informative to examine stratified subsamples of *Sb* in order to identify any temporal trends. Horizontal variation in particle size or composition or in thickness of laminations might indicate the direction of the source(s).

The Upper Breccia bed

This unit represents the best preserved debris flow yet examined. It also shows the most developed structure, including many of the features noted above in the survey of the literature on this subject. There is marked lateral sorting of both coarser elements and platy or elongate elements, the central region being composed almost exclusively of small, compact limestone clasts floating in the fine matrix. In Area D(C), the flow occupies a channel, *c.* 50 cm. deeper than the normal tabular occurrences and *c.* 175 cm. across, situated roughly in the middle of the chamber along the same vertical axis as the troughs occupied by *Ic* and *LBb*. The nature of the substratum seems to have had little effect upon the erosive power of the flow; in places the uncemented silts of *Sb* are intact, whilst in others *UBb* has cut deeply into the coarse material of *LBb*. In Area B, the flow has eroded underlying deposits right across the Fissure and at a relatively steep angle, suggesting that there was a significant increase in gradient towards the south. It seems possible that *UBb*, with its greater organisation, may have been a more fluid event than *LBb* or the components of *Ic*.

This deposit contains a much higher proportion of limestone fragments than the units beneath it. C:3 and the base of D:2 have very high fine sand and silt contents, material clearly derived from reworking of *Sb*. However, the matrix of *UBb* is generally much finer than that of *LBb*, even in Area B which was presumably 'upstream' of the pool. Limestone clasts in a matrix of such fine material would form a typical cold climate entrance facies.

The Red Cave-Earth bed

Sadly, this unit is only present as an extremely restricted deposit in Area B. It is exactly the sort of entrance facies sediment referred to above. That its present position is again due to debris flow, or perhaps slightly slower mass movement, is shown by the rare fractured siliceous pebbles and by the rounded edges of the otherwise unaltered and angular limestone clasts. The matrix is so rich in silt (*cf*. Fig.III.17c) that there is a good possibility of an aeolian source. The insoluble residue of the local limestone has a similar particle size distribution and many of the extant slope deposits in the Pontnewydd area have high silt contents. The silts in *RCEb* are probably extremely local wind sorted material rather than sediments of any regional importance.

The lack of cementation and alteration in *RCEb* is of interest, especially since the exposure is very close to the cave wall. It seems highly unlikely that the cave could have remained generally dry after the emplacement of *RCEb* if this unit is of any great antiquity. Bull (*pers. comm.*) has remarked upon the apparent absence of desiccation cracks throughout the deposits. Some shrinkage may have helped to open up the gaps between the stratified deposits and the walls, gaps which are now full of younger sediment, but preferential drainage is much more likely to have been responsible for the main development of these features. It is therefore inferred that *RCEb* is significantly younger than *UBb* and, furthermore, that it is a relatively recent deposit.

The Upper Deposits

The *Pan lithozone, Upper Clay and Sand beds, Laminated Travertine lithozone* and the *Earthy lithozone* form a sequence that is extremely common in British caves. During a glaciation, permafrost, or even actual ice-sheets and their associated basement till, seal off the influent sections of a cave system. Water, which would normally be quickly absorbed into fissures and sink-holes, flows overland. Major influent systems are rapidly blocked by mass movement of various types. What little water that still penetrates the cave can only carry the finest material, sediment which is quickly deposited, clogging the formerly active drainage system. When the permafrost breaks down, for example near the end of a glaciation, masses of water are released, pushing sediment chokes deeper into the system. In order to re-establish the old drainage pattern and equilibrium with the local geomorphology, streams must excavate down through the choked conduits, much as surface streams must clear their choked valleys. This will be quite a lengthy process. In the mean time, streams will flow out to the surface through high, previously long abandoned sections of the system. Even if deep conduits are in fact open, the vadose zone may remain 'perched' if valleys are still buried under relatively impermeable sediments.

This is clearly what has happened at Pontnewydd. At the onset of stream flow, the immediately subjacent deposits were violently altered *(Pl)*, a process which was quickly inhibited by the deposition of clays by the stream itself (*cf*. D(E):4). The presence of clay pellets shows that the stream was eroding existing clayey deposits and that it was probably rather more energetic than the particle size distribution would at first suggest. That this phase of sedimentation was quite rapid is shown by the later contortion of these clays, which probably resulted through loading of originally badly compacted material. Had the majority of the older deposits not been cemented, much more considerable erosion might have occurred. It is not clear whether the stream flowed right out of the present entrance, but it certainly flowed at some time into the South Fissure, removing all but the threshold occurrence of the uncemented *RCEb*. No fine stream deposits or water-worn rock surface have been encountered on the rock platform outside the cave. As stream flow became more efficient, and perhaps as new source sediments were reached, sand sized and larger material began to arrive in the study areas (*cf.* D(E):3). The presence of only superficially altered, angular limestone particles, both as sand and fine gravel, indicates that the stream was downcutting through immature sediments somewhere further back in the system. However, these sands contain a holocene fauna (p.179). When some of the water began to find an outlet at a lower level, stream flow in the study areas became sporadic, with the deposition of more clay as flow waned (*cf.* D(E):2). Between flows, thin stalagmite laminae were precipitated, formations which became thicker as water flow became rarer. Eventually, flow ceased altogether and a thick travetine was formed (*LTl*). The presence of *El* in the cave probably indicates that, by that time, a nearby entrance was open, allowing the accumulation of organics and earthy material, washed and blown in or brought in by animals.

The general lack of diagenesis in these deposits would indicate that the period covered was the end of the last glaciation and the present interglacial.

5 – DISCUSSION

The following discussion concerns certain stratigraphic and contextual aspects of the sequence at Pontnewydd that are best seen in the light of a combination of data from the various chapters of this report.

The case for the present lithologic correlation of the deposits has been argued in detail above. Inference concerning the lithogenesis of each deposit supports this correlation. If the discussion is widened to include information presented by the other specialists, the majority of suggested links would appear to hold in those cases where relevent data are available. However, some measure of uncertainty (*cf.* p.30), which the present author believes to be slight but which should properly be assessed by the team as a whole, remains in the case of Area B (South Fissure).

Several dates on fragments of speleothems from Area B do not fit the proposed correlation (see Chapter IV). The most extreme case is sample B396, which has given both U-series and TL dates (see Table IV.5) that would suggest that lithozone B:8 may be the approximate chronological equivalent of lithozones C:3, D:2 and D(E):6. Thus the deposit which first received the name 'intermediate' would appear to date from some period within the Devensian, as do other deposits which, after lithologic correlation, have been grouped with lithozone B:5 as the *Upper Breccia bed*.

Schwarcz has indicated that one sample from Area B may have been subject to such processes as recrystallisation (p.91) but this does not automatically imply that all these samples are suspect. As for the sediment bodies, it should not be forgotten that Area B presents considerable difficulties with respect to stratigraphic definition. However, these difficulties were very quickly recognised and extreme care was then taken to ensure accurate sampling of both sediments and fragmented stalagmite. The present author does not believe that the apparent chronological problem is the result of sampling error.

The South Fissure does not contain large quantities of fossiliferous deposits and, as has been said, the stratigraphy is difficult to follow. Normally, one might be justified in leaving such a problem in order to concentrate upon the much more promising sequence in Area D. However, there are reasons why such a step might be unwise in this case.

First, many of the lithostratigraphic units were originally defined (informally) in Area B. The present author is totally in agreement with the proposition (p.211) that the Area D sequence will eventually provide the most suitable stratotype for the *Pontnewydd Cave formation*. Nevertheless, to abandon Area B on the grounds that there are problems with its correlation with Area D would seem to be contrary to the spirit, if not the letter, of the *International Stratigraphic Guide*.

Second, if the problem is not resolved, there will always be the possibility that the present lithologic correlation is in fact wrong. If it were wrong, there would be irrefutable evidence that such correlation cannot avoid homotaxial error in the context of the site as a whole (*cf.* p.49).

Third, if the correlation were wrong, doubt would be cast upon the very concept of debris flows at Pontnewydd. At present, the main flows of the *Lower* and *Upper Breccia beds* are seen as regular, generally tabular bodies, a concept supported by all the available literature on such phenomena. Any other correlation would suggest much more tortuous sediment bodies and would necessitate a radical rethinking of the processes involved. Furthermore, any alternative correlation could only be geochronologic, not chronostratigraphic; there is no conceivable way that a lithozone such as B:8 could be part of, or even strictly contemporary with, the same sediment body as evidenced by lithozones C:3, D:2 or D(E):6. Consequently, the taphonomic situation would become infinitely more complex.

There is another case where combined data have a bearing upon the overall stratigraphy of the site, this time with a rather more positive result. It was suggested in the Summary to this section (p.31) that much of the total time span of the Pontnewydd sequence was not represented by extant clastic sediments. One of the major gaps appears to follow the emplacement of the *Lower Breccia*. The only material deposited over an extremely long period, perhaps as long as 200,000 years (p.113), was stalagmite; the various occurrences are grouped here as the *Stalagmite lithozone*. However, the dating evidence has shown that useful chronostratigraphic subdivision can be made of this unit. The dates fall into two main groups, *c.*225–160 ka and *c.*95–80 ka (p.210). Comparison of this information with the faunal data shows that at least one more subdivision must be present. The *Silt beds* contain a Late Devensian fauna (p.179), yet these beds are clearly interstratified towards the base with stalagmite (p.40, D(C):4). This material is usually very heavily corroded but it is to be hoped that samples good enough for dating will eventually be found. It would be useful if these three groups could also be differentiated on grounds of detailed lithology or micropalaeontology.

The context of the archaeological material is discussed in some detail elsewhere in this Report. The present author is in complete agreement with the proposition that the occupation site must have been in or near the original cave entrance, as well as with the arguments set out to support this proposition (p.208). Similarly, the information available from the sediments would lend no support whatsoever to a suggestion that the archaeological material represents a mixture with a range of any great temporal significance (*cf.* p.114).

The sedimentary and topographic context of the site is of interest in any discussion of the exact nature of the archaeological occupation. It is quite clear that the area of the cave now under investigation was not the precise site of occupation. Apart from the fact that this areas must have been most inhospitable (dark, cold and very damp), the recovery of archaeological material from debris flows entails the assumption that it came from elsewhere. The fact that we have good reason to believe that the original site was close by does not mean that we can necessarily characterise the physical limits acting to restrict the size of the occupation; the exact site has been totally destroyed by a combination of processes, including glaciation. Estimates of the potential living area within the present cavity (*cf.* p.147) would seem to be of doubtful relevance. Ford has indicated most reasonably that there is no evidence to suggest that the ancient cave entrance was any more extensive than the present one (p.217). However, it would also seem difficult to rule out the possibility that the entrance was in fact as large as the "Archway" (a huge natural arch with a complex of avens, passages and rockshelters, lying near the present Elwy below Cefn Rocks) or, conversely, that it was a restricted vertical shaft unsuitable for any sort of occupation. Indeed, there is no reason to reject the possibility of a site on open ground just outside the cave entrance.

The fact that the raw materials from which many of the artefacts were made are also naturally present in the earlier cave deposits (p.194) might appear to strengthen the association between cave and occupation. However, allowing that the cave was indeed accessible to man, the presence of nodules in sufficient numbers and of sufficient size has yet to be demonstrated. Since these rock types must also have been present in surface deposits throughout the valley, would stream beds not have provided exposures at least as attractive?

Green has proposed that the range of artefact types, together with the low proportion of waste flakes, suggest a hunting encampment rather than an 'industrial' site (p.147). Newcomer has convincingly demonstrated the difficulty of recognising human manufacture with waste from some of these raw materials (p.157). He also notes the chemical vulnerability of fine waste (p.158), to which must be added the possibility of mechanical comminution during transport in debris flows. Even if fine waste has survived – and no such material has been recognised by the present author despite microscopic scanning of all sediment samples for this very purpose –, the deposits should contain natural chips totally indistinguishable from true retouch debris, since it is accepted that pseudo-retouch is present on some artefacts (p.146).

Discussion of the sedimentary context may be taken further. An archaeological living floor is an areal entity with little significant thickness, whilst a debris flow is very much a volumetric entity. The incorporation of the former into the latter involves not only the obvious dilution factor but also complex relationships between debris discharge rate and rate of mobilisation of the archaeological material. For instance, if the debris flow were actually initiated in the sediments which contained the artefacts, the immediate dilution factor would simply be the depth of failure in the deposit. However, if initiation occurred up-flow of the occupation material, dilution would also depend upon the velocity of the flow and how quickly artefacts in its path were eroded. Once the occupation material had been incorporated, further overall dilution might occur, both by additional input of archaeologically sterile sediment and also due to the sorting capabilities of debris flows, with respect to both shape and size of particles (artefacts). Of course, these same sorting phenomena, coupled with varying flow parameters and cave micromorphology, could also lead to localised concentrations of particles, which would be dimensionally non-random. How far is the present collection representative of the original industry? How many artefacts remain to be excavated from deposits of unknown extent and how much of the original occupation material was incorporated into the debris flows in the first place? The fact that only some 22 kilos of stone artefacts had been excavated by the end of the 1981 season (Table VIII.4) may have little bearing upon the duration of the occupation (cf. p.147).

The temporary and small scale occupation of this site would certainly seem to be a most reasonable proposition on the general grounds of what is currently known about the archaeology of Britain during this period. Nevertheless, the present author remains to be convinced that Pontnewydd Cave has yet provided any strong internal evidence to support this view.

ACKNOWLEDGEMENTS

This work was funded through the National Museum of Wales, by the Donald Baden-Powell Quaternary Research Centre (University of Oxford) and from private sources. Thanks are due to R.N.E.Barton for taking the photographs in Plates XII and XIII and to J. Dumont for processing them.

PART B
SCANNING ELECTRON MICROSCOPE STUDIES OF SEDIMENTS
by
Peter A. Bull

INTRODUCTION

Samples taken from a number of sites in Pontnewydd Cave were analysed by means of the scanning electron microscope (SEM) in order that the palaeoenvironmental history of the samples could be determined. The precise analytical and interpretative procedures are well documented in the geological literature and are presented here in Appendix III.1 (p.86). The technique is capable, under optimum circumstances, of throwing some light upon the past sedimentary events through which the deposits have passed before final emplacement in the cave. Particularly important in this study is the inference made regarding the varied provenance of the materials found within Pontnewydd Cave. Information is also obtained of events including the final cave emplacement mechanism and various weathering phases which have subsequently altered the deposits.

Care must be taken, however, in the interpretation of SEM results on their own. The technique is a powerful environmental reconstruction tool but should be viewed along with the results of as many other comparative studies as possible which use other means of reconstruction. This study relies exclusively upon quartz grain studies (through logistical restraints) but the results, particularly of inferred weathering conditions, should be compared with those of clay mineral and heavy mineral investigations.

RESULTS

The various environmental modification procedures outlined in Appendix III.1 give rise to numerous discrete surface textures on quartz grains. This study quantitatively assesses the abundance of thirty-four features and textures. These results are presented (Fig. III.19) in diagramatic form and need some explanation. The presence or absence of 34 surface textures was noted on 50 grains from each sample and percentage values were calculated. These figures were then grouped for ease of visual comparison between samples. The resultant surface feature occurrence chart was divided into those textures caused by mechanical breakage (categories 1–17), those textures derived from chemical alteration (precipitation or solution of silica, categories 25–34) and the derived morphological qualities of grain relief and roundness (categories 18–24). Thus, as each line represents the complete characteristics of the sample, visual comparisons between samples (and even down-section variations) can easily be undertaken.

PALAEOENVIRONMENTAL HISTORIES OF THE SAMPLES

General inspection of the surface texture suites present on all of the samples analysed suggests that none of the deposits shows evidence of having been derived from sub-glacial debris. The classic texture suites present on glacially modified debris include large percentages of all textures in categories 3–15. Whilst some samples exhibit some of these textures it is unlikely that the material was ever part of a ground glacial sediment of classic type. The fact that not all of the samples exhibit roughly the same pattern of conchoidal fractures and breakage blocks suggests that the material does not derive from one source

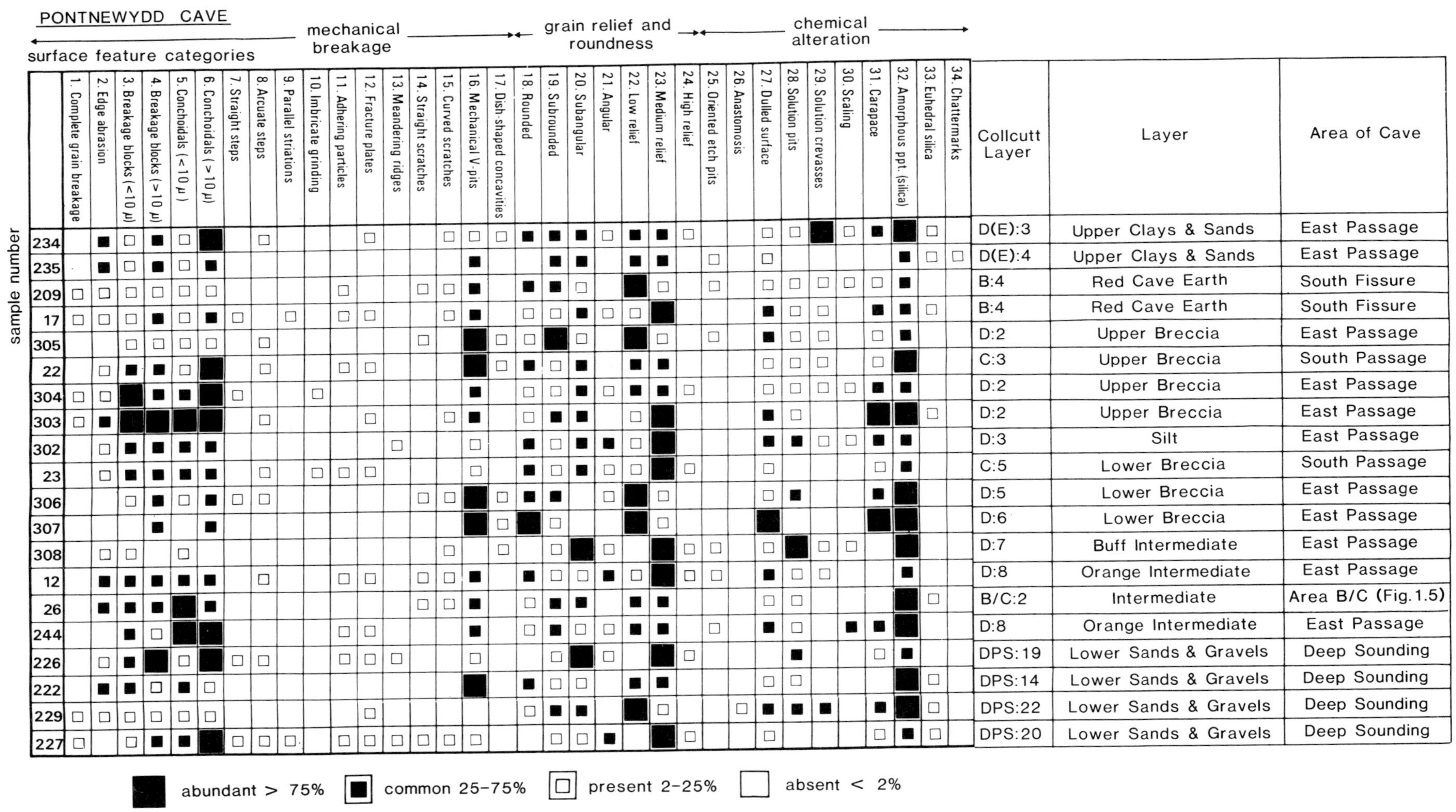

PONTNEWYDD CAVE — surface feature categories

Area of Cave	Layer	Collcutt Layer	sample number
East Passage	Upper Clays & Sands	D(E):3	234
East Passage	Upper Clays & Sands	D(E):4	235
South Fissure	Red Cave Earth	B:4	209
South Fissure	Red Cave Earth	B:4	17
East Passage	Upper Breccia	D:2	305
South Passage	Upper Breccia	C:3	22
East Passage	Upper Breccia	D:2	304
East Passage	Upper Breccia	D:2	303
East Passage	Silt	D:3	302
South Passage	Lower Breccia	C:5	23
East Passage	Lower Breccia	D:5	306
East Passage	Lower Breccia	D:6	307
East Passage	Buff Intermediate	D:7	308
East Passage	Orange Intermediate	D:8	12
Area B/C (Fig.1.5)	Intermediate	B/C:2	26
East Passage	Orange Intermediate	D:8	244
Deep Sounding	Lower Sands & Gravels	DPS:19	226
Deep Sounding	Lower Sands & Gravels	DPS:14	222
Deep Sounding	Lower Sands & Gravels	DPS:22	229
Deep Sounding	Lower Sands & Gravels	DPS:20	227

Surface feature categories (grouped):

chemical alteration:
- 34. Chattermarks
- 33. Euhedral silica
- 32. Amorphous ppt. (silica)
- 31. Carapace
- 30. Scaling
- 29. Solution crevasses
- 28. Solution pits
- 27. Dulled surface

grain relief and roundness:
- 26. Anastomosis
- 25. Oriented etch pits
- 24. High relief
- 23. Medium relief
- 22. Low relief
- 21. Angular
- 20. Subangular
- 19. Subrounded
- 18. Rounded
- 17. Dish-shaped concavities

mechanical breakage:
- 16. Mechanical V-pits
- 15. Curved scratches
- 14. Straight scratches
- 13. Meandering ridges
- 12. Fracture plates
- 11. Adhering particles
- 10. Imbricate grinding
- 9. Parallel striations
- 8. Arcuate steps
- 7. Straight steps
- 6. Conchoidals (>10 μ)
- 5. Conchoidals (<10 μ)
- 4. Breakage blocks (>10 μ)
- 3. Breakage blocks (<10 μ)
- 2. Edge abrasion
- 1. Complete grain breakage

Legend:
- ☐ absent < 2%
- ☐ present 2–25%
- ■ common 25–75%
- ■ abundant > 75%

Fig. III.19 A surface feature variability chart for deposits from Pontnewydd Cave.

rock (whether it be acid igneous or sedimentary). Indeed, the varied nature of the grains suggests a mixed provenance for the material (Plates XIV a–d). Similar conclusions are reached by analysis of the occurrence and relative abundance of many other surface textures. The lack of minor mechanical features (categories 7–15) does not, then, augur well for a well-crushed sub-glacial source for the original material. Although post-depositional chemical modification may have masked some of the textures it is unlikely that *any* of the deposits originated sub-glacially, and perhaps a source in englacial, supra-glacial or even medial deposits is more likely.

The presence of mechanical V-pits (category 16), often in very high percentages on the grains examined (Plate XIVe) indicates a quite extensive fluvial transport phase for a number of layers. Generally it would appear that the Breccias (Upper and Lower) contain more deposits which have been fluvially transported (Plate XIVf) than other layers. Of course, this could reflect derivation from local fluvial deposits outside the cave, but it could also merely reflect selective deposition into the cave by debris flow of a layer on the surface (perhaps a moraine), which at one time in its past history, had undergone fluvial transportation. It would be tempting, however, to correlate these fluvially modified sediments with temperate conditions on the surface.

Acting as a complementary check, the degree of grain rounding (catagories 18–21), closely reflects in its diversity the multisource nature of the sediments depicted in the variation of conchoidal fractures and breakage blocks described above. Equally, the rounding, most likely fluvial (although some post-depositional activity *has* rounded grains), compares well with the occurrence of mechanical V-pits mentioned above. Charateristic, however, of the samples from Pontnewydd is the very mixed nature both of the degree of rounding and of general relief. Whilst this latter group of features (categories 22–24) shows a great degree of variation between grains of low relief and of high relief, it would be wrong to consider this pattern indicative of mixed provenance material. This variation is likely to be derived and related to the occurrence of conchoidal patterns and breakage blocks.

The chemical features (categories 25–34), notorious as they are for their independence of any discrete environmental modification, show at least that the samples have undergone very little chemical modification. Before this leads to ideas that the deposits were unaltered it is important to realise that these results apply to *quartz* grains only, and a less rigorous SEM examination of other mineral types suggests that feldspars have been particularly heavily weathered. It is unlikely, however, from the results presented (Fig.III.19) that any of the deposits were incorporated in a true soil horizon on the surface before introduction into the cave, as pedogenic features are few. Possible exceptions include PN307 (Lower Breccia) and PN209 and PN17 (Red Cave Earth); but the latter may well be *in situ* cave weathering phenomena. The lack of pedogenic features can be interpreted in at least two ways. Firstly, the sediments may not have been deposited on the surface for a long enough time for an extensive soil profile to develop. Secondly, the conditions on the surface may not have been conducive to soil formation; cold tundra-like environments may have prevailed.

The variable presence of euhedral silica (category 33 and Plate XIVb,g) on grain surfaces also suggests a mixed provenance for the material since the features recognised in this study relate to a diagenetic phase of grain alteration, most probably in a coarse-grained sandstone. Edge rounding of at least some of these features further suggest fluvial activity since removal from the parent body.

Most of the surface textures so far mentioned are common enough on many grain surfaces from any number of environments. There is, however, one texture which is characteristic of only a few discrete environments and furthermore is present in a significant number of grains from the Pontnewydd deposits. Complete grain breakage (category 1) (Plate

XIVd,h) is to be found in six samples in significant numbers (approximately 14% of the grains in each sample exhibit this feature). The phenomenon portrays, as its name suggests, grains which have been broken in half by mechanical fracturing. Necessary energy levels to promote grain fracture are so specific as to be known in only a few environments. It is unlikely that glacial grinding has caused this breakage: although such energy conditions exist in glacial grinding, associated grinding phenomena (categories 3–14) would normally be produced on the grain surface. Ice loading may cause fracturing by imparting local stress high enough to cause grain breakage but such energy levels are normally associated with grinding and crushing (again represented by categories 3–14). Grain breakage has also been noted as a phenomenon associated with high energy grain saltation and collision in underwater sediment chutes in the deep seas, but such an explanation does not apply here! If the association of grain breakage with mechanical crushing is not convincing, neither is a chemical origin for these features. Certainly, the general chemical activity exhibited on all grain surfaces does not support intense chemical activity (categories 25–34). Problematic, too, is the occurrence of these distinctive modification events within the sediment sequence; they are to be found in the Red Cave Earth (two samples) (Plate XIVh) the Upper Breccia (two samples) (Plate XIVd) and the Lower Sands and Gravels. The importance of grain breakage should be stressed; it is not a random event and has developed in response to some specific environmental condition. Perhaps the emplacement mechanism in the cave was sufficiently extreme to effect grain breakage; if this is so the event was locally very extreme and the textures represent the first documental evidence of specific environmental modification by debris flow transportation.

Thus, the general picture portrayed by the SEM analysis is one of a deposit which almost uniformly derives from a mixed provenance. Glacial debris seems to be evident, although not through specific texture assemblages but rather through the mixed nature of the general characteristics of all the deposits. There are, undoubtedly, deposits which at one stage or other were derived from fluvial sediments; whether these deposits were initially fluvial and then incorporated in a glacier is a moot point. If this is indeed the case then this sequence represents the first documentation of *any* sediment which has passed through glacial transportation whilst retaining previous environmental modification features. Perhaps this rarity testifies to the likelihood that the deposits were a discrete fluvial deposit incorporated into the glacial debris on the surface. This would involve a topographic context in which the river flowed at the height of the cave, a matter for geomorphological interpretation.

The deposits, however they were mixed on the surface, contain evidence that they once derived from acid igneous rocks, coarse-grained sandstones, rivers and, by involuted reasoning, from glaciers. Perhaps, too, the emplacement mechanism is recognised in the grain breakage: certainly weathering, or the relative lack of it is noted. As to other post-depositional modification to the sediment, there appears to be no record upon the quartz grains themselves that anything extreme has occurred since emplacement. Perhaps this reflects the relative protection afforded to such sedimentary sequences within the sheltered cave environment, compared with outside.

Some Detailed SEM Comments

Following the sequence of sedimentation identified (Fig. III.19) some useful comment can be made concerning the micromorphology of grains from layers in the various areas of the cave.

a) Lower Sands and Gravels

The sample is characterised (Fig.III.19) by a varied assemblage of both chemical and mechanical modification features on the quartz grains (sample numbers 227, 229, 222 and 226). Plate XIVi shows three grains, two well rounded and one angular (exhibiting euhedral

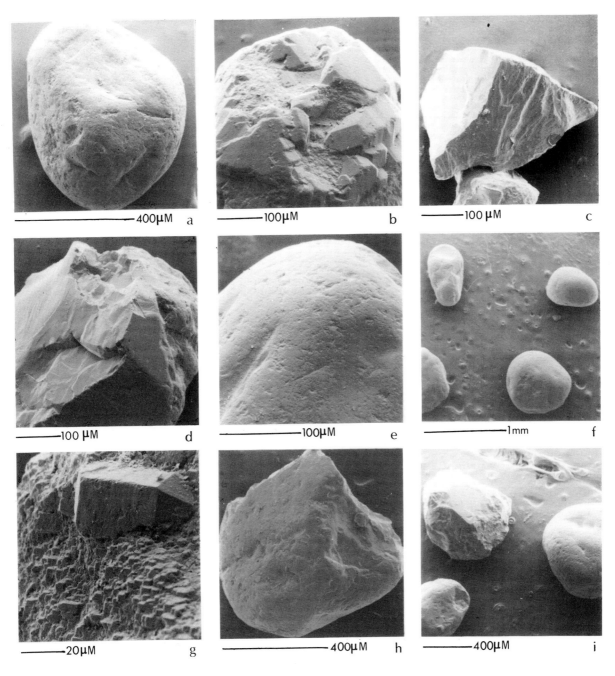

a SEM photo of well rounded quartz grain from the Upper Breccia, East Passage (PN 305). Note original background breakage blocks and conchoidal fractures. V-pits (category 16) are present on the grain surface.

b Quartz grain with euhedral crystal growth (category 33). The crystals are dulled (category 27) and slightly edge rounded. The sugary surface elsewhere on the grain is as a result of silica precipitation (category 32) and solution (categories 25, 26, 28, 30). The grain is from sample PN 235. Upper Clays and Sands, East Passage.

c An angular quartz grain from PN 304 (Upper Breccia, East Passage). Fracture planes are evident (category 12) and a small conchoidal fracture can be seen on the top of the grain (category 6). There is no edge rounding or abrasion (category 2), nor any post-depositional chemical modification (categories 25–34).

d A quartz grain, rounded both by chemical precipitation and by mechanical abrasion with complete grain breakage (category 1).

There has been no subsequent modification to the grain. From PN 303 Upper Breccia (East Passage).

e Small indentations on the surface of a well rounded quartz grain are mechanical V-pits (category 16). From PN 307, Lower Breccia (East Passage).

f General view of well rounded, fluvially transported quartz grains from the Lower Breccia (PN 307, East Passage.

g Euhedral quartz crystal growth on the surface of a grain from the Intermediate complex (PN 26, Area B/C).

h Complete grain breakage of an originally well rounded quartz grain (PN 209, Red Cave Earth, South Fissure).

i Three quartz grains showing rounding and euhedral crystal growth (PN 222, Lower Sands and Gravels, Deep Sounding).

Plate XIV Pontnewydd Cave. SEM photographs of quartz grains.

crystal growth; grain top left). These grains have clearly, at some time in the past, undergone different amounts of fluvial transportation and/or represent grains from different provenances (it is most likely that all of the grains are from sedimentary environments). Plate XVa shows a close up of the grain pictured bottom right in Plate XVi which is well rounded with numerous fluvial V-pits on the grain surface. The mixed nature of grains from this layer (Lower Sands and Gravels) may readily be seen from comparison of Plate XVa with Plate XVb (subdued dulling (category 27) of the surface of an angular grain), Plate XVc (a fresh, angular grain with very little edge rounding) and Plate XVd which provides a close-up view of the fresh surface of one of the grains from this layer. Finally it should be noted (Plate XVe) that the grains with euhedral crystal growths have been edge abraded in a fluvial environment prior to emplacement in the cave. Since the emplacement followed abrasion, the crystal growth is most likely to be a diagenetic effect associated with the lithification of the parent sandstone. There is, therefore, strong evidence for fluvial transportation of material with mixing, perhaps by stream erosion, of other superficial deposits (perhaps tills or other glacially derived debris). Since field observations suggest that emplacement was by a debris flow, the whole must have been deposited on the surface above and about the cave by fluvial agencies.

b) Intermediate complex

The Intermediate deposits represent a complicated set of sediments which, under SEM examination, have revealed surface feature characteristics, equally as varied as those found in the Lower Sands and Gravels. Grains from these "intermediate" layers consist of well rounded fluvial sands (Plate XVf) together with grains which have undergone much chemical alteration but yet exhibit a late phase of conchoidal fracturing (Plates XVg–h). Since this late fracturing is only very gently smoothed by subsequent chemical action (Plate XVh), it is most likely that this fracture phase occurred immediately prior to or during emplacement in the cave. It is a record of the last phase of mechanical fracturing which has effected this change to the grains. The survival of the fresh surfaces is testimony to the chemically stable environment at the level of these layers within the cave since deposition. Generally, these deposits lack the frequent grains present in the underlying strata which are derived from the same coarse grained sandstone which yielded the grains with euhedral crystal growths.

c) Lower Breccia

These deposits are broadly similar to the underlying strata, exhibiting a large range of grain types (Plate XVi) but varying in two main respects from the previously mentioned deposits. Grain surfaces from the Lower Breccia generally have mechanical V-pit densities and grain shapes which suggest *extensive* fluvial transportation (Plate XVIa). There are, however, grains which have obviously not undergone this degree of transportation (Plate XVIb), and such a mix seems quite characteristic of the deposits in Pontnewydd. Interestingly those grains which are more angular are almost totally lacking in any edge abrasion which suggests that they have not travelled any distance by river action and are more likely to be derived from local superficial deposits.

Secondly, the Lower Breccia is characterised by having grains with significantly lower amounts of conchoidal fractures and breakage blocks than from overlying deposits. Such variation suggests a strong likelihood of provenance or environmental change.

d) Silt ("Pond deposit")

This deposit yields quartz grains which were particularly angular, of low relief (similar to the Lower Breccia) with few signs of any fluvial modification (Plate XVIc). (Those grains which were water-worn may well have been reworked from lower stratigraphic layers). These deposits appear to be the most likely, of all those examined, to have derived from

a   Rounded quartz grain with mechanical V-pits (PN 222, Lower Sands and Gravels, Deep Sounding).

b   Quartz grain with chemical action which has dulled the surface of an originally angular grain (PN 226, Lower Sands and Gravels, Deep Sounding).

c   An angular quartz grain with fresh, unaltered surface (PN 227, Lower Sands and Gravels, Deep Sounding).

d   High magnification of a quartz grain surface unaffected by any post depositional modification (PN 227, Lower Sands and Gravels, Deep Sounding).

e   An edge-abraded euhedral crystal face on a quartz grain (PN 222, Lower Sands and Gravels, Deep Sounding).

f   A well-rounded, fluvial sand grain. Note subdued breakage blocks and conchoidal fractures (PN 244, Orange Intermediate, East Passage).

g   Late phase conchoidal fracturing and edge abrasion on a quartz grain (PN 12, Orange Intermediate, East Passage).

h   Late phase conchoidal fracturing on an already heavily altered quartz grain surface (PN 244, Intermediate, East Passage).

i   Quartz grains displaying varied shapes and macrotexture assemblages (PN 23, Lower Breccia, South Passage).

Plate XV.   Pontnewydd Cave. SEM photographs of quartz grains.

cold climates since they are not only very angular and mechanically fresh, but also relatively free of chemical alteration (which appears to be a "surface" phenomenon in other deposits).

e) Upper Breccia

The Upper Breccia samples are, as a group, quite distinct from those underlying Silt and Lower Breccia units, for they contain grains which represent a return to environmental conditions similar to those which must have occurred in the Lower Sands and Gravels and Intermediate deposits.

The grains have relatively high relief, exhibiting surfaces with many conchoidal fractures and breakage blocks (Plate XVId). The grains, like those from the lowermost units, are very well rounded and show evidence of much fluvial transportation in relatively high energy rivers (see V-pits on Plate XVIe) Grains which are not obviously rounded by river tranportation are as fresh as any others viewed but some are edge abraded, suggesting that there has been a small degree of transportation (Plate XVIf).

f) Red Cave Earth

The name for this unit is not technically correct as the grains exhibit evidence of fluvial transportation (Plate XVIg) showing that the deposit is not a true Cave Earth. The deposit contains an assemblage of long-distance travelled grains with a few more angular grains. It is most likely that this angular suite derives from underlying deposits. The relative lack of chemical activity within the cave since deposition can be seen in Plate XVIh. Here, a feldspar grain, most often one of the easiest minerals to be chemically etched, remains practically as fresh as the day it was eroded from its granite parent body.

g) Upper Clays and Sands

Stratigraphically, the highest unit examined by SEM, this deposit is very similar in nature to the underlying Red Cave Earth. It represents a fairly even mix of water transported grains and more locally-derived angular grains (Plate XVIi). The uppermost layers of this unit are heavily affected by chemical solution and precipitation indicating, perhaps, the depth of chemical alteration of the quartz grains within the cave environment.

Summary

The SEM investigation of quartz grain surface textures from samples taken from Pontnewydd Cave suggests that many of the deposits are assemblages of sediments derived from various sources. Far travelled fluvial deposits are mixed with sediments derived from sandstones which are not located near the cave site. An angular suite of material has been mixed with rounded grains probably both outside and inside the cave. The angular material shows no sign of appreciable water transportation but some slight water movement is indicated. It is likely, though by no means certain, that this angular material derives from glacial debris.

The most strikingly characteristic of these materials taken as a whole is the big differences of surface texture assemblages which are noticeable between sedimentary units. The Intermediate complex deposits are similar to the Upper Breccia in many respects and equally are different from the units of Lower Sands and Gravels, Lower Breccia and Red Cave Earth. The Silt (Pond) deposit, too is very different from overlying or underlying beds. As such, field designated sedimentology units seem to be identical to sedimentary units identified by SEM analysis.

I have indicated in the text where I consider that provenance variations have affected the nature and characteristics of the deposits. However, environmental factors too, must also be considered even though they are of uncertain importance in this study, due to the very

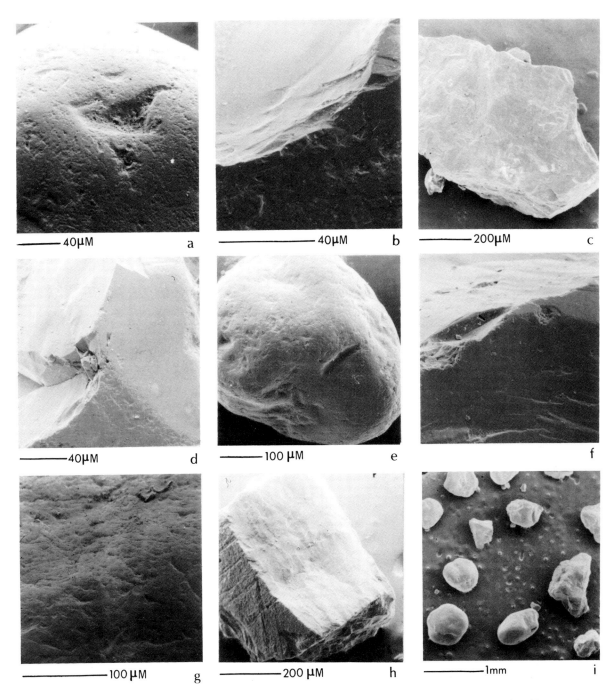

a A well rounded fluvial quartz grain with percussion chips and V-pits (PN 306, Lower Breccia, East Passage).

b A fresh grain surface with angular edges. Edge abrasion is absent on this grain (PN 23, Lower Breccia, South Passage).

c An angluar, fresh quartz grain of medium relief (Silt deposit PN 302, East Passage).

d A high relief quartz grain with late conchoidal fractures (grain breakage) and breakage blocks. Note selective chemical solution. (PN 303, Upper Breccia, East Passage).

e A well-rounded quartz grain with mechanical V-pits on the grain surface (PN 304, Upper Breccia, East Passage).

f An angular, fresh surface of a quartz grain with some edge abrasion caused by transportation. (PN 304, Upper Breccia, East Passage).

g Low relief surface textures on a quartz grain. Note the general rounding and mechanical V-pit assemblages (PN 209, Red Cave Earth, South Fissure).

h A fresh, unaltered feldspar grain exhibiting slight surface dulling due to quartz precipitation (PN 17, Red Cave Earth, South Fissure).

i A general view of quartz grains showing the varied shapes and macro-texture assemblages on grain surfaces (PN 234, Upper Clays and Sands, East Passage).

Plate XVI. Pontnewydd Cave. SEM photographs of quartz grains.

varied nature of the material and the subtle differences between samples which have to be unravelled from the strong background trends attributable to provenance differences. Nevertheless the environmental histories described above stand although a *caveat* must be introduced: this study is but one means by which environmental histories can be elucidated. The results of this work must be placed in context of the results obtained from all other studies employed in this project.

Perhaps the major problem of SEM studies as employed in this project is the possibility that the surface textures are all inherited from a previous sedimentary cycle. It may be imagined that if the source of the grains in the cave was a sandstone rock which itself contained both angular and rounded grains, that examination of the grains from the cave would show nothing of the phase of the latest sedimentary cycle, involving erosion from the parent sandstone, transportation and finally deposition in the cave. It has been, therefore, with much care that this study concludes that most of the surface texture now examined on the quartz grains does represent the last cycle of erosion and sedimentation before entry into the cave but inherited textures do exist and include the background conchoidal fracturing, breakage blocks and steps together with euhedral crystal growth. Indeed, these textures are used to identify variations in source of the respective sedimentary units in the cave.

Perhaps the most important evidence for dismantling the idea of the textures being mostly inherited is the variation which occurs in the percentage of sedimentary surface features occurring successively through the deposits (i.e. through time). These textures do not occur at random but recur together as minor surface texture assemblages which, in turn, reflect the small scale environmental changes which have modified the grains. These are *small* features which do not readily survive sandstone diagenesis: neither can selective sorting of particular features within the cave be readily explained. Absolute certainty as to the origins of the surface textures can only be achieved by a more comprehensive sediment collection exercise particularly of the superficial deposits and outcropping sedimentary rocks of the area around the cave.

Appendix III.1

The samples analysed from Pontnewydd Cave by SEM analysis were studied in order that the palaeoenvironmental history of the samples could be determined. By identifying the suite, and type, of textures which are present on the surfaces of quartz grains in each sample, it is possible to reconstruct the environments in which the grains had been modified. Each major environmental type (e.g. glaciers, rivers, sea, wind, etc.) exhibits its own type of modification processes whether it be mechanical crushing (glacier), severe grain turbulence (rivers and beach action), or grain saltation (deserts). Correspondingly, these processes impart particular types of textures (up to 40 or 50 of which can be identified) upon the grain surfaces. For more detail, see published works such as Krinsley and Doornkamp (1973).

Whilst the fundamentals of the technique are quite straightforward, the analytical procedure is more complex. Early work was often criticised for its qualitative nature, but recent trends advocate a more quantitative approach. Thus, this report presents the *conclusions* of the study in a qualitative manner, but derives all of its conclusions from statistical analyses and interpretations. These data are presented in diagramatic form (Fig.III.19).

Sample Preparation

Each sample to be analysed was subdivided into 10 gramme sub-samples and lightly boiled in 10% hydrochloric acid for twenty minutes. Each treated sediment was then washed in distilled water, further boiled in stannous chloride and thoroughly washed in sodium hexametaphosphate. The remainder, free of carbonates, iron staining and clay particles, was further washed in distilled water and then oven-dried.

Next 50 unicrystalline grains of sand-size were randomly picked and mounted on viewing stubs. In addition, a fraction of the smaller grains was also mounted in order to give an impression of grain characteristics throughout the whole sediment size range in each sample. The grains, mounted on double-sized adhesive tape, were sputter coated with gold and viewed on a Cambridge 150 stereoscan at magnifications ranging from 20 to 20,000.

Thirty-four surface textures were identified from the samples studied and their relative presence or absence on all fifty grains in the sample were noted. The results are presented in Figure III.19.

CHAPTER IV

ABSOLUTE AND RELATIVE DATING

The absolute dating programme has been the work of a number of individuals and institutions. The different techniques used are relatively new and one – thermoluminescence dating of calcite – is only now moving out of its experimental stage. Five necessarily separate papers on uranium-series, thermoluminescence and relative dating follow. The results as a whole are discussed in Chapter IX (p.208).

H.S.G.

PART A
URANIUM-SERIES DATING AND STABLE ISOTOPE ANALYSES OF CALCITE DEPOSITS
by
H.P. Schwarcz

INTRODUCTION

Calcite which has been deposited from fresh water is found in the cave:
a) as discrete layers of flowstone (horizontally laminated stalagmitic travertine) interstratified in the sequence of detrital layers;
b) as fragments of flowstone or stalagmite enclosed within debris flow units which partly comprise the sedimentary fill sequence;
c) calcite crystal (spar) coatings on clasts in debris flow layers.

Some of this calcite has grown contemporaneously with the filling of the cave by detrital sediments. Therefore, through dating these calcite deposits, it is possible to establish a time scale for the evolution of the detrital fill and its enclosed archaeological and palaeontological record.

This report describes the dating of these calcite deposits (which we shall collectively describe as travertine) by the uranium-series method. The application of these methods to travertine in caves and spring deposits has been summarised earlier by the author (Schwarcz, 1980). In brief, the methods take advantage of the observation that uranium in the 6+ oxidation state is quite soluble in ground-waters, while two of its daughter isotopes, ^{230}Th and ^{231}Pa are not. Therefore, pure calcite precipitated from ground water contains traces (0.1 to 10 ppm) of U but is virtually devoid of thorium and protactinium. The half lives of these daughters are such that their subsequent ingrowth can be used as a monitor of the age of deposits formed over the last 350,000 years (Fig.IV.1). The activity ratio ^{230}Th/^{234}U increases from zero at the time of deposition to unity at the upper age limit of the method, at which time the two isotopes are said to be in secular radioactive equilibrium. Note that this ratio is measured by counting the number of disintegrations per minute per gram of rock for each isotope and determining the ratio of these quantities. To do this, the Th and U in the calcite are chemically extracted and plated onto separate steel discs which are placed in an alpha particle spectrometer that separates the energies of the various alpha particles emitted, and determines their rate of emission. Typically it is possible to determine the age on a sample of 20 grams containing 0.2 ppm U. The ratio ^{231}Pa/^{235}U can be used analogously; however the specific activity of ^{231}Pa in a sample of a given age is only 5% of that of ^{230}Th. Therefore ^{231}Pa can only be used to date samples of relatively high U content (> 1 ppm). None of the samples in the present study contained sufficient U for this purpose.

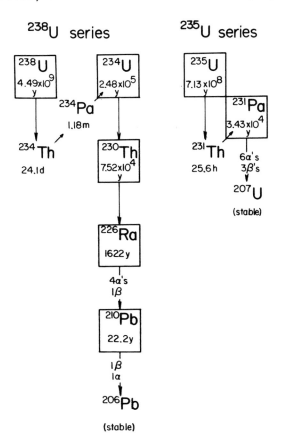

Fig. IV.1   Decay schemes of daughter isoptopes of ^{238}U and ^{235}U. Heavy-lined boxes signify isotopes useful in dating of archaeological sites.

Various problems can arise in the application of this method of dating. If the calcite sample contains any significant amount of detrital impurity, then this component will contribute Th and U that will give the sample a spuriously great age; but the presence of such an impurity can usually be deduced from the presence in the alpha spectrum for Th of a peak for ^{232}Th, and this isotope (which is not a daughter of a U isotope) must have been present at the time of deposition and thus was accompanied at that time by a certain amount of ^{230}Th (since these two isotopes are chemically indistinguishable). If the initial ^{232}Th/^{230}Th ratio is known, a rough correction for the "detrital" ^{230}Th component can be made. Unfortunately, no analagous correction for detrital U can be made since it has no distinctive tracer isotopes, and the Th correction is only used for samples which have a ^{230}Th/^{232}Th ratio less than 20.

Another problem which can plague the method is that the calcite may have been recrystallised some time after its original precipitation from ground water dripping into the cave. This effect can sometimes be recognised through characteristic changes in the microscopic texture of the travertine, or by the development of solution cavities and a porous texture in otherwise compact, impermeable travertine. The higher the initial porosity of the travertine, the greater the likelihood of its subsequently being recrystallised; indeed, recrystallisation is probably unavoidable in such deposits as they remain buried in water-saturated sediments for much of their history, but it is hoped that recrystallisation terminates relatively soon after deposition, due to loss of all significant porosity.

The precision of the method of dating depends on the U content of the sample, since precision increases with the number of alpha particles actually counted. For samples containing 0.5 ppm, the error is about 5% of the age, for ages up to 200 ka (1 ka = 1000 y B.P.).

THE SAMPLES

The samples largely consist of loose fragments of travertine encountered as clasts within the various units of detrital fill. A few critical samples were actually found growing *in situ*, as stalagmites whose bases rested on top of one of the detrital units, and could therefore provide a strict *ante quem* date to the unit. For the derived fragments, however, the age significance is more problematic. In general, the excavators believe that much of the detrital fill was transported into the cave as debris flows. Any fragments of travertine found embedded in these deposits would presumably have been stripped off earlier deposits *in situ* within the cave. They could therefore have been deposited at any time prior to the emplacement of the debris flow, including times prior to deposition of underlying units. Therefore ages obtained on such material can give only a *post quem* date for the emplacement of the debris flow, and give no age information about underlying units.

The samples which have been analysed so far are described in Table IV.1. They consist principally of broken, rounded fragments of flowstone. Fragments of stalagmites, some still attached to flowstone bases, are also represented. Stalactites occur both as broken fragments cemented into the flowstone blocks by subsequent overgrowths of travertine and as discrete stalactite fragments in the debris. One slab of flowstone broken from the roof of the cave (B 285) was found in the Red Cave Earth.

Besides these types, one other kind of sample recovered from Pontnewydd, is calcite, found as a sparry overgrowth on limestone clasts embedded in the detrital fill at several localities (samples B162, C133). Such coatings may have formed after emplacement of the fill and, if so, would give an *ante quem* date for the fill.

In general the travertine samples were quite pure with respect to detrital contaminants but possessed varying degrees of porosity. Wherever possible, sub-samples of the specimens were extracted from the least porous, least recrystallised portions. Samples were prepared by cutting the specimens with a diamond saw, and by chipping away contaminated or porous material with an air-driven tool. Some specimens were studied in thin section to estimate the degree of recrystallisation.

The stratigraphically youngest samples analysed in this study come from the Red Cave Earth. Samples of the capping stalagmite floor have been analysed by N. Debenham *et al.* (p.105).

ANALYTICAL RESULTS

The results of analyses of samples up to the present date (January, 1982) are shown in Table

IV.2. In general we note that the uranium content of all the travertine samples is quite uniform, having an average value of 0.52 ± 0.21 ppm, roughly normally distributed about the mean. The $^{234}U/^{238}U$ ratio of the calcite samples is only moderately variable, ranging from 1.00 to 1.40 (with the exception of B275 which gave a value of 3.88; in all other respects this sample is normal). When corrected for their age, the initial $^{234}U/^{238}U$ ratios have an average value of 1.221 ± 0.192. This initial ratio is sufficiently uniform to be used to estimate the age of samples older than 350,000 years (and hence too old to date by the $^{230}Th/^{234}U$ method). No such samples have yet been encountered at this site, however. This method of dating is described in Thompson et al., 1976.

Very few of the samples contained sufficiently large contents of detrital thorium to require any form of correction. A more serious problem appears to be erratic discrepancies between replicate dates on the same samples. Sample BOb consisted of one piece of finely laminated flowstone from the South Fissure section of the Lower Breccia and two samples from it gave ages of 130 ± 7 and 204 ± 20 ka respectively. Both samples were somewhat porous and although care was taken to select sample material from the least porous, least altered portions, we may be seeing the effect of localised post-depositional recrystallisation. I am indebted to Nicholas Debenham (in litt., January 1983) for details of his Thermoluminescence measurements of these same samples, which gave respective archaeological doses (A.D.) of 17.3 ± 2.0 krads and 13.4 ± 2.3 krads. He comments that "both [samples] exhibited exceptionally low TL sensitivities, hence the poor precision of the A.D. measurements. The one standard deviation limits of the measurements overlap, and it cannot be said that they are significantly different". Debenham's own replicate dates on BOb are to be found below (Chapter IVc).

A sample with similar problems is D534, found deposited in situ on the Lower Breccia. This stalagmite, approximately 25cm high, was divided into four portions representing successive growth layers. However, the $^{230}Th/^{234}U$ ratios of the top and the base of this deposit are definitely disturbed (i.e., > 1.1), leading one to suspect the validity of the central two samples. The uranium content of each sample is surprisingly uniform, as is the $^{234}U/^{238}U$ ratio, so that we cannot attribute the discrepancies to loss of U alone. Petrographic study shows that the calcite comprising the inner part of this deposit has probably been recrystallised, because it is composed of an aggregate of amoeboid equant crystals, whereas the outer layers are composed of radiating, prismatic calcite crystals. It is possible that all samples were somehow contaminated with excess ^{230}Th. The two grossly discrepant analyses (01 and 04) both give low $^{230}Th/^{232}Th$ ratios although the initial ratio that would have been required to account for the discrepancy (i.e. to produce a corrected age comparable to those of the middle samples) is much higher than normally encountered in detritus. As the sample both rests on and underlies limestone breccia in a situation very close to the cave wall, it is possible that some radiogenic ^{230}Th was leached from the limestone and introduced into the stalagmite.

The remainder of the data is mutually consistent, and allows the construction of a chronology of filling of the cave with the sediment in which these stalagmitic fragments were embedded or on which they were deposited. The following is a summary of the ages obtained for the different layers (Tables IV.2A–C).

Lower Breccia   Stalagmite deposits found certainly or probably growing *in situ* on the upper surface of the Lower Breccia range from 215 to 83 ka (East Passage) with single dates of 177 ka from the South Passage and 217 ka from near the South Fissure. The East Passage date, 215 ± 36 ka, is the mean of three determinations on a sample of stalagmitic floor (D1288B) discovered *in situ* on the Lower Breccia of the East Passage in 1982. A series of dates determined by Miro Ivanovich (pp.98–99) give a grand average of 224 ka for another sample from this same floor. The reader is referred to p.98 for a description of the floor.

Sample D1288B as received consisted of a saw-cut slab with planar surfaces essentially perpendicular to the pronounced sedimentary layering. A futher section was cut from this slab, and this section was divided into three equal portions representing the base, middle and top of the slab, and labelled D1288B:01, 02, 03 respectively. The analytical results are given in Table IV.2C. The absolute ages obtained from the bottom and top layers of this flowstone are identical. The middle layer, while resembling the other two in terms of its U-isotope ratio and U concentration, gives a significantly larger age, although overlapping the age of the top layer at the 1 sigma level. Considering the agreement between the top and bottom layers, and the high degree of recrystallization displayed by the sample, it seems likely that the difference between the ages of the middle and the outer layers is due to some minor chemical disturbance of the sample after deposition. The entire flowstone layer was probably deposited within an interval of a few tens of thousands of years, centred around the average age of the three sub-samples, 215,000 years before the present. This result agrees closely with the date of 217ka from sample B274, found *in situ* at the same stratigraphic level near the South Fissure.

It is gratifying to note that these results on D1288 do not differ significantly from those reported in the following paper (Ivanovich *et al.*), showing that two independent laboratories using somewhat different analytical methods are able to arrive at very similar analytical results. The estimates of probable error of the analyses in our work are comparable to those obtained after replicate analyses by the Harwell group, suggesting that the error is essentially limited by the radiochemical properties of the samples and not by the precision of analytical procedures.

The dates here listed (Table IV.2) imply that the cave was sealed off at the time of the introduction of the Lower Breccia and subsequently received no sedimentary fill for some 100,000 years. Faunal analysis (p.179) suggests that, in fact, the next sedimentary influx did not occur until towards 10ka. The sealing of the cave is confirmed in part by the stable isotope analyses of stalagmite D312 (reported below).

Fragments of derived stalagmite described as coming from the base of the Lower Breccia have been dated from the South Fissure area only (Green, 1981a; p.30 here). The dates on these samples present several problems. First, there are the discrepant readings, discussed above, of 204 and 130 ka from the same block (sample B0b). A result of 209 ± 16 ka (B148) is obviously compatible with the results obtained on stalagmite *in situ* on the Lower Breccia, but the age of 149 ± 9 ka (B0a) seems a little young. Sample B162 is a calcite coating on a fragment of limestone within "Breccia". Unless incorporated as a clast within the debris flow, its formation must post-date emplacement of the deposit. Its date of 225+89/−47ka, whilst not very precise, is consistent with our dates on the stalagmites and flowstones found *in situ* on the lower Breccia. (See also note to Table IV.2A)

Upper Breccia   Unfortunately, only broken fragments from within this unit have been recovered; and no overlying *in situ* deposits have been dated. The two ages obtained (227 and 125 ka from the South Fissure and East Passage respectively) are consistent with the formation of this deposit sometime after 83 ka but do not give any clue as to the actual date of emplacement.

Red Cave Earth   This breccia of angular rock fragments in a poorly sorted matrix is also believed to be the product of a debris flow. As in the case of the Upper Breccia, only derived fragments have been dated, which give *post quem* estimates for the time of deposition of the stratigraphic unit (307 to 123 ka), but do not add to our knowledge of the chronology of this layer. Some of the stalagmite fragments in this unit may have been reworked from underlying breccia units or more likely, broken from remnants of older stalagmitic floors adhering to the wall of the cave, thus accounting for their great range in age.

STABLE ISOTOPE STUDIES

If stalagmites are deposited in a closed cave chamber where humidity is close to 100% and there is very limited circulation of air, then it is possible for the calcite to be formed in isotopic equilibrium with the water from which it is deposited, and some palaeoclimatic information can be obtained from the oxygen isotopic composition of the calcite (Gascoyne *et al.*, 1978; Schwarcz *et al.*, 1976).

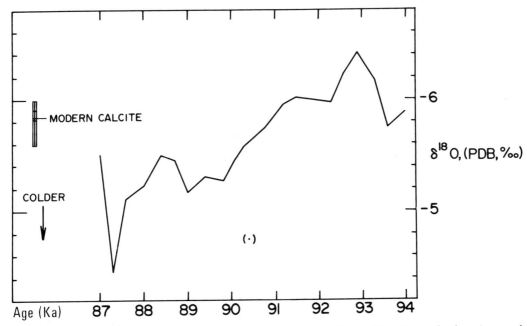

Fig. IV.2   Variation of $\delta^{18}O$ of calcite in stalagmite D 312 versus time of deposition. Base of stalagmite was dated at 96± 4, top at 89 ± 3 ka. Age spectrum shown on diagram extends beyond these ages to take into account averaging effect when a significant thickness of stalagmite is sampled for dating.

Inspection of stalagmite D 312 which had probably grown *in situ* on the Lower Breccia in the East Passage, suggested to the author that it had formed in a closed system, and might be in isotopic equilibrium. A series of profiles of the $\delta^{18}O\star$ values of single- growth layers on this stalagmite was prepared. The uniformity of oxygen isotopic composition along each analysed growth layer was taken as evidence that the stalagmite had formed in oxygen isotope equilibrium (Hendy, 1971). For comparison of the isotopic composition of this "fossil" stalagmite, samples of modern seepage water in the cave and soda-straw stalactites of very young age broken from the roof were analysed for their oxygen isotopic composition. Then a profile of $\delta^{18}O$ of calcite was analysed along the axis of the stalagmite, to provide a record of changes in the isotopic composition of the calcite over the interval from 96 to 89 ka. This profile is shown in Fig. IV.2. In general we have observed in other localities (Harmon *et al.*,1978) that $\delta^{18}O$ decreases with increasing temperature, as a result of the decrease of the oxygen isotope fractionation factor between calcite and water. It is not possible to convert a curve such as that in Fig. IV.2 directly into a temperature scale, but the general tendency of the record is however clearly indicative of a cooling trend over the

$\star$ The $^{18}O/^{16}O$ ratio is reported in the $\delta^{18}O$ notation:

$$\delta 18O_{ct}= \left(\frac{(^{18}O/^{16}O)_{ct}}{(^{18}O/^{16}O)_{std}} -1\right)\cdot 10^3$$

where ct = calcite and std = standard. The units are per mil (‰); the standard used here is PDB.

history of this deposit. A stalagmite formed over approximately the same interval in a cave in Lancashire shows a comparable trend, although displaced to lower overall temperatures (Gascoyne, 1980). Note that over part of the record preserved in D 312, the isotopic composition of calcite being deposited was more ^{18}0-depleted (lighter) than modern calcite (for which $\delta^{18}0 = -5.8\%$). This would imply that temperatures in the cave were even warmer than at present. The temperature inside a sealed cave such as this one would be equal to the average temperature on the ground above the cave. Thus we have here a record of the deterioration of climate, possibly at the end of oxygen isotope stage 5c.

CONCLUSIONS

At various stages in the development of Pontnewydd Cave chemically precipitated calcite deposits have formed on the floor and roof of the cave. Fragments of these deposits are present in at least four of the detrital sedimentary units of the cave-filling sequence. Ages obtained from these fragments have allowed us to provide maximum estimates of the time emplacement of the host units. In a few instances deposits of calcite formed *in situ* on the upper surfaces of one of the sedimentary units (Lower Breccia) have allowed more precise estimates for the time of deposition. These data are summarised in Fig.IV.3, where the dates are shown as bars of width equal to 1 sigma, the error in the age as estimated from the statistical analysis of the alpha-particle counting data.

The Lower Breccia was emplaced, presumably in a single brief pulse as a debris-flow deposit. Superimposed on the top of the Lower Breccia in the East Passage of the cave are *in situ* calcite deposits that range in date from 215 ± 36 ka to 83 ± 9ka. One similar *in situ* deposit adhering to the wall of the cave near the entrance, where it capped and cemented a lump of Lower Breccia onto the wall of the cave, gave a comparable date of 217 + 24/−20 ka.

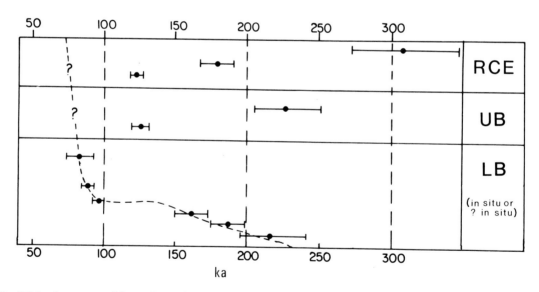

Fig. IV.3 Summary of dates obtained in this study and estimate of time of deposition of each stratigraphic unit up to Red Cave-Earth. Dashed line shows inferred date of top of detrital fill at each stage. LB = Lower Breccia; UB = Upper Breccia; RCE = Red Cave-Earth. Samples B0a, B0b, B148, B162 and D1288 are not shown here.

The cave appears to have been quiescent, and devoid of active sediment transport during the interval from 215 ka to 83 ka. Stable isotopic data from the youngest *in situ* deposit on the Lower Breccia confirms that the cave was sealed, and marks a cooling episode at the end of the last interglacial. Deposition of clastic sediments in the cave was renewed with the formation of the Pond Deposit, resting on the Lower Breccia. Some time thereafter the Upper Breccia was introduced into the cave as a debris flow. It is important to remember that clasts of travertine from within it give ages older than those of *in situ* deposits lower in the sedimentary sequence. They therefore do not inform us as to the maximum age of the Upper Breccia. A similar problem is encountered in the overlying Red Cave Earth.

The hope of this study was initially to provide an estimate for the time of occupation of the cave by hominids. It appears that most or all of the artefacts and hominid fossil materials were carried into the cave enclosed in debris flows. Therefore it is not expected that the archaeological evidence would be found in a stratified context capable of treatment by normal methods of U-series dating of travertines. Nevertheless, we have been able to place some limits on the human record. Most of the artefacts were recovered from the Lower Breccia, which is shown here to be at least 217 ka old. The artefacts are described as representing an Acheulian tool kit (Green, this volume); artefacts of similar typology are found in both the underlying Intermediate and the overlying Upper Breccia (where they are believed to be derived from the Lower Breccia). Hominid finds have come from the Intermediate and Lower Breccia layers of the East Passage. A TL study of a burnt flint core from the former unit places the probable age of the artefact and nearby hominid adult molar at 200 ± 25 ka. It is important to note, however, that we have not yet been able to place a maximum limit on the age of these deposits based on a dated sample from an unambiguous context. This would require dating of some *in situ* deposit in a layer beneath the

B0a:	Fragment (15 × 8 × 10 mm) of pale-tan flowstone, finely laminated; pods of porous material locally; columnar calcite crystals, 2 cm long, normal to layers; mound-like layering.
B0b:1	Fragment of finely laminated, pale-tan flowstone; lenses of porous rock with prism-lined vugs; dated material is from non-porous layers.
B0b:2	Second fragment of the same block which yielded date B0b:1. Finely laminated flowstone, with porous lens-shaped patches 2–5 mm long; coarse xtals normal to bedding. Vugs, sand-filled, cemented tight.
B 148:	Rounded block of flowstone, 4 cm thick with fine laminations; partly non-porous; locally up to 20% porosity, with fine rhombs growing into cavities.
B 162:	Calcite, stalagmitic coatings chipped from pebbles and boulders; non-porous, or locally vuggy; finely laminated.
B 260:	Rounded clast of flowstone, tan-white; 0.2 mm laminae, locally comprised of fine prisms normal to bedding. Very porous.
B 262:	Small slab of flowstone topped by small stalagmites. Top layers brownish with clay and stalactite fragments; lower 2/3: honey-tan and white layers, translucent.
B 274:	Fragment of flowstone enclosing two large stalactites, pebbles of limestone and small stalactites (soda-straws). Dated sample includes some of stalactite (< 10%).
B 275:	Rounded chunk of massive flowstone, very porous, recrystallised; vugs lined with fine stal. Relict stalactites (?) *in situ* suggest origin as roof deposit.

B 279:	Rounded fragment of flowstone, coarsely crystalline (recrystallised?), very low porosity.
C0:	Flowstone fragment, with stalagmite growing on it; pure, finely laminated, white, non-porous; dated sample from base.
C 133:	Very pure calcite encrusting pebbles of dark grey limestone. One piece of flowstone (older generation) encrusted by calcite (not dated).
D 187:	Stalactite, slightly rounded, found embedded in breccia.
D 312:	Stalagmite, possibly growing *in situ* on breccia. Pronounced hiatus in growth in middle of deposit. Samples :02 from below hiatus, :01 from above it (extending to base).
D 534:	Stalagmite attached to flowstone apron. Central parts of stalagmite show recrystallisation to amoeboid 1–2 mm calcite grains, while outer parts and base are of prismatic, radiating xtals. Deposited on limestone breccia.
D 604:	Calcite-cemented breccia of limestone fragments, covered by flowstone (draped over irregular surface) containing thin stalactites. Sample taken from youngest layer.
D 642:	Large mass (3 kg) of flowstone with erratically swirled, tan, non-porous travertine, 5% porosity as discrete 2–10 mm holes. Patches of crumbly stalagmite.
D1288B:	See description given by Collcutt in Ivanovich *et al* (p.98).

Table IV.1   Description of samples

Intermediate. Note also the wide range in ages of clasts within each breccia unit, which leaves open the possibility that the true age of any of the hominid and artefactual material from the various detrital layers may be *as old* or *older* than the maximum age indicated by U-Th dating of any enclosed stalagmitic fragment. Indeed, because of the transported, redeposited nature of the breccia units in which these archaeological materials have been found, even absolute dating of an underlying (pre-Intermediate) *in situ* stalagmite would not ultimately rule out the possibility that the artefacts are older yet. However, this is perhaps a counsel of despair and there are, in fact, a number of sound reasons (p.208) for believing the human occupation of the site to have taken place after the deposition of the Upper Sands and Gravels and before the emplacement of the Lower Breccia.

ACKNOWLEDGEMENTS

This work was supported by research grants from the Social Science and Humanities Research Council at the Natural Science and Engineering Research Council. Analytical assistance was provided by M.M. Russell, N. Cesar and Martin Knyf. McMaster Isotopic Nuclear and Geochemical Contribution 128.

Sample No.	$\dfrac{^{234}U}{^{238}U} \pm 1\sigma$	$\dfrac{^{230}Th}{^{234}U} \pm 1\sigma$	$\dfrac{^{230}Th}{^{232}Th} \pm 1\sigma$	U conc., ppm	Age (uncorr.)	Age (corr.)	Description
Red Cave Earth							
B 260	$1.137 \pm .021$	$0.977 \pm .026$	> 1000	0.77	$307 \begin{smallmatrix}+44\\-35\end{smallmatrix}$	–	porous flowstone
B 262	$1.085 \pm .025$	$0.821 \pm .022$	170	0.59	179 ± 12	–	stalactite
B 275	$3.879 \pm .078$	$0.756 \pm .015$	> 1000	0.26	123 ± 4	–	stalagmite (interface RCE/UB)
Upper Breccia							
B 279	$1.140 \pm .029$	$0.904 \pm .027$	36 ± 4	0.51	$227 \begin{smallmatrix}+24\\-20\end{smallmatrix}$	–	stalagmite (rounded fragment)
In situ on Lower Breccia							
B 274	$1.092 \pm .018$	$0.899 \pm .025$	11 ± 0.9	0.65	$230 \begin{smallmatrix}+21\\-20\end{smallmatrix}$	$217 \begin{smallmatrix}+24\\-20\end{smallmatrix}$	stalagmite
Derived fragments at or near base of Breccia							
B148	$1.001 \pm .017$	$0.855 \pm .022$	78 ± 9	0.72	209 ± 16	–	stalagmite
B0a (HPS-78850)	$1.039 \pm .017$	$0.752 \pm .021$	85 ± 21	0.88	149 ± 9	–	flowstone (base of LB)
B0b:1 (HPS–78851)	$1.066 \pm .017$	$0.706 \pm .019$	50 ± 11	0.88	130 ± 7	–	flowstone
B0b:2	$1.047 \pm .035$	$0.857 \pm .030$	70 ± 19	0.65	204 ± 20	–	(base of LB)
Calcite coating on clast in Breccia							
B 162	$0.930 \pm .050$	$0.886 \pm .048$	52 ± 7	0.63	$255 \begin{smallmatrix}+89\\-47\end{smallmatrix}$	–	calcite coating on block

Note: Age (corr): corrected for detrital ^{230}Th assuming initial $^{230}Th/^{232}Th = 1.25$

TABLE IV.2A   Uranium-series ages for travertine from Pontnewydd cave. Area B (from Deep Sounding to cave-entrance, including South Fissure); RCE = Red Cave Earth; UB = Upper Breccia; LB = Lower Breccia; Int = Intermediate.

NB   Samples B0a, B0b, B148 have previously (Green, 1981a) been ascribed to the interface of LB/Int. Greater knowledge of the very complex stratigraphy in this area (p.30) shows that most or all of these samples have probably come from the base of the Upper Breccia. Samples B0a and B0b, however, certainly came from the interface of Lower Breccia and Intermediate sediment but the LB is locally cemented and it is possible that the LB sediment in question was in one or both cases in the form of large clasts transported by UB.

Sample No.	$\dfrac{^{234}U}{^{238}U} \pm 1\sigma$	$\dfrac{^{230}Th}{^{234}U} \pm 1\sigma$	$\dfrac{^{230}Th}{^{232}Th} \pm 1\sigma$	U conc., ppm	Age (uncorr.)	Age (corr.)	Description
In situ on Lower Breccia							
CO							
(HPS–78852)	1.146 ± .018	0.849 ± .021	9 ± 1	0.49	189 ± 12	177 ± 12	stalagmite
Lower Breccia							
C 133							
(root of CO)	1.166 ± .029	1.011 ± .030	19 ± 2	0.39	> 350	–	calcite crust

Note: Age (corr): corrected for detrital ^{230}Th assuming initial ^{230}Th/^{232}Th = 1.25

Table IV.2B Uranium–series ages for travertine from Pontnewydd cave. Area C (South Passage)

Sample No.	$\dfrac{^{234}U}{^{238}U} \pm 1\sigma$	$\dfrac{^{230}Th}{^{234}U} \pm 1\sigma$	$\dfrac{^{230}Th}{^{232}Th} \pm 1\sigma$	U conc., ppm	Age (uncorr.)	Age (corr.)	Description
Upper Breccia							
D 187	1.312 ± .024	0.710 ± .019	87 ± 16	0.47	125 ± 6	–	stalactite
Lower Breccia							
in situ or ? in situ deposits on L.B.							
D 642	1.151 ± .017	0.594 ± .030	6.6 ± 0.4	0.58	95 ± 7	83 ± 9	flowstone
D 534:1 – 4							
(top) : 1	1.195 ± .030	1.452 ± .078	3.0 ± 0.2	0.28	-	–	
: 2	1.282 ± .021	0.927 ± .018	86 ± 12	0.28	227 ± 13	–	stalagmite
: 3	1.044 ± .021	0.953 ± .025	23 ± 2	0.28	$300 ^{+54}_{-37}$	–	
(base): 4	1.317 ± .036	1.668 ± .074	4.7 ± 0.4	0.25	-	–	
D 312: top	1.384 ± .021	0.579 ± .012	79 ± 12	0.47	89.3 ± 2.7	–	stalagmite
D 312: base	1.401 ± .029	0.607 ± .018	38 ± 12	0.52	95.7 ± 4.3	–	
D 604	1.151 ± .028	0.794 ± .023	62 ± 11	0.24	161 ± 11	–	stalagmite
D1288B:03 (top)	1.233 ± .039	0.874 ± .042	113.7	0.28	$196 ^{+27}_{-22}$	–	stalagmite
D1228B:02 (middle)	1.254 ± .035	0.958 ± .049	76.2	0.26	$257 ^{+60}_{-40}$	–	stalagmite
D1288B:01 (lower)	1.374 ± .045	0.883 ± .036	35.2	0.20	$193 ^{+21}_{-18}$	–	stalagmite

(Sample D1228B: average age = 215 ± 36)

Note: Age (corr): corrected for detrital ^{230}Th assuming initial ^{230}Th/^{232}Th = 1.25

Table IV.2c.   Uranium–series ages for travertine from Pontnewydd Cave. Area D (East Passage)

PART B

BRIEF REPORT ON DATING THE
IN SITU STALAGMITIC FLOOR FOUND IN THE
EAST PASSAGE IN 1982

by

M. Ivanovich, A.M.B. Rae and M.A. Wilkins

A stalagmitic floor sample, D1288C, obtained during the 1982 autumn season was received in October. The sample was in one piece with a clearly labelled top orientation. The *in situ* floor (Pl.XXXIX a) was found (p.205) underlying the Silt beds and on top of a localised roof fall on Lower Breccia at the entrance to the South East Fissure (grid square J7). The bulk of the sample was a rather pure, milky calcite and only its upper and lower sides were dirty, containing pieces of detrital cave material and limestone embedded in the calcite. We are indebted to Simon Collcutt *(in litt., 21/12/82)* for the following detailed description of another sample from the same floor (D1288D):

"The stalagmite sample is relatively pure. No organic matter could be identified under the microscope, but there is a little iron oxide that does not appear to be totally detrital. The calcite itself has been considerably recrystallised in places, although this has probably happened mostly in a closed system. Chemical tests for organic matter showed no measurable amounts (i.e. less than 0.2%)."

The 'contaminated' upper and lower faces were carefully removed and the remaining 'pure' calcite was cut into three horizontal (with respect to the top orientation) layers which were then labelled UPPER, MIDDLE and LOWER samples. Each layer sample obtained in this manner was crushed to particle size less than 120μm and homogenised. Aliquots of between 10 and 15 gm were then used for the uranium series disequilibrium analyses. The radiometric results and the derived ages are presented in Table IV.3. Each part of the stalagmitic sample (UPPER, MIDDLE, LOWER) was analysed at least three times in order to establish the reliability of the measurement through repetition and to demonstrate the homogeneity of the sample derived from each section. It was also hoped that, in the event of sufficient age resolution between the three sections, the rate of the stalagmitic growth could be estimated from the data.

Only one analysis reported in Table IV.3 has failed to produce a date (HAR 5609) because the $^{230}Th/^{234}U$ activity ratio was higher than unity, indicating, therefore, post-depositional contamination. The same sample has also yielded a higher uranium content than the other nine. The uniformity in the measured uranium content is remarkable. Similarly, $^{234}U/^{238}U$ activity ratios are all well within the quoted one standard deviation of each other in each layer. The thorium isotopic ratios are all greater than 50, indicating that the material is free of detrital thorium. However, the apparent variations from one measurement to another are either due to very low thorium specific activities resulting in large statistical errors, or due to inhomogeneous distribution of resistate minerals containing detrital thorium (^{232}Th), or due to the combination of the two.

The spread of the reported ages in each layer is within the quoted two standard deviations and average values for each layer shown in the last column of Table IV.3 cannot be distinguished statistically from each other. Because of this apparent poor resolution of the dating method the three individual averages should also be averaged to yield the grand average of 224+41/−31 ka. This age can be taken to represent an average age of formation of the *in situ* stalagmitic floor discovered in East Passage of the cave. The archaeological implication is that the hominid remains found beneath the stalagmitic floor from which sample D1288C derives must pre-date the quoted age of 224,000 years before present. The results reported by Henry Schwarcz (p. 92) and Nicholas Debenham (p. 105) are statistically consistent with our own mean date.

Sample Number	$[^{238}U]$ (ppm)	$^{234}U/^{238}U$	$^{230}Th/^{234}U$	$^{230}Th/^{232}Th$	$[^{234}U/^{238}U]_O$	Age ± 1σ (ka)	Av. Age (ka)
UPPER							
HAR 2255	0.26 ±0.01	1.30 ±0.06	0.857 ±0.046	51	1.50 ±0.11	184^{+26}_{-22}	
HAR 5612	0.26 ±0.01	1.32 ±0.06	0.996 ±0.047	715	1.72 ±0.13	285^{+71}_{-45}	225^{+44}_{-32}
HAR 5624	0.27 ±0.01	1.28 ±0.07	0.893 ±0.049	1000	1.50 ±0.12	205^{+35}_{-27}	
MIDDLE							
HAR 2256	0.27 ±0.01	1.29 ±0.07	0.969 ±0.054	101	1.61 ±0.16	262^{+69}_{-44}	
HAR 5610	0.29 ±0.01	1.44 ±0.07	0.960 ±0.049	88	1.85 ±0.14	238^{+44}_{-33}	218^{+39}_{-29}
HAR 5622	0.27 ±0.01	1.28 ±0.05	0.853 ±0.036	422	1.46 ±0.08	183^{+20}_{-17}	
HAR 5623	0.28 ±0.01	1.40 ±0.06	0.875 ±0.044	244	1.68 ±0.11	188^{+25}_{-21}	
LOWER							
HAR 2257	0.26 ±0.01	1.43 ±0.06	0.961 ±0.045	129	1.84 ±0.11	239^{+41}_{-31}	
HAR 5609	0.31 ±0.01	1.36 ±0.06	1.085 ±0.049	217	-	-	229^{+41}_{-32}
HAR 5621	0.26 ±0.01	1.39 ±0.08	0.926 ±0.054	320	1.71 ±0.15	218^{+42}_{-31}	

All ± errors quoted are one standard deviation due to counting statistics only.

TABLE IV.3. Harwell radiometric data and derived ages for sample D1288C, Pontnewydd Cave, 1982

PART C
THERMOLUMINESCENCE AND URANIUM SERIES DATING OF STALAGMITIC CALCITE
by
N.C. Debenham, M.J. Aitken, Alan J. Walton and M. Winter

SAMPLES

Twelve samples of stalagmitic calcite were dated by the thermoluminescence method. Their locations and stratigraphy are given in Table IV.4. An interior portion was cut from each sample (the surface layer of at least a few mm being discarded) and slices (approximately 10 mm × 10 mm × 0.6 mm) were prepared from it for spectroscopic and spatial distribution studies (Walton and Debenham, 1980; Debenham et al.,1982). The remainder of the portion was crushed in a vice, and the granular fraction between 90 μm and 150 μm collected, etched in 1% acetic acid for 2 minutes, and washed in acetone. The dried grains were finally sieved to separate the 90 μm–125 μm fraction. For insertion in the TL oven, quantities of the grains were sprinkled onto stainless steel discs (10 mm dia. × 0.5 mm thick) which had been coated with a thin layer of silicone oil to provide adhesion and thermal contact between the disc and the grains. When the disc was held face down in a pair of tweezers and lightly tapped, grains not in direct contact with the disc were knocked off, and a single layer of grains was thus achieved. This configuration gives optimum conditions for heating and β-irradiation.

TL EQUIPMENT AND METHODS

The sample discs were glowed with a heating rate of 5°C/sec. The oven atmosphere was an oxygen-free gas (<3 ppm O_2 in argon), which was introduced after evacuation to 20 mtorr.

Sample Lab. Ref.	Site Ref.	Location	Metre Square	Area of Cave
226a1	D188	Upper stal. floor	H6	East Passage
226e9	D446	In Upper Breccia	H8	East Passage
226e13	D292	In Upper Breccia	K10	East Passage
226e6	D471	In top of Lower Breccia	H7	East Passage
226e14	D604	On Lower Breccia (? *in situ*)	J9	East Passage
226h21	D1711	On Lower Breccia (*in situ* floor)	J7	East Passage
226h3	D1693	On Lower Breccia (*in situ*)	G10	East Passage
226a8	B111	Interface Int/Breccia	K21	South Fissure
226f1	B0b:2	Interface Intermediate/Breccia	K21	South Fissure
226f2	B0b:1	Interface Intermediate/Breccia	K21	South Fissure
226e4	B396	Probably base of Breccia	K20	South Fissure
226g1	B409	Lower Sands and Gravels 3	K17	Deep Sounding

TABLE IV.4 Details of samples of stalagmitic calcite from Pontnewydd.
LB = Lower Breccia   Int = Intermediate
N.B. Since initial publication of some of these dates (Green, 1981a), there has been reassignation of layers for the South Fissure samples (*cf.* p.30 and Table IV.2a)

Measures were taken to reduce the water vapour content of the oven, including the use of a drying agent (P_2O_5). By these means it was possible virtually to eliminate spurious TL, even in fine-grain samples. The photomultiplier tube was an EMI 9635 QA with a bialkali photocathode and was fitted with a Chance-Pilkington HA3 infra-red absorbing filter and a Corning 5-60 blue filter. The latter gave a sensitivity to radiation-induced TL emissions while rejecting interfering emissions characterised by a localised origin (Debenham *et al.*, 1982).

Each disc was normalised by the Zero Glow method (Aitken *et al.*, 1979), i.e. by the response of the 80°C peak to a small beta test dose under standard conditions of storage time and temperature. The normalisation glow, which does not exceed 130°C, does not produce optical transparency changes in the sample or measurable drainage of the 280°C dating peak. Thus the subsequent high temperature glow, whether of the natural TL or with an additional β induced signal, is effectively the first glow.

TL ANALYSES

The principal data concerning the samples of stalagmitic materials, are presented in Table IV.5. The lower TL response of the calcites to a given deposited dose from α-particles compared to that for the same dose from β or γ radiation is described in terms of the a-value (Aitken and Bowman, 1975). Samples for α-irradiation were prepared as thin layers of 5μm grains, etched in 0.2% acetic acid, on Al discs. Measured a-values varied between samples from 0.18 to 0.53 as shown in Table IV.5.

Also presented in Table IV.5 are the environmental γ-dose rates incident on each sample. These were measured using two methods: (i) by γ-counting on site with a γ spectrometer capable of determining levels of U, Th and K, and (ii) by the burial *in situ* of copper capsules containing a drained sensitive phosphor (natural CaF_2) for about one year.

The β-dose intercepts of the first and second glow growth curves, Q and I respectively, define the palaeo-dose, P, by P = Q + I (see Fig.IV.4). The added β-doses for the first glow measurements ranged to > 280 Gy. All growth curves were linear except where initial supralinearity was observed with second glows or with the first glows of the youngest

Oxford TL ref.	Site ref.	a-value	Gamma Dose-rate Gy/ka	Q Gy	I Gy	P=Q+I Gy	TL Age ka BP	Layer
226a1	D188	0.29	0.68 ± 0.07	−15±10	37± 4	22±11	25±13	Upper stal. floor (EP)
226e9	D446	0.21	0.67 ± 0.07	134±25	−4±22	130±33	177±48	UB (EP)
226e13	D292	0.24	0.80 ± 0.15	112± 5	18±18	130±19	128±27	UB (EP)
226e14	D604	0.19	0.90 ± 0.15	187±11	15±16	202±19	201±35	LB (EP)
226h21	D1711	0.18	0.95 ± 0.10	158±10	10± 9	168±14	157±20	LB (EP)
226h3	D1693	0.21	0.75 ± 0.15	148± 9	22± 7	170±12	165±27	LB (EP)
226e6	D471	0.27	0.85 ± 0.15	206±26	15± 7	221±27	176±32	LB (EP)
226a8	B111	0.33	1.05 ± 0.15	142±18	14± 7	156±19	108±19	Int/Breccia (SF)
226f1	BOb:2	0.35	1.15 ± 0.15	133±11	7±12	140±17	105±18	Int/Breccia (SF)
226f2	BOb:1	0.53	1.15 ± 0.15	149±12	9±12	158±17	102±16	Int/Breccia (SF)
226e4	B396	0.49	1.20 ± 0.15	167±12	28± 9	195±15	102±14	Probably base of Breccia
226g1	B409	0.29	1.30 ± 0.15	223±16	15± 6	238±17	154±19	LSG3 (DPS)

TABLE IV.5 TL measurements and dosimetric data on stalagmites from Pontnewydd. Layers: UB – Upper Breccia, LB – Lower Breccia, Int – Intermediate, LSG – Lower Sands and Gravels. Areas: EP – East Passage, SF – South Fissure, DPS – Deep Sounding.

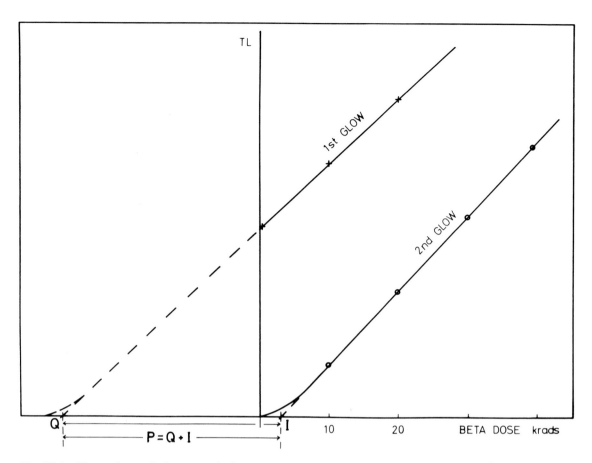

Fig. IV.4   First and second glow growth characteristics of calcite, defining the quantities Q, I and P (paleodose).

sample (a1). The errors result from the reproducibilities of the growth curve measurements which varied between a 2% and 8% standard deviation depending on the material studied. Poor reproducibility was associated with high levels of localised TL emission (Debenham *et al.*,1982), which were not completely suppressed by the filter used. It has been found that the reproducibility of the measurements is greatly improved by using the 100 μm grains resulting from a prolonged crushing procedure, probably because the mineral particles giving the interfering TL lie on lines of structural weakness in the calcite. Thus they would be freed in the first stages of crushing, whereas later stages would yield relatively uncontaminated calcite.

The TL date calculations were based on the following assumptions:

(i) that the gamma-ray dose to the calcite was derived entirely from the activity of the surrounding rock and/or sediment (i.e. that the dimensions of the sample were small compared to the characteristic gamma-ray range).

(ii) that the alpha- and beta-doses to the calcite were derived from its internal U-activity and that of its daughters. The effects of U-234 decay and Th-230 growth were included, but it was assumed that no Rn-222 was lost from the system (see Appendix B of Wintle, 1977).

(iii) that the α- and β-dose rates were not spatially correlated with TL intensity.

The first assumption is considered valid for the majority of stalagmitic samples from Pontnewydd, which were commonly found in the form of small fragments of floors dispersed through soil of fairly uniform gamma activity. Exceptions to this pattern are some of the *in situ* stalagmites. Sample a1 is an example, deriving from an *in situ* floor approximately 20 cm thick.

The calculation of the accumulated internal dose, according to the second assumption, was based on measurements of the uranium content of the samples and the present-day activity ratios, Th-230/U-234 and U-234/U-238. These measurements were carried out in the course of the uranium disequilibrium age determinations, which are described in the next section. The assumption that Rn-222 is not lost from the chain requires further investigation. Alpha-counting tests carried out with a gas cell (Aitken, 1978) on a single 8 gm portion of stalagmite implied that 17% of the internal α-dose was lost due to radon emanation. This would lead to a maximum error of 7% to the TL dates of the Pontnewydd samples, the true ages being older than calculated. Gamma-spectroscopy of the individual samples would allow more reliable assessments of this effect to be made.

The possible effects of spatial correlation between TL and uranium contents were investigated. The spatial distributions of radiation-induced TL emissions were observed using an image-intensifier tube (Walton and Debenham, 1980). No pronounced non-uniformities were found, and any correlation with the internal dose-rate would therefore be small. The effects on the calculated ages of these calcites would be further attenuated by the generally low proportions of the total dose-rates which are internally derived.

URANIUM DISEQUILIBRIUM ANALYSES

The states of U-234/U-238 and Th-230/U-234 disequilibria in the stalagmitic samples were determined by α-spectrometry of thin depositions of uranium and thorium extracted from spiked solutions of the calcites. Results of the analyses are summarised in Table IV.6. The extraction of the uranium and thorium was carried out by a slightly modified version of the method used at the Institut für Kernchemie, Cologne University. Dissolution of the calcite was by hydrochloric acid. Thorium was removed from uranium by two passes of the solution through an anion column. Thorium was extracted on a cation column, and removed from it with oxalic acid. The deposition on to the counting discs was by the method developed by Miro Ivanovich (AERE Harwell) in which Tetra Ethylene Glycol is used as a spreading agent. The extraction efficiencies of uranium and thorium, η_u and η_{Th} respectively, are given in Table IV.6.

The concentrations of U-238 were calculated knowing the activity of the added spike. The values of the ratio Th-230/Th-232 indicate the extent of contamination by non-radiogenic thorium which is leached from insoluble detritus held in the stalagmites when they are dissolved. All these values are high enough to have almost negligible effects on the Th-230/U-234 measurements, except in the case of 226a1. This sample held high levels of detrital material, and its dating by uranium series disequilibrium is consequently difficult.

The measured activity ratios, U-234/U-238 and Th-230/U-234, are listed in Table IV.6. The latter are uncorrected for detrital thorium contamination. The resolutions of the α-spectra, measured with a solid-state barrier detector, were usually less than 160 keV (full width half maximum). Where the resolution was poorer, a correction was made for interference by nearby peaks. The values of the U-234/U-238 ratios, ranging between 1.01 and 1.31, are all consistent with the uranium being derived only from ground water sources. The quoted errors of the U-234/U-238 ratios are statistical in origin. Those of the Th-230/U-234 ratios also include uncertainties in corrections to the Th-228 activities, whereby allowance was made for interference by the 5.44 MeV component of Ra-224, the decay of Th-228 activity since its separation from the supporting U-232, and the presence of Th-228 activity derived from Th-232.

We now consider the effects on the measured ratios of the leached detrital Th-230 levels in the sample solutions. To make an estimate of the possible errors, we have assumed a value for the leachable Th-230/Th-232 ratio in the detritus at the time of the stalagmitic formation, $B_0 = 2.0$. With reference to other work (Turekian and Nelson, 1976; Schwarcz,

Sample Lab. Ref.	Site Ref.		ηU	ηTh	U-238 ppm	Th-230/Th-232	U-234/U-238	Th-200/U-234	Detrital Th Corrn. ka	Corrected U-Series Date ka
226a1	D188	(i)	24%	53%	0.51	3	1.08 ± 0.04	0.157 ± 0.009	11	13 (7 – 20)
		(ii)			0.40	4.6	0.97 ± 0.04	0.30 ± 0.03	13	32 (21 – 44)
		(iii)			0.64	3.4	1.11 ± 0.05	0.167 ± 0.016	10	15 (8 – 22)
226c9	D446		67%	79%	0.22	>39	1.03 ± 0.07	1.125 ± 0.093	–	∞
226c13	D292	(1)	30%	44%	0.62	>39	1.13 ± 0.03	0.794 ± 0.035	5	160(142–182)
		(ii)	19%	24%	0.58	>16	1.18 ± 0.03	0.858 ± 0.53	9	185(154–230)
226h21	D1711		47%	42%	0.36	>33	1.27 ± 0.05	1.004 ± 0.064	5	302(228– ∞)
226h3	D1693		49%	74%	0.66	>73	1.20 ± 0.03	0.834 ± 0.045	2	176(153–205)
226c6	D471	(i)	26%	–	0.82	–	1.15 ± 0.03	–	–	–
		(ii)	34%	28%	0.72	>44	1.31 ± 0.05	0.843 ± 0.054	4	174(147–209)
226a8	B111	(i)	21%	24%	0.98	>27	1.06 ± 0.02	0.630 ± 0.037	5	104 (91–118)
		(ii)	28%	13%	0.92	>27	1.09 ± 0.02	0.751 ± 0.037	6	143(126–163)
226f1	B0b:2		35%	59%	0.61	>36	1.11 ± 0.04	0.922 ± 0.051	4	244(198–332)
226f2	B0b:1		38%	28%	0.68	>19	1.11 ± 0.03	0.916 ± 0.052	9	236(190–316)
226c4	B396	(i)	13%	51%	1.36	>26	1.01 ± 0.02	0.673 ± 0.037	9	118(103–135)
		(ii)	32%	13%	1.23	>18	1.06 ± 0.02	0.642 ± 0.034	7	106(93 –121)
226g1	B409		58%	52%	0.54	>68	1.17 ± 0.05	0.931 ± 0.059	3	243(195–334)

TABLE IV.6   Uranium series disequilibrium analyses of stalagmites from Pontnewydd.

1980), this value may be considered the maximum likely. The corrected Th-230/U-234 ratio was obtained from the measured ratio by subtracting $B_0 \exp (\lambda_0 t)$ (Th-232/U-234), where λ_0 is the Th-230 decay constant, and t is the stalagmite's age. The resulting decrease of the 1 standard deviation lower limit of each sample is given in Table IV.6. Except for sample 226a1, the correction amounts to only a few percent. The ages presented in the last column have their lower limits corrected in this manner, while no correction has been made to their upper limits. (Central values are shifted by an intermediate amount).

The U-232 spike solution was supplied in concentrated form by Miro Ivanovich (A.E.R.E. Harwell). Measurements of its activity ratio Th-228/U-232 have been repeated by various workers during the last two years, including ourselves. These measurements yield a ratio of 1.00 within an error of ±2%, and this value has been used in our evaluation of Th-230/U-234. The U-Series dates are compared with corresponding TL dates in Fig.IV.5.

RESULTS

The TL date for stalagmite a1 is consistent with its supposed Holocene formation. Best estimate ages for the main stratigraphic units are calculated from the TL measurements as follows:

Upper Breccia in East Passage   (2 dates on derived fragments), maximum age = 140±42 ka;

Lower Breccia in East Passage   (4 dates from calcite certainly or probably *in situ* on its surface), minimum age = 169±21ka.

Interface of Intermediate Breccia, all dates South Fissure,   (4 dates from derived calcite), maximum age = 104±14ka.

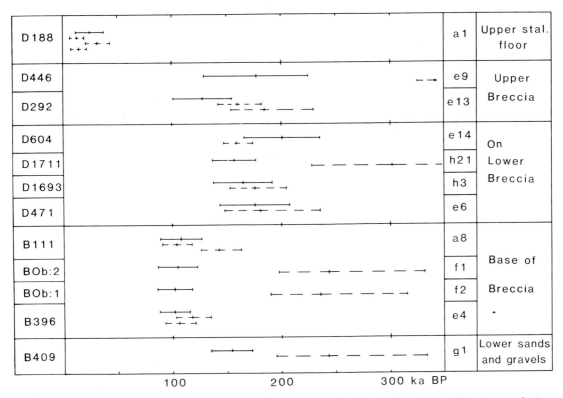

Fig. IV.5   Graphical presentation of TL(——) and Uranium series (– – –) dates ± 1σ. Uranium analysis on sample e14 carried out by Henry Schwarcz.

The last date is clearly consistent with the reconsideration of the provenance of most or all of the samples (p.30 and Table IV.2A) as coming from the interface of the Upper Breccia/Intermediate and not the Lower Breccia/Intermediate as originally proposed (Green, 1981a).

It is suspected however that some recrystallisation of the stalagmites in the South Fissure area has taken place, causing a re-zeroing of the TL signal. This interpretation is supported by visual examination of these and adjacent samples (*cf.* observations by Henry Schwarcz in Table IV.1 above). The TL date of stalagmite g1, in particular, may have been affected in this way.

The stalagmitic floor overlying the Lower Breccia has been dated with the U-Series method by Henry Schwarcz (sample D1288B) and by Miro Ivanovich (D1288C). The data from these analyses have been combined with our U-Series data for samples h21, h3 and e6, and with the data on e14 (= D604) measured by Henry Schwarcz. They form a fairly consistent set (minimum χ^2 = 24.4 on 16 measurements) and yield a mean date of 204 ka with the 1 standard deviation range 174 − 248 ka. This does not differ significantly from the mean TL date (169 ± 21 ka).

ACKNOWLEDGEMENT

We acknowledge financial support from the Science-Based Archaeology Committee of the Science and Engineering Research Council.

PART D
THERMOLUMINESCENCE (TL) STUDIES ON BURNT FLINT AND STONES
by
J. Huxtable

The dating of crushed flint samples has been reported in detail elsewhere (Huxtable and Jacobi, 1982), but a brief resumé of the technique follows. The material must have been heated to a sufficiently high temperature (in excess of 500°C) to reset its TL signal to zero; the sample then starts to reaccumulate TL signal due to its exposure to ionising radiation from the natural radioactive environment in which it is buried. There is also some contribution from the internal radioactivity of the sample, but in the case of flint this self dose is very low and the environmental contribution is usually 80% or more of the total dose. It is therefore essential to collect the exact sediment which surrounds the dating sample, and it is preferable that samples should come from a uniform stratum.

There is a limit, the 'saturation value', to the amount of radiation which can be absorbed by any sample before it shows no change in output with increasing age. All saturated samples are valueless, because it is impossible to tell whether the material was, despite appearances, burnt at all, or how much time has elapsed since the specimen became saturated. The saturation value varies for different materials, and it seems likely that cherts are among the best materials for TL dating of the Palaeolithic, because they have high saturation values, which permit the study of old samples and the establishment of dates from them.

The samples are prepared from flints which had the outer 2 mm of surface removed using a diamond wheel saw, leaving a disc about 3 cm across and 0.5 cm thick in order to extract sufficient grains by crushing in a vice; the sample of artefact removed is destroyed in the process of preparation.

A total of five burnt samples was analysed from three different areas within the cave, B, C and D (Fig. I.6). Petrological details are given in Table IV.7.

Site B (South Fissure)

One burnt stone core (B302; lab. ref. no. 226b2) from the Upper Breccia had a high internal radioactivity with a thick source (42 mm diameter ring) α count of (12.1 ± 0.3) counts per kilosec, and K_2O value of 4.41%. The material was saturated, with a saturation value of about 55 krad.

Site C (South Passage)

Two stones from site C were submitted – a burnt stone flake (C13; lab. ref. no. 226b) and a natural pebble fragment (C249; lab. ref 226c1) both from the Lower Breccia.
i) 226b: This was not flint but a mudstone: Internal radioactivity measurements: α count (3.5 ± 0.04) counts per kilosec, thick source (42 mm diameter ring), K_2O 0.61%. It was saturated, the quartz fraction appearing to have a saturation value around 20 krad. It was also investigated by Don Robins, using ESR techniques, at the Institute of Archaeology, University of London and he concluded that it had been burnt (personal communication); and further by Alan Walton and Dr. Nicholas Debenham using the image intensifier at the Open University Research Unit, Boars Hill, Oxford, with a similar conclusion.

ii) 226c1. Internal radioactivity measurements are α count (11.7 ± 0.2) counts per kilosec, thick source, 42 mm diameter ring, K_2O 2.52%. The TL signal from this sample was not very reproducible, but it appeared to be saturated.

Site D (East Passage)

Two samples were submitted from Site D. They were a burnt flint core (D687; 226d1) from the Buff Intermediate, and one burnt pebble (D620; 226d2) from the junction of the Buff and Orange Intermediate layers.

i) 226d1. This burnt flint gave good responses to all the parameters measured. It had an archaeological dose of (29.6 ± 1.0) krad. The total dose rate for the sample was made up of the internal dose .025 rad a^{-1}, and the soil γ + cosmic dose of .120 rad a^{-1}, the latter derived from fluorite dosimeter measurements in the layer. The calculated TL age for the sample is (200 ± 25) ka, Lab. ref. no. OX TL 226d1, the error quoted being the total predicted error at the 68% confidence level.

ii) 226d2. This pebble was again in saturation, the saturation value being about 40 krad. Internal radioactivity measurement: alpha count (6.8 ± 0.2) counts per kilosec, thick source, 42 mm diameter ring, K_2O 2.14%.

Sample PN78 C13. Oxford TL reference 226b.

Lithology: Mudstone.
Components: Quartz, white mica, hematite, rare chlorite and rare apatite.
Features: The white mica crystals show a preferred orientation, probably defining a penetrative cleavage.

Sample PN80 C249. Oxford TL reference no. 226c1.

Lithology: Mudstone/fine siltstone.
Components: Quartz, white mica, biotite mica, chlorite and rare ore.
Features: A parallel alignment of white mica crystals probably defines a penetrative cleavage.

Sample PN80 B302. Oxford TL reference no. 226b2.

Lithology: Vitric tuff.
Components: Quartzo-feldspathic aggregates replacing shardic fragments are set in a fine grained quartz-rich matrix, with minor amounts of ore.
Features: Very delicate glass shards are well preserved in this rock, showing very little evidence of tectonic deformation. This specimen bears a strong resemblance to tuffaceous rocks of Ordovician age exposed in central Snowdonia.

Sample PN80 D620. Oxford TL reference no. 226d2.

Lithology: Mudstone.
Components: Quartz and oxidized mica.
Features: Extensive oxidation of the iron-mica has occurred at some stage, possibly as a result of a tectonic event, such as shearing.

TABLE IV.7. Brief petrological descriptions of burnt rock specimens (by R.E. Bevins).

PART E
RELATIVE DATING AND ASSESSMENT OF DEPOSITIONAL ENVIRONMENT FROM TRACE ELEMENT ANALYSIS OF FOSSIL BONES
by
T.I. Molleson

INTRODUCTION

It has long been accepted that, since bone or teeth become altered when buried in the ground for any length of time, the chemical composition of a fossil provides a guide to the burial history. Differences in concentration of certain elements can be used to ascertain the relative ages of groups of fossils and have often proved the basis for accepting or rejecting hominid material of doubtful antiquity.

Some fossils found during the recent excavations at Pontnewydd are of doubtful antiquity either because of the nature of the deposits (old excavation-dumps), or because of the complexity of the depositional environment (reworked beds). The elucidation of some of the contextual problems has been explored in this pilot study.

MATERIALS AND METHODS

To test the feasibility of assessing the material by trace element analysis, five bone samples were selected from the different horizons recognised. In addition, three bones found out of context and a modern bone were also tested. Wherever possible, bear phalanges of similar size and completeness were chosen. The bones were sectioned midshaft, and were submitted to Graeme Coote of the Institute of Nuclear Sciences, Lower Hutt, New Zealand, for proton microprobe profiling (Coote & Sparks, 1981). One gramme of powdered sample was also taken and measured for uranium uptake as indicated by beta activity (Oakley, 1980). Part of the powdered sample was used to determine the conversion of bone hydroxyapatite to fluorapatite by X-ray diffraction techniques (Niggli et al.,1958).

RESULTS AND DISCUSSION

The results of the three series of tests are summarised in Table IV.8.

The uranium values (expressed as eU_3O_8 ppm) have already been discussed (Molleson in Green et al.,1981). Of the bones tested only the modern bone showed no radioactivity and gave no indication of post-mortem uptake of uranium. It can therefore be inferred that all of the other bones tested, including those deriving from the old excavation dumps, had been buried for some time. This includes the human vertebra recovered from the East Passage and the human mandible recovered from the World War II excavation dump. The uranium value for the bear phalange PV found in the Upper Breccia fell within the range of the values obtained for phalanges from the Lower Breccia and Intermediate. It is therefore not possible to use this technique to distinguish material from the different Pleistocene levels nor can the material found out of context be referred to a particular Pleistocene horizon.

The fluorine assessments using X-ray diffraction techniques appear to indicate little or no post-mortem uptake of fluoride in the modern dog bone nor in some of the older bones. A

Lab No.	Sample	Excavator's Reference No.	Preservation Type	Fluorine % X-ray	Fluorine % probe average	Uranium (eU308) ppm
QA	Modern dog, domestic	PN79 D2	Modern	0.3	0.05	nil
PV	Bear phalange, Upper Breccia	PN80 D567	III	1.19	0.60	13
PY	Bear phalange, Lower Breccia	PN80 D634	II	0.45	0.33	27
PU	Bear phalange, Lower Breccia	PN80 D504	II	0.86	0.15	17
PW	Bear phalange, Intermediate	PB80 D584	I	0.72	0.03	10
PX	Bear phalange, Intermediate	PN80 D616	I	0.23	0.03	15
PR	Bear phalange, World War II Dump	PN80 A122	?	1.58	0.10	15
PT	Human vertebra, East Passage, Unstratified	PN78 C5	?	0.86	–	8s
PZ	Human mandible, World War II Dump	PN80 A80	?	0.23	–	17s

TABLE IV.8 Pontnewydd Cave. Fluorine and uranium analyses of bone. (s = solid sample)

higher level of fluorine was recorded in the bone from the albeit younger Upper Breccia than in bones from the underlying Lower Breccia and Intermediate. Whilst the high level of fluorine in the bear phalange from the World War II dump might be indicative of a provenance from the Upper Breccia, many more samples need to be tested to ascertain the pattern of fluorination in the different levels.

The degree of fluoride uptake is believed to be a function of time and the concentration of fluorine in ground waters. Temperature and pH affect the mobility of the fluoride ion. Permeability and compaction of the sediment, sealing by an overlying impermeable deposit, or even water-logging in stagnant waters are factors that can slow or arrest fluoride exchange. It follows that the fluorine content of fossilized bone is a result of the interaction of a number of factors which may not apply equally to all the bones in a given bed; nevertheless the interpretation of the results can only be in terms relative to the other bones analysed. This said, if several bones are tested from each horizon a pattern of alteration often emerges (Molleson and Oakley, 1966); but the interpretation is complicated where, as in the Pontnewydd sequence, many of the bones in the deposits are derived by reworking skeletonized but incompletely altered material.

Bones in layers of the Intermediate complex and from the Lower Breccia are in consolidated debris flows which probably moved in a waterlogged condition from deposits, nearer to the cave entrance, where the bones had been degraded and fossilized to a greater or lesser degree depending on exposure time before re-emplacement. (There are also some bones derived from the Intermediate in the Lower Breccia). The Upper Breccia, a much younger deposit, contains faunal remains in part transported from the direction of the cave-mouth, in part derived from the Lower Breccia and in part derived from the Silt beds which were laid down by flowing water. The Silt beds are porous and permeable and the Upper Breccia contains a lot of silty material in the matrix. The bone from the Upper Breccia tested is determined from the nature of its preservation to have been derived from the Silt beds, but *in situ* Silt bed material was not available for the analysis at this stage.

The proton microprobe scans for fluorine distribution carried out by Dr Coote produced distinctive profiles that can most probably be related to the mode of emplacement of the bone as described above. Certainly, the fluorine levels themselves are not correlated directly with age as was already clear from the studies by X-ray diffraction. Whether the fluorine level is more determined by ambient levels of fluorine in the ground-waters, or by the duration of exposure of the bone to exchange from the ground-waters, can to some extent be inferred from the shape of the proton scan profiles.

Spiky profiles – that is profiles in which the fluorine concentration jumps abruptly from a high level to a low level (QA, Fig. IV.6a) – suggest that there was not enough time or enough water present for the fluorine to build up across the bone before the consolidation of the deposit or the recovery of the bone. Such spiky profiles were observed in the outermost regions of the modern bone QA, and in the bone that had been recovered from the modern dumps as well as in the bone, PO, from the Lower Breccia; but a gradient (PX, Fig.IV.6b), as in sample PX, suggests a longer exposure of the bone to ground-waters. The shallower the gradient, the longer the exposure time, so that the development of a plateau (sample PY) (PY, Fig. IV.6c) suggests a very long exposure to ground-waters.

A preliminary assessment of the material is as follows. The two bones PW and PX from the Intermediate beds have almost identical profiles which show an even distribution of fluorine that is doubtless the lifetime level. An increase in the fluorine level towards the outer side of the cortex indicates a small amount of *post-mortem* uptake of fluorine. The gradient is very steep, and this suggests a short exposure time. The overall indication is of rapid burial and no ground-water movement through the sediment, which could have been waterlogged or sealed by the overlying Lower Breccia. Available fluorine in the ground-waters was minimal.

The profiles of the two specimens PY and PU from the Lower Breccia both reveal increased levels of fluorine throughout the bone sections, but there are certain differences between the two profiles which may be significant. The bear phalange (sample PU (D504)), has an increased level of fluorine in the outermost layer of the cortex which should indicate recent exposure. The profile then drops rapidly to about 0.06% for about 2.5 mm., then rises again to about 0.15% for the innermost 1.5–2.0 mm. of the scan. It shows no resemblance at all to PY, in which the level of fluorine has increased to about 0.32% and the distribution is constant across the section so that the profile presents a high plateau. There is no marginal gradient and this is the sort of distribution to be expected from lifetime uptake of the element; however, such levels (0.3%) are on the high side and it seems probable that the plateau has been established after long exposure of the bone to fluoride in percolating ground-waters. Uptake of fluoride across the bone has occurred, and equilibrium was achieved before compaction of the sediment enclosing the bone. The lower level of fluorine in PU and the very spiky nature of the profile would be due to a shorter exposure to ground-waters before the enclosing sediment dried out or was compacted – diffusion of fluoride across the bone has been arrested. The outer spike should indicate a renewal of fluorine uptake.

The sample PV from the Upper Breccia also shows an outer spike imposed upon an evenly distributed increased level of fluorine. All the indications from the profile are for an increased level of fluorine in the ground-water, long exposure of the bone in a permeable sediment and the possibility of renewed uptake at the time of redeposition of the bone or more recently (*cf* PU). The failure of the outer spike to develop a gradient suggests that if there was a renewed uptake at the time of redeposition, diffusion was arrested by the rapid compaction of the Upper Breccia. The character of the surface spike, however, suggests recent exposure.

The modern dog femur QA shows the expected distribution of life-time fluorine across the bone cortex. In addition, there is a narrow spike of increased fluorine in the outermost cortical layer on the medial side of the shaft. This marks *post-mortem* uptake of short duration such as Coote has shown in bones buried for no more than two years. A diffusion gradient has not developed, because of the short time interval.

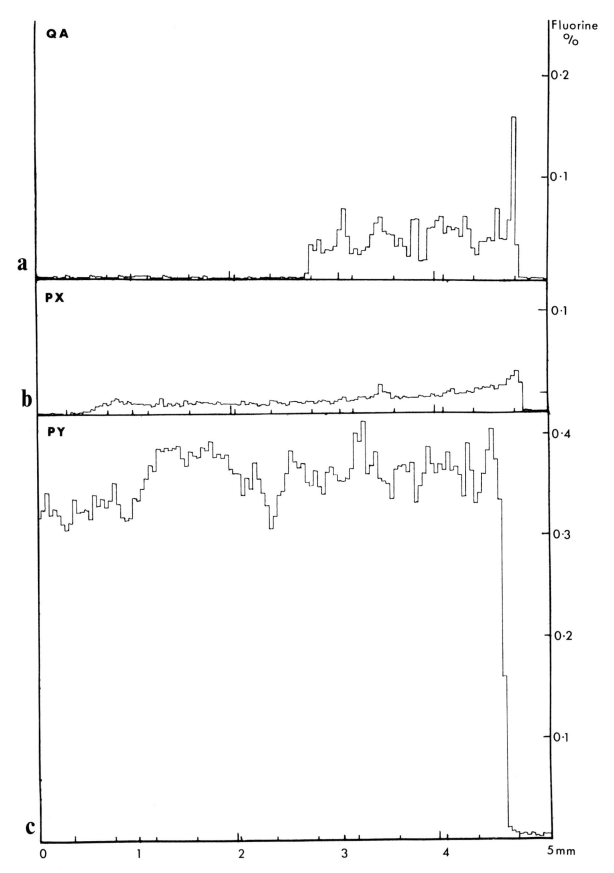

Fig. IV.6   Distribution of fluorine in bones from Pontnewydd Cave as revealed by PIXE scans made across the cortex of the bone. (a) outermost spike of increased fluorine in recently buried dog femur. (b) steep gradient in the outermost region of the cortex in bear phalange from Intermediate complex. (c) increased level of fluorine distributed throughout the thickness of the bone in bear phalange from Lower Breccia.

The profile of the bone PR from the modern dumps (A122) is most like that for the bone PU from the Lower Breccia or possibly PW and PX from the Intermediate beds. There is an outermost spike, then an outer layer having a small evenly distributed increase in fluorine that increases to higher values towards the innerside of the cortex. This suggests a depositional history and environment of deposition similar to that of the bone from the Lower Breccia.

The detection of fluorine in bone by the proton microprobe seems to be less sensitive than determination from X-ray diffraction patterns, but the distribution of fluorine in the bone is clearly demonstrated. Coote and Holdaway (1982) discuss the interpretation of the scan profiles. Throughout the above discussion I have ignored the small scale variation in fluorine due to bone structure. Indeed, the profiles reveal the heterogeneity of the bone, and some of the discrepancies between the determination of fluorine by the probe and X-ray diffraction may be explained by the very small size of the samples required by the latter technique. Because of the heterogeneous nature of bone many samples should be taken to obtain a reliable pattern (Molleson, 1981).

CONCLUSION

The moderately high beta counts obtained from the bone samples, including the two human bones that were recovered from modern contexts indicate that these bones are of some antiquity. Neither fluorine nor uranium can be used to distinguish Upper Breccia from Lower Breccia material. Uranium can probably be used to differentiate Pleistocene from Recent material. Fluorine profiling shows potential as a new technique for the elucidation of burial environments.

ACKNOWLEDGEMENTS

I am most grateful to Eva Fejer and John Francis, Department of Mineralogy, for preparing and reading the X-ray diffraction films; to Andy Currant for selecting the bone samples and discussion; Graeme Coote for collaborating on the interpretation of the fluorine profiles.

CHAPTER V

THE ARCHAEOLOGICAL DISCOVERIES

Necdum res igni scibant tractare neque uti
pellibus et spoliis corpus vestire ferarum,
sed nemora atque cavos montis silvasque colebant,
et frutices inter condebant squalida membra
verbera ventorum vitare imbrisque coacti.

Lucretius *De Rerum Natura* 5. 953–7.

PART A

THE PALAEOLITHIC ARTEFACTS
by
H. Stephen Green

INTRODUCTION

The following interim account is largely restricted to finds from the 1978–81 seasons and to the nineteenth century finds in the Sedgwick Museum of Geology in Cambridge. Use is made of data from the 1982–3 seasons where this is available. A simplified distribution of the stratified artefact finds by context is shown in Table V.1. and an analysis of the density of finds in the artefact-bearing deposits of the East Passage has produced the results shown in Table V.2.

Table V.2 demonstrates that artefacts are twice as common in the Lower Breccia per unit volume of deposit dug as in the Upper Breccia and this would support my view that the artefacts in the Upper Breccia may have been redeposited, as a result of natural processes, from either the Lower Breccia or its original source-material. A similar picture is shown by the distribution of the bones (Table V.2) and it is clear from a variety of evidence that the main, and probably the only, human occupation must pre-date the emplacement of the Lower Breccia.

One or more industries?

There appears to have been a very long time-gap between the two Breccias, perhaps of the order of some 200,000 years, and there is some evidence (H.P. Schwarcz, p.93) that the

	South Fissure	South Passage	East Passage	Totals
Upper Breccia	–	1	31	32
"Breccia"	30	–	–	30
Lower Breccia	4	20	56	80
Intermediate	0	1	2	3
Totals	34	22	89	135

TABLE V.1   Distribution of stratified artefacts by principal context. Finds 1978–1982

	Relative % volume of deposits	Expected no. of artefacts	Observed no. of artefacts	Observed % of artefacts	Observed % of bones
Upper Breccia	51.58%	37	31	35	25%
Lower Breccia	42.94%	30	56	63	69%
Buff Intermediate	5.48%	4	2	2	6%

TABLE V.2   East Passage. Relative density of artefacts relative to volume of deposits (total of artefacts = 89; volume of deposits based on section CD (Fig. IX.2)) and comparative density of bones (computed by number of bone-finds (total = 1212), whether single bones or bulked fragments). Finds 1978–1982.

cave-mouth may have been blocked for at least a part of this interval. There is no sign of any occupation of Later Upper Palaeolithic age to go with the Late Glacial fauna. Furthermore, as Tables V.3A–B show, no typological differences may be discerned between the two breccias and the same is true of the raw materials (R.E. Bevins, p.198). I do not believe, therefore, that more than one broad phase of occupation - however seasonal or intermittent it might have been – can be distinguished. Furthermore, we must take note of the widely accepted view (*cf.* Roe, 1981, 268–9) that the north and west of Britain were mostly outside the area of regular Palaeolithic settlement. If this view is broadly valid (as I accept (Green, 1981b)), then it is a corollary of it – applying Occam's Razor – that the settlement at Pontnewydd Cave is inherently likely to have been a single event, a conclusion which is not at variance with the composition and size of the assemblage (see also p.208).

TYPOLOGY

A full assessment of the significance of the typology of the artefacts can only be made in the light of a programme of experimental knapping of the raw materials used (see Newcomer, p.153). The typology used here follows Bordes (1961) and the English names for types, given in Table V.3A–B, likewise follow those of Bordes (1972, 152–7). The reference numbers of the finds quoted in the text and given in the figures (e.g. C382; A66/12) are the original site find-numbers. The capital letter prefixes A, B, C and D represent the following: A = Boyd Dawkins and World War II dumps; B = South Fissure; C = South Passage; D = East Passage. Reference numbers from the Sedgwick Museum of Geology collection – like some of the Pontnewydd find numbers, prefixed by the letter "D" – are here prefixed by SMG (e.g. SMG-D2913) to avoid confusion. The use of the "D" preface by the Sedgwick Museum has no implications for the provenance of the nineteenth century finds within the cave. A few old finds came to the National Museum of Wales in 1968 from the collection kept by the Williams-Wynn family at Plas-yn-Cefn (Accession No. 68.88). These are prefixed NMW. A key is given in Fig. V.1 (top) to the orientation of profiles and of views of the striking platforms, where present. Areas of modern damage have been left blank on the drawings.

Bordes type no.	Artefact class	Totals
1.	Typical Levallois Flakes	33
3.	Levallois Points	3
5.	Pseudo-Levallois Points	3
6–7.	Mousterian Points	1
9.	Single Straight Side-Scrapers	7
10.	Single Convex Side-Scrapers	3
23.	Convex Transverse Scrapers	4
26.	Abrupt Retouched Side-Scrapers	1
27.	Side-Scraper with Thinned Back	2
28.	Side-Scraper with Bifacial Retouch	2
31.	Atypical End Scrapers	2
–	Scraper Fragments	3
38.	Naturally Backed Knives	9
40.	Truncated Flakes and Blades	1
42.	Notches	4
43.	Denticulates	2
45.	Retouches on Ventral Face	2
46–7.	Abrupt and Alternate Retouches (Thick)	6
48–9.	Abrupt and Alternate Retouches (Thin)	60
54.	End Notched Pieces	1
59.	Choppers	1
	Chopping Tools	1
	Flake Cleaver	1
	Handaxes	32
	Crude Cores	19
	Disc Cores	12
	Levallois Cores	18
	Indet. Core Fragments	7
	Flakes etc.	97
	Total	337

TABLE V.3A   Typology of Artefacts from Pontnewydd Cave. Excavations 1978–81 plus Sedgwick Museum of Geology Collection.

Natural Damage to the Artefacts

The artefacts have been described as damaged by "natural chipping and abrasion . . . received during transport in the mud-flow" (Green, 1981a, 190). This possible natural damage takes the form both of rounding of ridges formed by the intersection of flake-scars ("rolling") and of edge-chipping. However, Peter Bull's pilot Scanning Electron Microscope study of possible rolling (on artefacts C61 and D702, both from the Lower Breccia), under magnification of X10,000, has shown the "rolling" to be almost certainly the result of solutional processes taking place *in situ*, for the flake ridges are simply rounded and do not after all exhibit the combination of rounding and scarring typical of water-rolled artefacts. I have not reached a definite view as to whether the artefacts have in general received this chipping during transport in the catastrophic conditions of the debris flow or whether natural damage to the artefacts has been largely occasioned by such other processes as frost-heaving and human (or animal) trampling.

Bordes type no.	Artefact class	Buff Intermediate	Lower Breccia	Upper/Lower Breccia Interface	Silt	Upper Breccia	Unstratified	Totals
1.	Typical Levallois Flakes	–	4	–	–	1	–	5
3.	Levallois Points	–	1	–	–	–	–	1
5.	Pseudo-Levallois Points	–	–	–	–	–	1	1
6–7.	Mousterian Point	–	1	–	–	–	–	1
9.	Single Straight Side-Scrapers	–	–	–	–	–	1	1
10.	Single Convex Side-Scrapers	–	1	–	–	–	–	1
27.	Side-Scraper with Thinned Back	–	1	–	–	–	–	1
38.	Naturally Backed Knives	–	–	–	–	1	1	2
46–7.	Abrupt and Alternate Retouch (Thick)	–	1	–	–	–	–	1
48–9.	Abrupt and Alternate Retouch (Thin)	–	7	–	1	4	1	13
–	Flake Cleaver	–	1	–	–	–	–	1
–	Handaxes	–	6	1	–	–	–	7
–	Crude Cores	1	1	–	–	1	1	4
–	Disc Cores	–	–	–	–	2	2	4
–	Levallois Cores	–	1	–	–	1	–	2
–	Indeterminate Core Fragments	–	1	–	–	–	–	1
–	Flakes etc.	–	11	1	–	8	2	22
	Totals	1	37	2	1	18	9	68

TABLE V.3B Typology of Artefacts from Pontnewydd Cave. East Passage Only. Excavations 1978–81.

Raw Material, Refinement and Technology

The raw materials used at the site (R.E. Bevins and C. Clayton, Chapter VIII) are all non-local and have probably reached the cave or its vicinity through the processes of glacial, periglacial and fluvial transport. The raw material was obtained in the form of pebbles or cobbles, generally of no great size, being not normally greater than 25-30 centimetres in maximum dimension. The size of the raw material and its quality have influenced the dimensions and refinement of the implements which could be produced (p.158 ff.). In particular, the rocks used frequently do not exhibit the clean conchoidal fracture of flint and may split instead along "fracture cleavages". Such fracture cleavages, in this case microfaults resulting from compression of the rock strata, take the form of parallel closely spaced fracture planes (Plate XVII). Unlike "slaty cleavage", fracture cleavage is non-penetrative and so may not continue throughout the thickness of the rock (Park, 1983, 20). Furthermore, such spaced cleavages may be complex, resulting from their creation at different times in the rock's history, and so may occur in more than one plane within a single pebble.

A further characteristic of the working of the hard volcanic rocks is the occurrence of a number of *accidents de Siret* (Tixier *et al.*, 1980, 103), both among the artefacts (Pl. XVII) and experimentally (p.153), in which flakes have split into two pieces more or less following the axis of percussion.

It is important to note Mark Newcomer's conclusion (p.157) that – notwithstanding the constraints of the raw material – it would have been possible for the knappers to have made tools, such as Quina-type scrapers, which exhibit a greater level of refinement than is

1   0   1   2   3 cm. **a**

0   2   4   6 cm. **b**

Plate XVII   Upper: Natural pebble of crystal tuff or rhyolitic lava from Pontnewydd Cave, broken open to reveal the laminar cleavage.

Lower: Levallois flake which has split naturally during knapping into two halves; a so-called *accident de Siret*.

actually seen in the assemblage. The raw material has, however, generally limited not so much the range of artefact types which could be produced, as their refinement in the sense of thickness relative to two-dimensional size parameters, symmetry and general elegance to our own eyes (see Table VIII.4 for the raw material types used). This is a necessary consequence not only of the spaced cleavage present in the raw materials, excepting of course flint and chert, but also of the hardness of the rocks requiring, as a general rule, the use of a hard hammer. Only a few of the flints recovered are of any size, even the largest being no more than 72 mm in length, and accordingly, it is not possible to gain an insight from the flint artefacts in the assemblage of the level of refinement which would have been achieved by the knappers, given a copious supply of flint.

THE ARTEFACTS

Crude and Discoidal Cores

Crude Cores (Fig. V.1, bottom)
The conversion of pebbles into cores has recently been described by John Wymer (in Singer and Wymer, 1982, 44) and his comments are, in general, applicable here. The cores may be divided into both crude examples, where the position and form of the main removals has not been carefully determined by previous blows (A59), and more specialised forms in which there has been deliberate preparation of the striking platform and sometimes also of the dorsal surface of the flake to be removed. Of the total of 49 classified cores found, 19 may be classed as crude, 12 as discoidal and 18 as Levallois.

Discoidal Cores (Figs. V.2–4)
Several sub-types may be determined:
1. Cores radially flaked over one surface but with only minimal trimming – confined to simple platform preparation – on the second, often cortical face (Fig. V.2).
2. Bifacially worked cores with a more or less regular pattern of small removals from each face (Figs. V.2–3).
3. Boldly flaked bifacially worked cores of slightly larger size with fewer and thicker removals per unit length of circumference (Figs. V.3–4).

Type 3 cores shade typologically into rough handaxes and indeed Roe (1981, pl. 34, no. 4, but with different orientation from Fig. V.4 here) has described SMG-D2897 as a handaxe. But the Pontnewydd handaxes proper, though crude, may nonetheless be readily distinguished by their more purposeful flaking, designed to create working edges. We may note in passing, also, that the piece described by Roe (1981, pl 34, no. 5) as a disc core is, in fact, a thick flake.

Levallois cores (Figs. V.5–8) and their products (Figs. V.8–11)

The problems imposed by the raw materials used are amply shown by the range of unfinished (C32 – not illustrated), unstruck (Fig. V.6) and mis-hit cores (Fig. V.7); and by the occurrence of so-called *outrepassé* flakes (Fig. V.11) which have run further than intended and, in consequence, incorporate, as a part of their edge, a small area of the margin of the core.

Centripetal preparation is the technique typically used here to pre-form the Levallois flakes on the core. The products range from the sub-circular (e.g. A66/23, Fig. V.9) to elongated (A66/12, Fig. V.11). In one case (B395, Fig. V.10), parallel preparation has been used to produce an elegant flake-blade with dihedral butt. Also present is a form of minimal preparation of some cores (A61, SMG-D2193, Fig. V.5; B315, Fig. V.8), the 'reduced Levalloisian technique' of Roe (1981, 199). The striking platforms of the flakes are typically facetted (80%) with a few dihedral (8%) and plain examples (12%).

The range of Levallois technology is extended by the occurrence of Levallois points of first order (A86/9 - not illustrated) and second order (Fig. V.8) (Bordes, 1961, Fig.4, p.19). Present also, but produced of course from discoidal cores, are Pseudo-Levallois points (Fig. V.11).

Evidence of the re-striking of some Levallois cores is present. We may note D306 and, more especially, C115 which has been re-struck after new preparation (both Fig.V.7). Among the Levallois flakes, B4 (Fig. V.9) bears clear evidence of an earlier removal at right angles to the blow which removed B4 itself from its parent core.

It is not possible, in general, to regard the discoidal cores as reworked Levallois cores. A simple plot of measurable cores restricted, for reasons of comparability, to the non-flint rocks, gives the results shown in Table V.4. These figures do not demonstrate a clear tendency for discoidal cores to be smaller than the Levallois cores, something which would be expected if the former were regularly derived from the latter.

	Size range (mm)	Median	Arithmetic mean	Sample size
Disc cores	35–103	64.5	63	11
Levallois cores	43–82	68.5	67	10

TABLE V.4 Pontnewydd Cave. Excavations 1978–81. Core sizes, excluding flint.

Handaxes (Figs. V.12–19)

Since the appearance of my *Antiquity* article (Green, 1981a) some of the miscellaneous handaxes have been reclassified leading to the revised picture shown in Table V.5.

The handaxes vary from coarse to relatively elegant examples. The commonest type represented is the amygdaloid with a few subtriangular examples in addition. Many display areas of original pebble surface but only a few have cortical butts. All display hard-hammer technique and whilst a number are quite crudely worked a few others, of which D930 (Fig. V.13) is perhaps the best example, show a much greater degree of refinement. Even on the latter, a large area of one face is composed of a fracture cleavage surface.

	Totals
amygdaloid	17
sub-triangular	3
cordiform	2
lanceolate	1
ovate	1
nucleiform	1
pick	1
miscellaneous	2
roughout	1
fragments	3
Totals	32

TABLE V.5 Pontnewydd Cave. Handaxes. Excavations 1978–81 plus Sedgwick Museum of Geology Collections.

Flake Cleaver (Fig. V.20)

One artefact may be considered here (D257). It is made on a flake probably but not certainly struck from its cortical edge (right hand view, left side in Fig. V.20, where the lines of the spaced cleavage of the rock are also shown). The blade of the cleaver has been retouched after removal of the flake from the core. The type compares with examples from the 'southern Acheulian' of the Perigord described by Guichard (1976, 915).

Choppers and Chopping Tools (Fig. V.20–21)

One artefact (B298) may be considered as a chopper (a tool with the cutting edge unifacially flaked) and several chopping tools (with cutting edge bifacially flaked) are present. Two such (A96/1 and D1088) are illustrated, of which the latter is one of the 1982 finds. All are made on pebbles.

Mousterian Point (Fig. V.22)

One Mousterian point, of a fine silicic tuff, comes from the Lower Breccia of the East Passage. The artefact is made on a double struck flake, most likely a handaxe trimming flake, and one edge of its ventral surface is composed of its facetted striking platform. It is clear, however, that at least some of the removals from the right hand edge (as illustrated) of the dorsal surface are secondary to the platform preparation and would appear to belong with the retouch seen not only on the distal edge of the dorsal surface but also around the tip on the ventral surface.

Scrapers (Figs. V.22–24)

A range of scraper-types (Table V.3A) is present at Pontnewydd including single side-scrapers (Figs. V.22–3); double sided-scrapers with ventral retouch (Figs. V.23–4); scrapers with thinned back and base (D9, Fig. V.23); transverse scrapers (Fig. V.23); and a few end-scrapers (Fig. V.24).

The following styles of retouch (based on de Lumley, 1972, 395–6 and Bordes, 1961) are present.

Thick retouch (retouches épaisses) This is a form of retouch where the removals have resulted in a perceptible reduction in the dimensions of the blank from which the scraper has been made (e.g. SMG-D2898, A66/32). Five examples in all are present.

Demi-Quina retouch The form of Demi-Quina retouch seen at Pontnewydd is scalariform, on a thin blank. Two examples, in all, are present. (B9).

Abrupt retouch This appears on two examples (B61 and A66/30).

Flat (or scalar) retouch (retouches plates) Short, typically scalar retouch which does not extend beyond one third of the width of the implement. This is the commonest form of retouch, seven examples being present (D9).

Invasive retouch (retouches envahissantes) Flat retouch which extends over greater than one third of the width of the scraper. Examples include NMW-68.88/2, A48 and A66/26. Four examples in all are present.

Denticulates and Notches (Figs. V.24–25)

These are categories whose number could possibly be increased as a result of detailed assessment of natural damage suffered by the artefacts. A68/5 exhibits a large Clactonion notch at its distal end; A86/12 is an end-notched piece; and A112/5 is a small denticulate of flint.

Naturally backed knives (Fig. V.25)

Several examples of this type are here illustrated (A66/16, B226). Their occurrence in the industry is probably no more than a reflection of the use of pebbles as raw material.

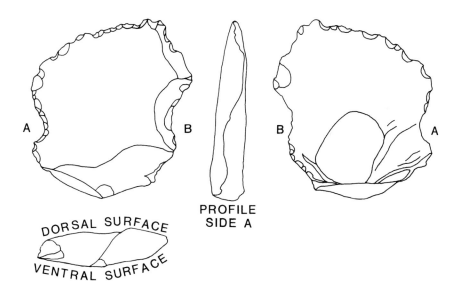

A   B   B   A

DORSAL SURFACE

PROFILE
SIDE A

VENTRAL SURFACE

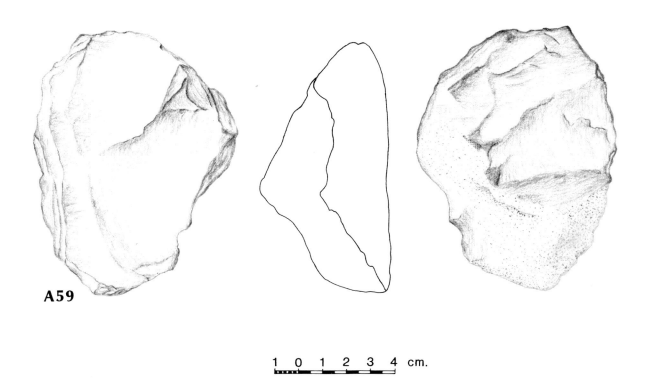

A59

1 0 1 2 3 4 cm.

Fig. V.1 Upper: The orientation of profiles and views of striking platforms on Figs. V.1–25.
Lower: Unspecialized core A.59, unstratified, feldspar-phyric lava. Scale 2:3.

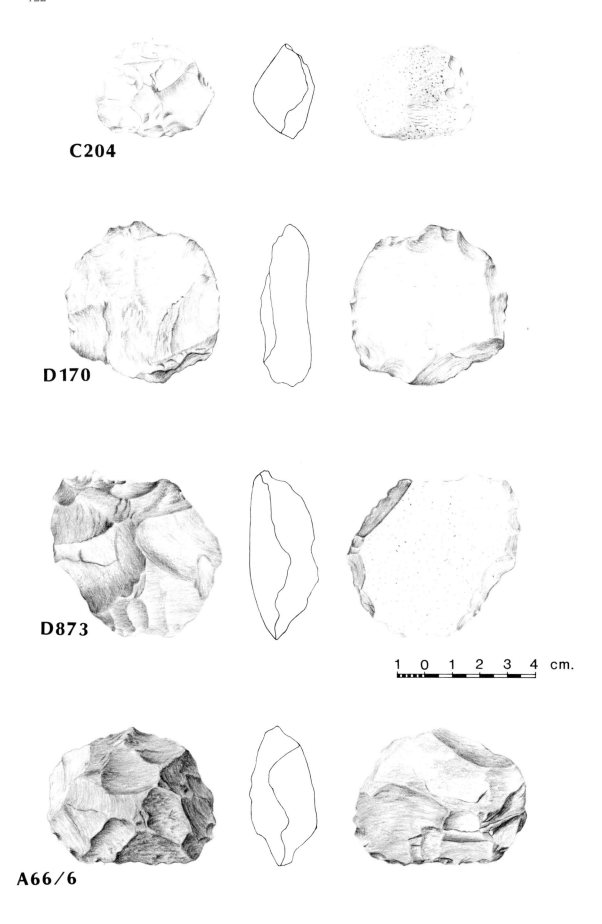

C204

D170

D873

1 0 1 2 3 4 cm.

A66/6

Fig. V.2 Pontnewydd Cave. Discoidal Cores. Type 1: C204, Lower Breccia, chert; D170, Upper Breccia, feldspar-phyric lava; D873, Upper Breccia, rhyolite; (Type 2): A66/6, unstratified, crystal tuff. Scale 3:4.

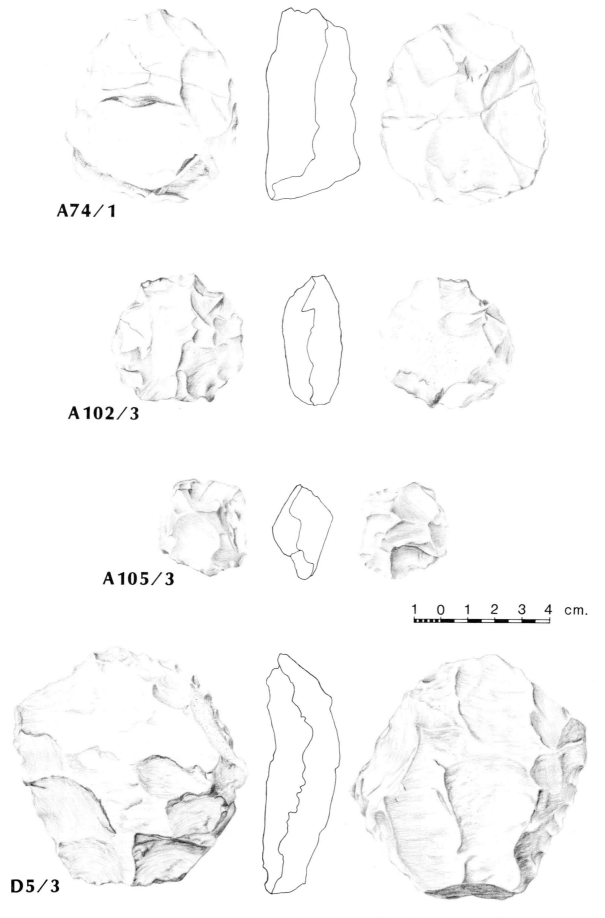

A74/1

A102/3

A105/3

1 0 1 2 3 4 cm.

D5/3

Fig. V.3   Pontnewydd Cave. Discoidal Cores. Type 2: A74/1, unstratified, ?microdiorite; A102/3, unstratified, fine silicic tuff; A105/3, unstratified, fine-grained silicic tuff; (Type 3): D5/3, unstratified, rhyolite. Scale 3:4.

124

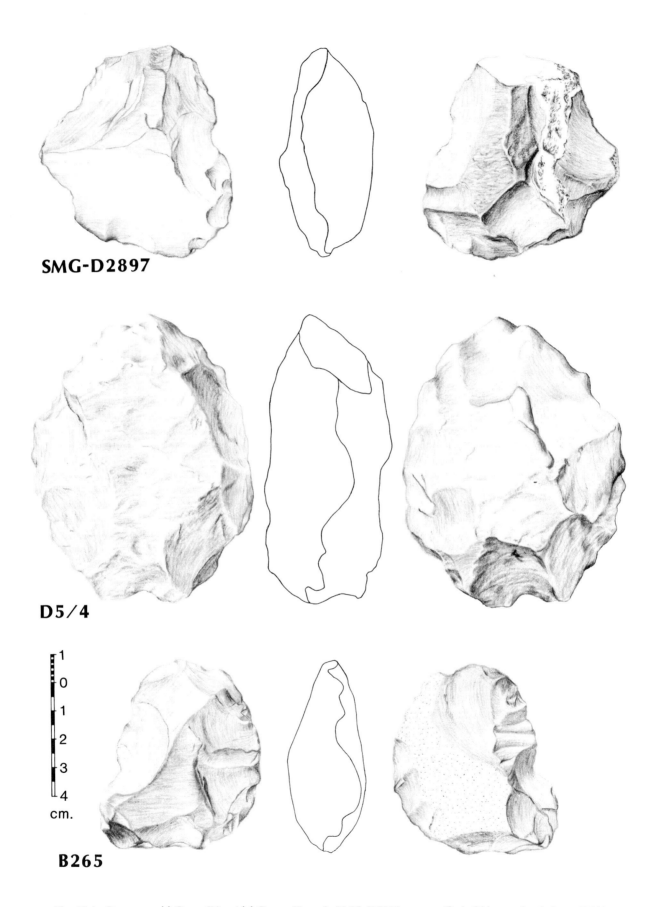

SMG-D2897

D5/4

B265

Fig. V.4   Pontnewydd Cave. Discoidal Cores. Type 3: SMG-D2897, unstratified, feldspar–phyric lava; D5/4, unstratified, crystal–lithic tuff; B265, Breccia, silicic tuff. Scale 3:4.

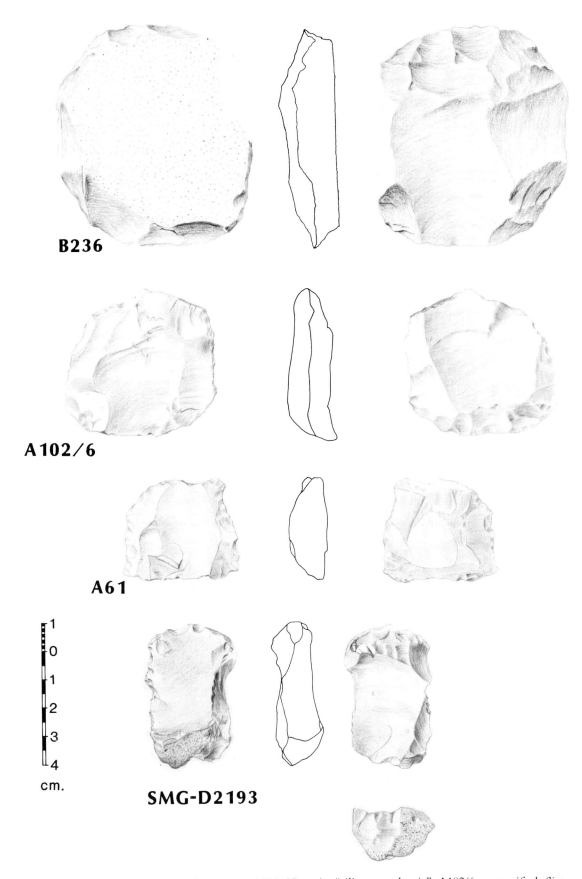

B236

A102/6

A61

SMG-D2193

Fig. V.5   Pontnewydd Cave. Levallois Cores: B236, ?Breccia, "siliceous volcanic"; A102/6, unstratified, flint. Levallois Cores showing minimal preparation: A61, unstratified, flint; SMG-D2193, unstratified, flint. Scale 3:4.

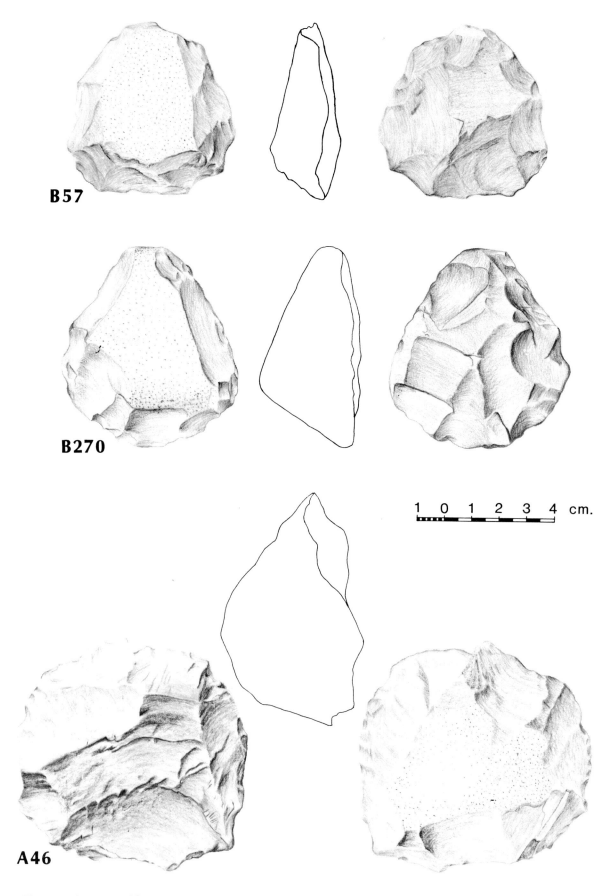

Fig. V.6 Pontnewydd Cave. Unstruck Levallois Cores: B57, Breccia, crystal lithic tuff; B270, Lower Breccia, "siliceous volcanic". Levallois core: A46, unstratified, flow banded perlitic rhyolite. Scale 3:4.

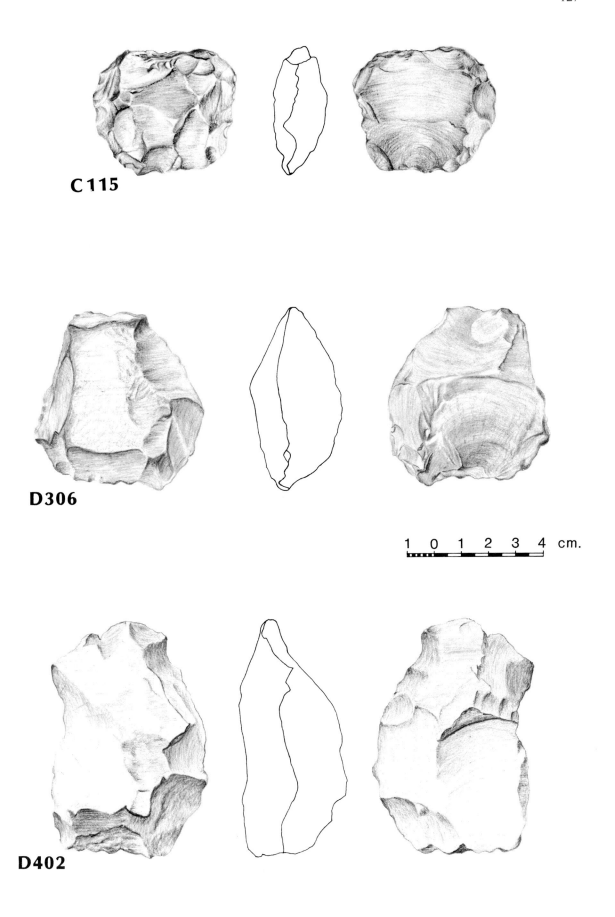

Fig. V.7 Pontnewydd Cave. Mishit Levallois Cores: C115, Lower Breccia, fine-grained silicic tuff; D306, Upper Breccia, rhyolite/fine crystal tuff; D402, Lower Breccia, feldspar-phyric rhyolite. Scale 3:4.

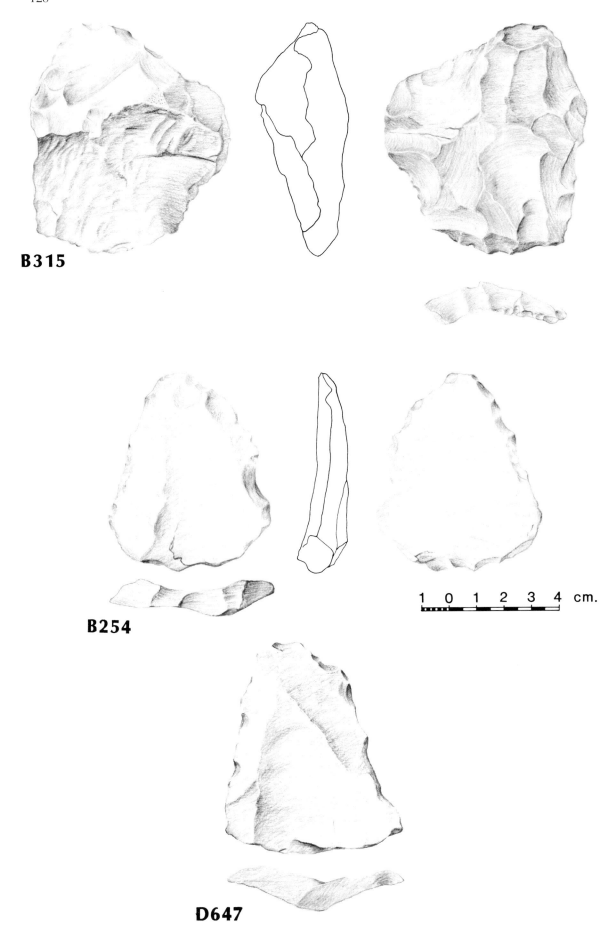

B315

B254

D647

Fig. V.8 Pontnewydd Cave. Levallois core showing minimal preparation: B315, Breccia, rhyolite. Levallois points (second order): B254. Breccia, crystal lithic tuff; D647, Lower Breccia, "siliceous volcanic". Scale 3:4.

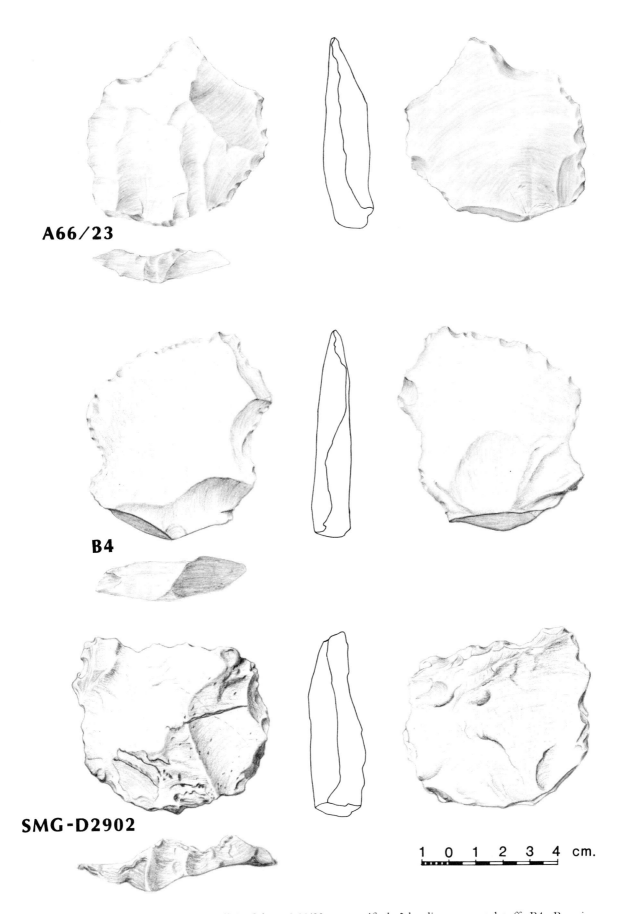

A66/23

B4

SMG-D2902

1 0 1 2 3 4 cm.

Fig. V.9 Pontnewydd Cave. Levallois flakes: A66/23, unstratified, ?rhyolite or crystal tuff; B4, Breccia, feldspar-phyric lava; SMG-D2902, unstratified, fine silicic tuff. Scale 3:4.

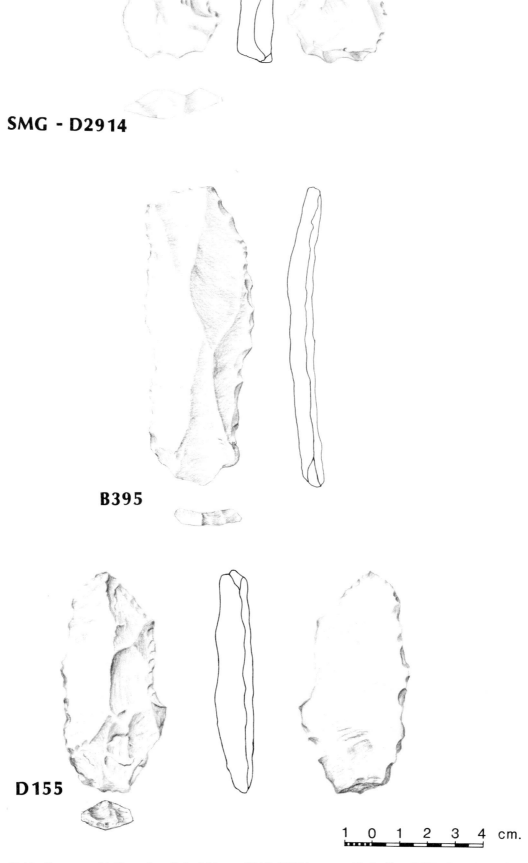

SMG - D2914

B395

D155

Fig. V.10 Pontnewydd Cave. Levallois debitage: SMG-D2914, unstratified, flint; B395, Breccia, "siliceous volcanic"; D155, Upper Breccia, crystal lithic tuff. Scale 3:4.

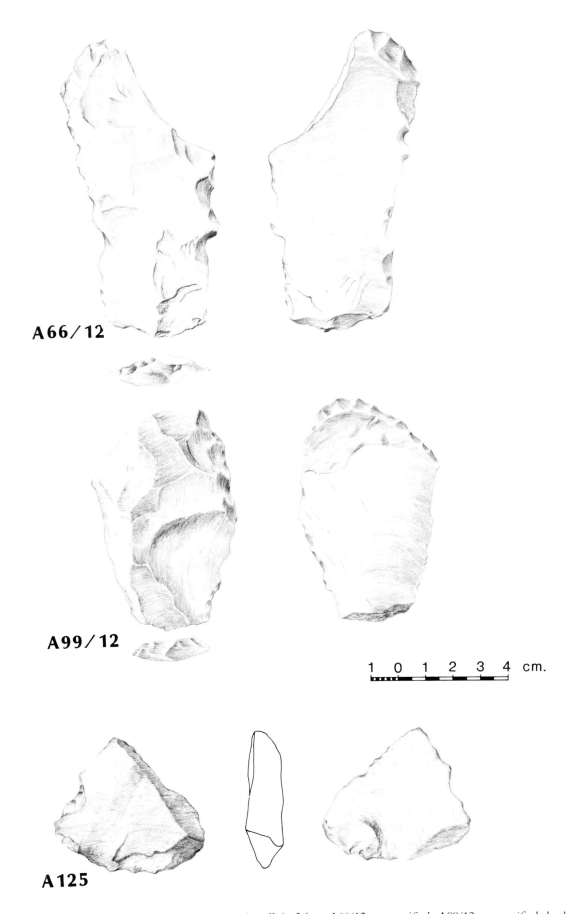

A66/12

A99/12

1 0 1 2 3 4 cm.

A125

Fig. V.11 Pontnewydd Cave. Outre-passé Levallois flakes: A66/12, unstratified; A99/12, unstratified; both "siliceous volcanic". Pseudo-Levallois point: A125, unstratified, feldspar-phyric lava. Scale 3:4.

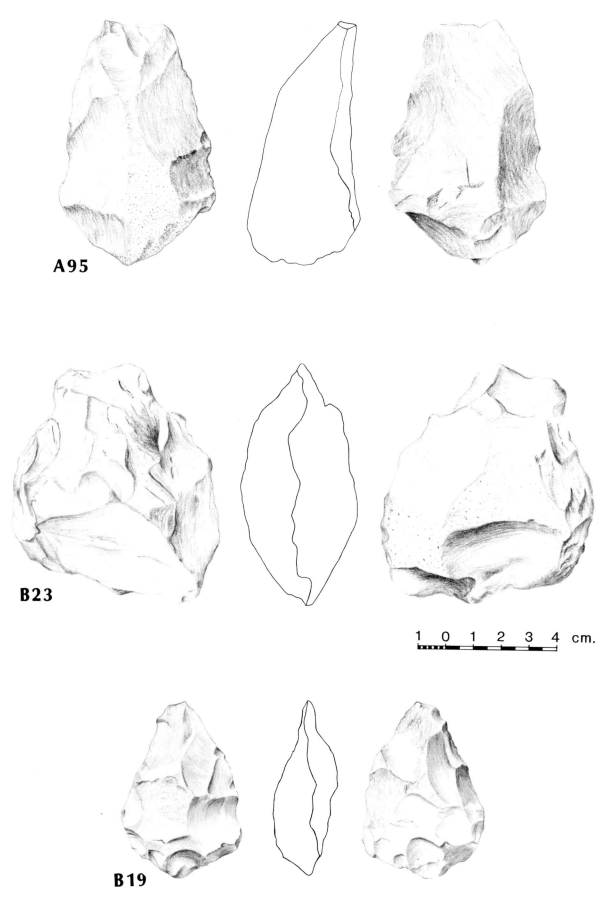

A95

B23

1 0 1 2 3 4 cm.

B19

Fig. V.12 Pontnewydd Cave. Handaxes (amygdaloid): A95, unstratified, feldspar-phyric lava; B23, Breccia, ?rhyolite lava/fine silicic tuff; B19, Breccia, "siliceous volcanic". Scale 3:4.

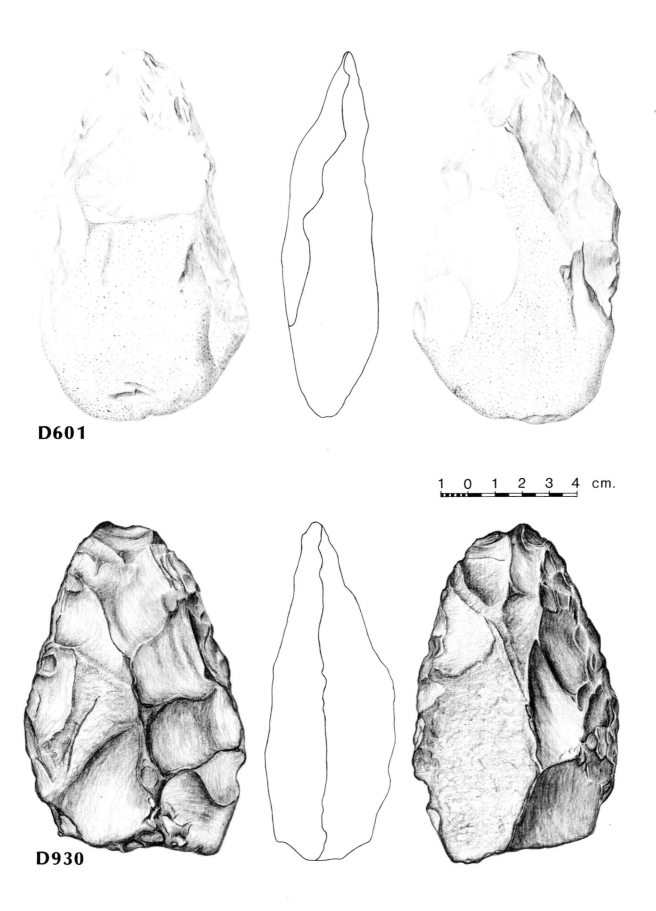

D601

1 0 1 2 3 4 cm.

D930

Fig. V.13   Pontnewydd Cave. Handaxes (amygdaloid): D601, Upper Breccia, rhyolite; D930, Lower Breccia, fine silicic tuff. Scale 3:4.

134

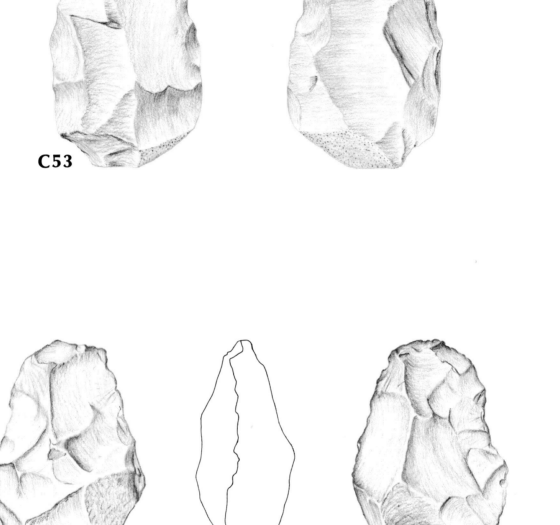

C53

SMG - D2894

1 0 1 2 3 4 cm.

Fig. V.14   Pontnewydd Cave. Handaxes (amygdaloid): C53, Lower Breccia; SMG-D2894, unstratified; both "siliceous volcanic". Scale 3:4.

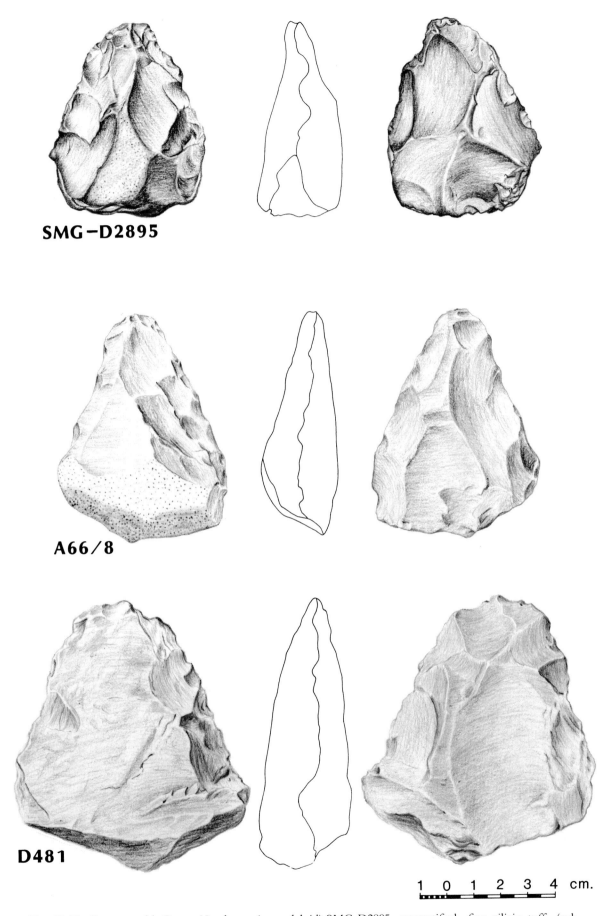

SMG–D2895

A66/8

D481

1 0 1 2 3 4 cm.

Fig. V.15 Pontnewydd Cave. Handaxes (amygdaloid):SMG–D2895, unstratified, fine silicic tuff; (sub-triangular): A66/8, unstratified, fine silicic tuff; (amygdaloid): D481, Lower Breccia, ignimbrite. Scale 3:4.

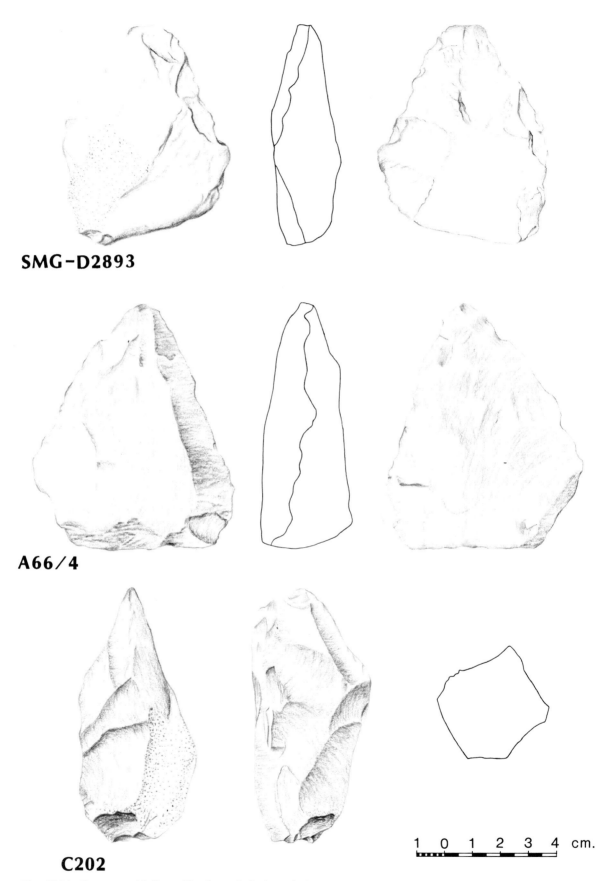

SMG-D2893

A66/4

C202

1 0 1 2 3 4 cm.

Fig. V.16 Pontnewydd Cave. Handaxes (subtriangular): SMG-D2893, unstratified, ?rhyolite; (amygdaloid):
A66/4, ignimbrite or rhyolitic lava; (pick): C202, Lower Breccia, "siliceous volcanic". Scale 3:4.

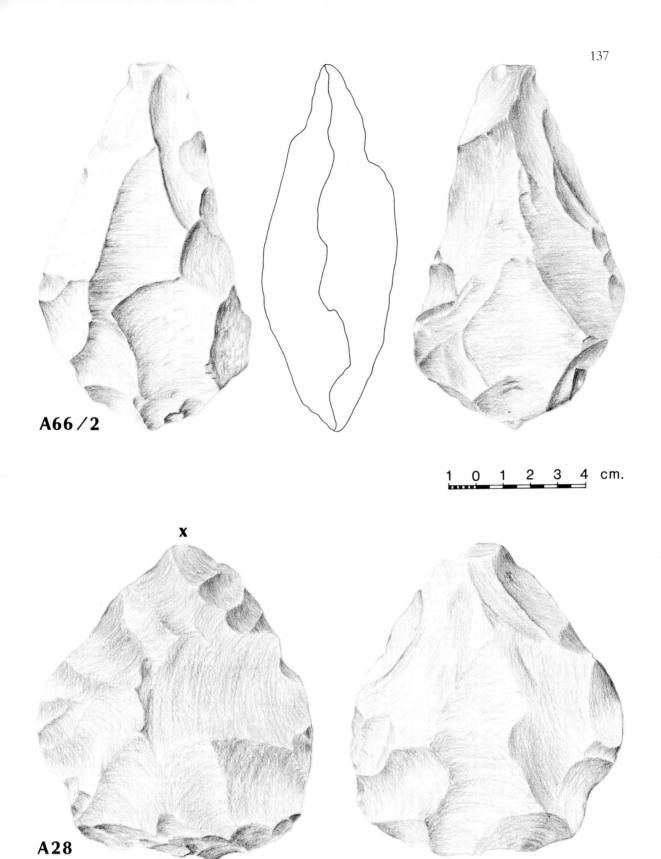

A66/2

1 0 1 2 3 4 cm.

x

A28

y

y   x

Fig. V.17 Pontnewydd Cave. Handaxes (lanceolate): A66/2, unstratified; (ovate): A28, unstratified. Both
siliceous "volcanics". Scale 3:4.

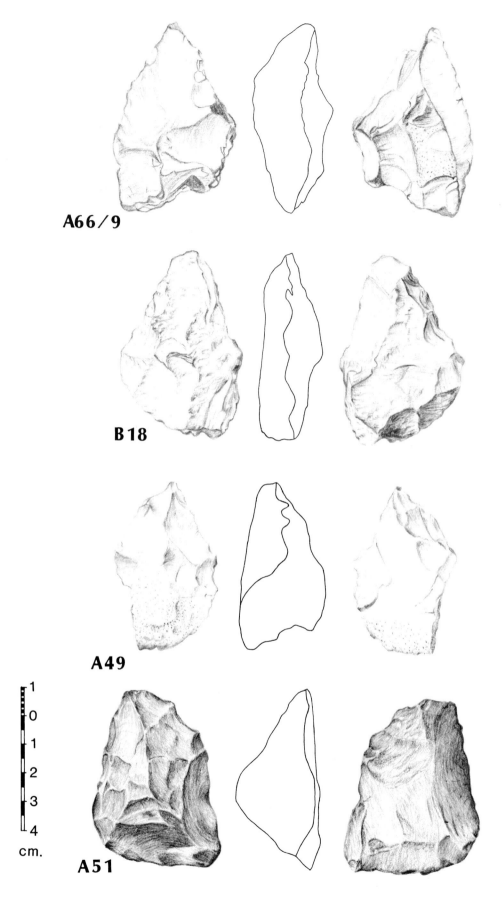

A66/9

B18

A49

1
0
1
2
3
4
cm.

A51

Fig. V.18 Pontnewydd Cave. Handaxes (amygdaloid): A66/9, unstratified, fine silicic tuff; B18, Breccia, ?crystal tuff; (nucleiform): A49, unstratified, silica vein; (unclassified): A51, unstratified, feldspar-phyric lava. Scale 3:4.

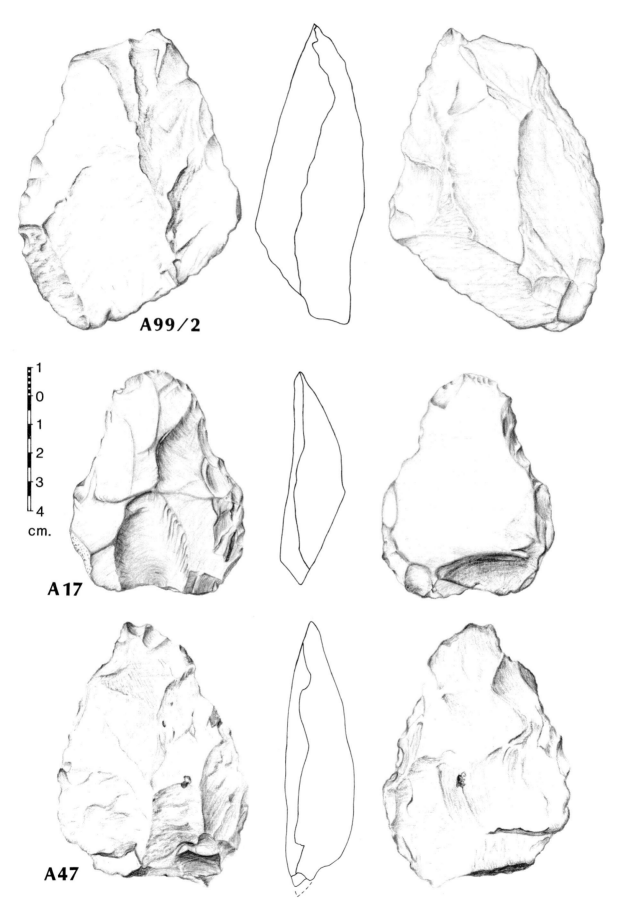

Fig. V.19 Pontnewydd Cave. Handaxes (amygdaloid): A99/2, unstratified, crystal lithic tuff; (partial cordiform): A17, unstratified, ?tuff; (cordiform): A47, unstratified, rhyolite. Scale 3:4.

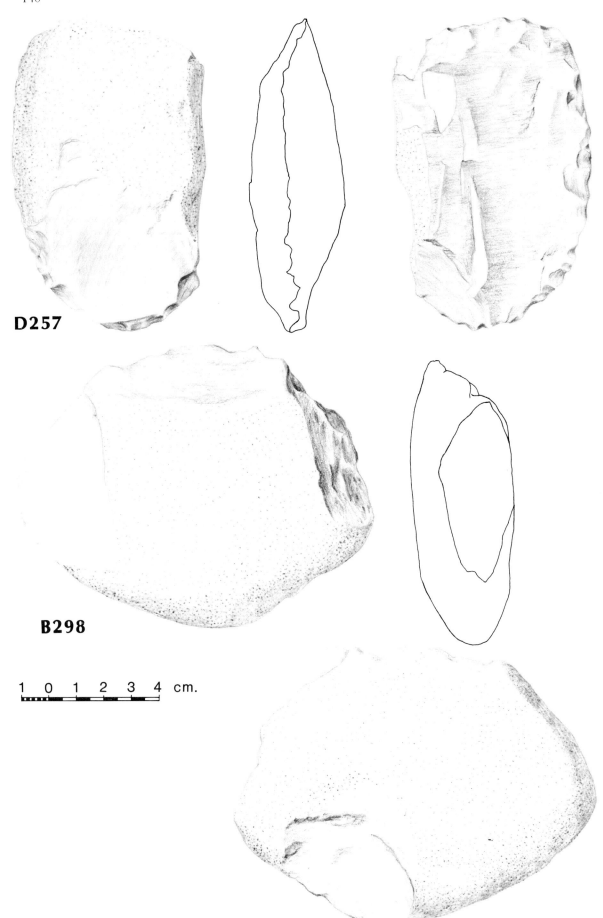

D257

B298

Fig. V.20 Pontnewydd Cave. Flake Cleaver: D257, Lower Breccia, rhyolite (ignimbrite). Chopper: B298, Breccia, crystal tuff. Scale 3:4.

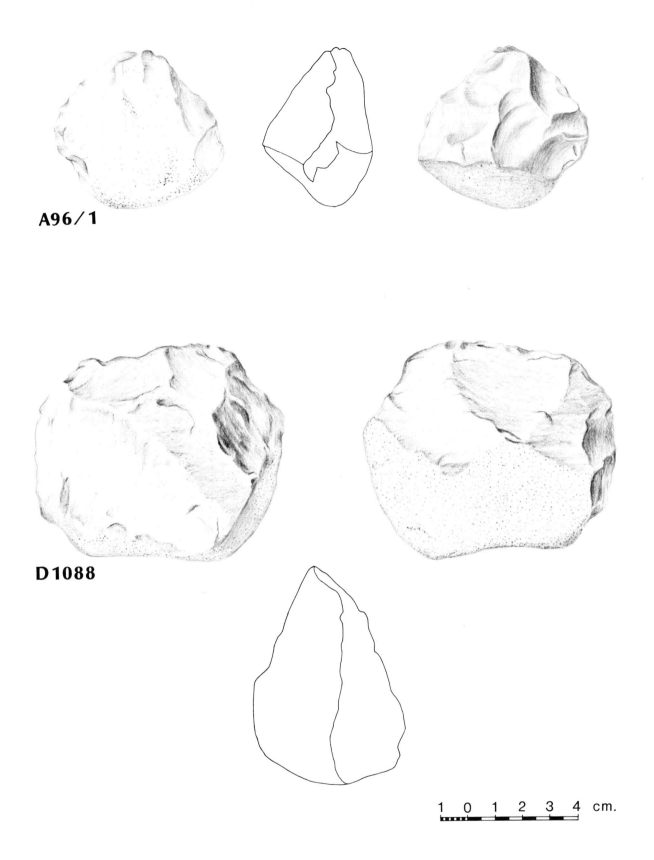

A96/1

D1088

1 0 1 2 3 4 cm.

Fig. V.21 Pontnewydd Cave. Chopping Tools: A96/1, unstratified, rhyolite/rhyolitic tuff; D1088, interface of
Upper and Lower Breccia. Scale 3:4.

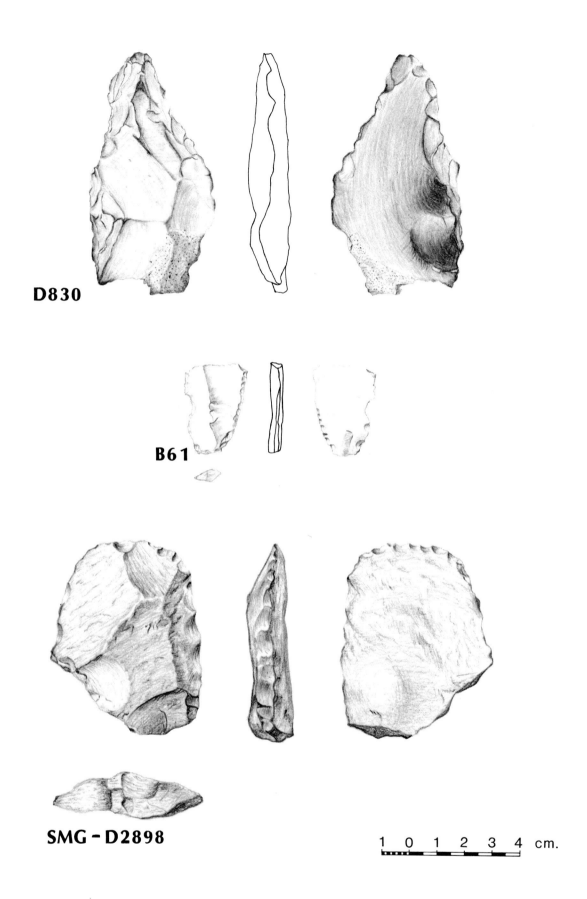

D830

B61

SMG - D2898

1 0 1 2 3 4 cm.

Fig. V.22 Pontnewydd Cave. Mousterian Point: D830, Lower Breccia, fine silicic tuff. Single side-scrapers; B61, Breccia, flint; SMG-D2898, unstratified, rhyolite. Scale 3:4.

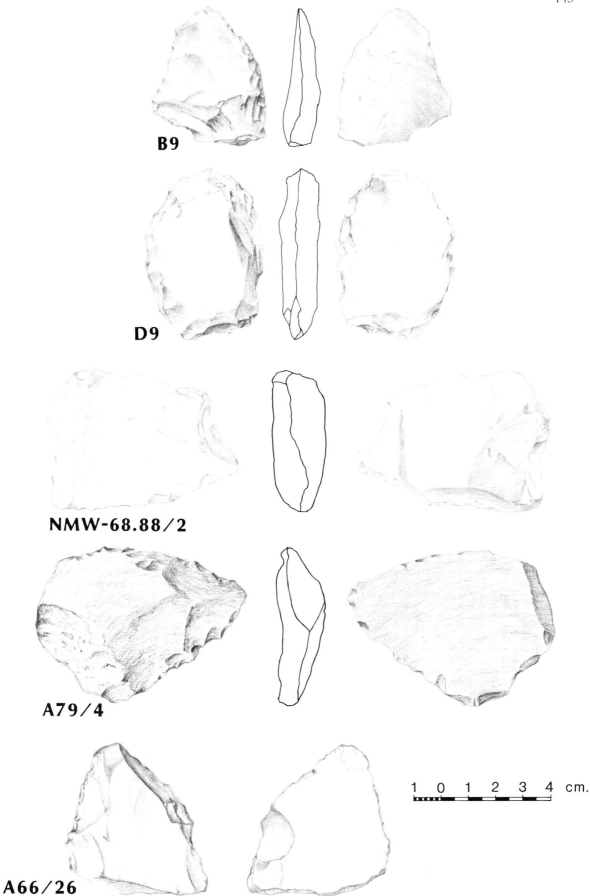

B9

D9

NMW-68.88/2

A79/4

A66/26

1 0 1 2 3 4 cm.

Fig. V.23 Pontnewydd Cave. Single convex side-scraper: B9, Breccia, fine silicic crystal tuff. Side-scraper with thinned back and base: D9, Lower Breccia, fine silicic tuff. Transverse scrapers: NMW-68.88/2 unstratified, fine silicic tuff; A79/4, unstratified, ignimbrite. Double side-scraper with ventral retouch: A66/26, unstratified, fine silicic tuff. Scale 3:4.

144

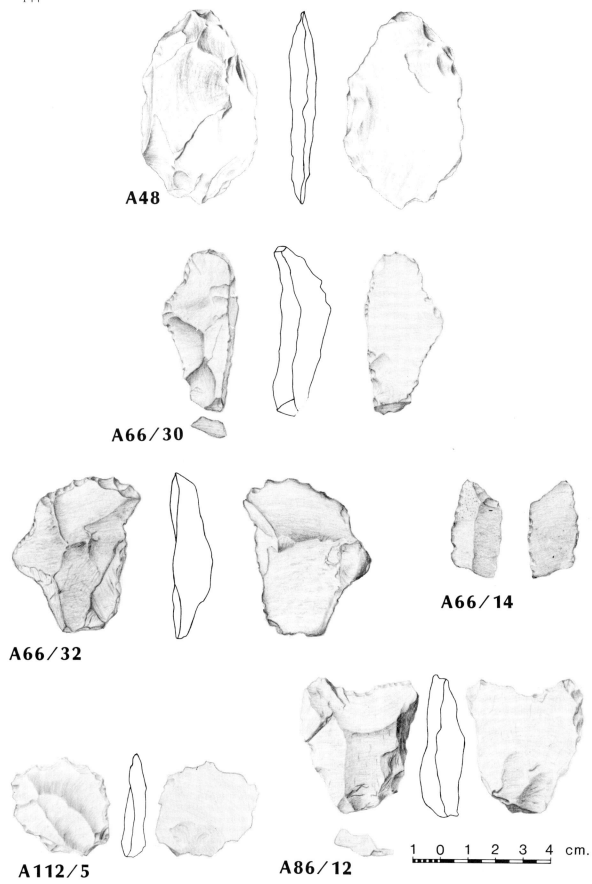

A48

A66/30

A66/32

A66/14

A112/5

A86/12

1 0 1 2 3 4 cm.

Fig. V.24 Pontnewydd Cave. Double side-scraper with ventral retouch: A48, unstratified, dark grey/black unlaminated siliceous fine-grained ?volcaniclastic. End-scrapers: A66/30, unstratified, fine silicic tuff; A66/32, unstratified, fine silicic tuff. Truncated blade: A66/14, unstratified. silicic tuff. Denticulates and Notches: A112/5, unstratified, flint; A86/12, unstratified, rhyolite. Scale 3:4.

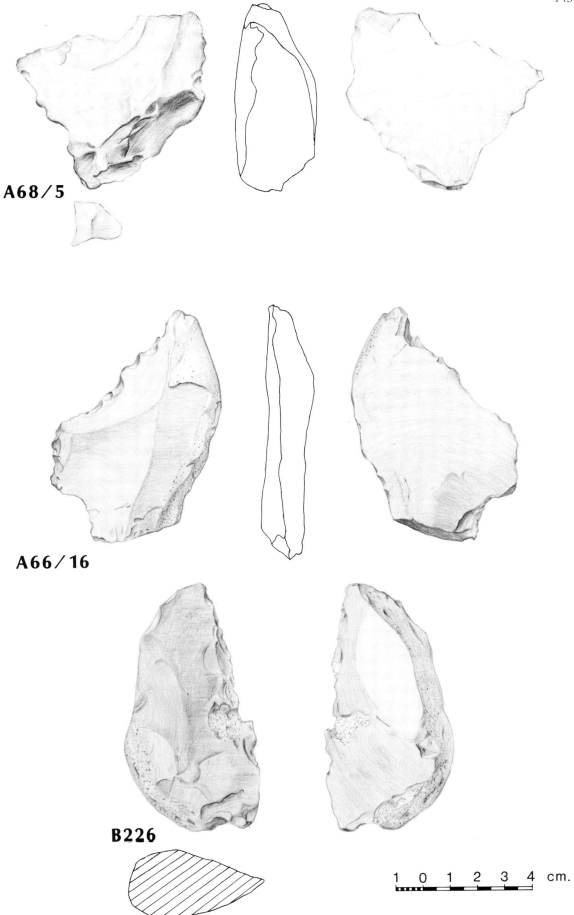

A68/5

A66/16

B226

1 0 1 2 3 4 cm.

Fig. V.25 Pontnewydd Cave. Notch:A68/5, unstratified, fine grained basic lava. Naturally backed knives:
A66/16, unstratified, silicic tuff; B226, Breccia, fine grained silicic tuff. Scale 3:4.

Truncated Blades (Fig. V.24)

There is one example of this type (A66/14) made on a blade which has been truncated by deliberate semi-abrupt retouch. The piece also bears natural damage on its long edges. Newcomer (p.157) comments below on a possible technological context for the appearance of occasional blades as part of the industry.

Utilised Flakes, Slightly Retouched Flakes and Pseudo-Tools

A good many flakes bear chipping which may be the result of transportation-damage in the debris flows, frost heaving or trampling but which may equally, in some cases, be either deliberate retouch or the result of use. Future research may admit of more confident recognition of these "pseudo-tools" (Bordes' types 45-50) either as tools or as naturally damaged pieces.

THE INDUSTRY AS A WHOLE

Principal Characteristics

The main characteristics may readily be reduced to the series of indices (Table V.6) devised by Francois Bordes (for the most accessible English account see Bordes (1972)).

Certain general features of the industry may be noted
  (i)   the importance of Levallois technique.
 (ii)   the important component of handaxes present.
(iii)   the important scraper component
(iv)   a low component of artefacts of Upper Palaeolithic★ type.
The typological indexes must be viewed with caution, however, because of the distortion imposed by the presence of a relatively large number of utilised/pseudo-tools, and the consequential difficulty in recognising some small retouched implements. It may be that the Denticulate Group is somewhat under-represented; it is improbable, however, that the relative importance of the Levallois, Mousterian★ or Upper Palaeolithic Groups★ has been seriously distorted. It is equally unlikely that the recorded frequency of handaxes is seriously in error.

Real Typological Levallois Index	=	22.16
Scraper Index	=	12.75
Handaxe Index	=	17.68
Unifacial Acheulian Index	=	0.00
Quina Index (strict)	=	0.00
I. Levallois Group (Types 1–4)	=	22.16
II. Mousterian Group (Types 6–29)	=	14.09
III. Upper Palaeolithic Group (Types 30–37, 40)	=	2.01
IV Denticulate Group (Type No. 43)	=	1.34

TABLE V.6   Real Typological Index and Characteristic Groups. Excavations 1978–81 and Sedgwick Museum of Geology Collections.

★These Groups are purely of typological significance and the presence of a small component of "Mousterian" or "Upper Palaeolithic" types at Pontnewydd should not be taken to possess chronological implications since implements from these groups may appear in Acheulian industries which predate the appearance of Mousterian or Upper Palaeolithic cultures.

The natural pebbles used as raw material, whilst very considerably harder to work than flint, were eminently suitable for the production of handaxes. The presence of a number of handaxe trimming flakes attests to the on-site production of handaxes. A flint handaxe (65 mm long) was found in the 1983 season.

Crude cores – so called *nucléus débités san prédétermination de la forme des éclats* – were used but cores in which the form of the flake was predetermined by previous removals are predominant. This is reflected in the fact that around 60% of all recognisable flake-butts are either dihedral or facetted.

Very little evidence of the remodelling of tools (for re-use) has been found. One artefact only has been made on an earlier patinated flake (D9) and this need not have been struck by human hand. The bifacial retouch seen on a few scrapers (p.120) might also be the result of such remodelling (Rolland, 1981, 28). If so, these artefacts may be the exception proving the rule that an absence of re-sharpened scrapers may result from the abundance of raw material relative both to the human population size at the site and to the duration of settlement there. This absence of evidence for the constant resharpening of tool cutting-edges would tend to reinforce our view of the transitory nature of settlement at the site. In general, then, the picture is one of unconstrained exploitation of readily available raw material.

DISCUSSION

Function

Some consideration has already been given to the role of the site within its contemporary social context and I have previously expressed my views on this (Green, 1981a). As already mentioned, there can be no doubt of the on-site production of a varied tool kit, while the presence of burnt natural pebbles and artefacts of flint and stone (J. Huxtable, p.106) indicates the lighting of fires. The cave is small in size at the present day and, like the remainder of north Welsh caves, was probably small also in ancient times (I am indebted to Trevor Ford for his view, expressed in the field, that this is indeed likely to have been the case). The size of the potential living area within the drip-line is no more than 30 square metres and such an area is unlikely to have accommodated more than half-a-dozen persons (Cook, 1972, 12–18). I have argued elsewhere (1981a, 192) against the cave having been used by Pleistocene hunters for long-term residential purposes. Such a view, in which the cave was used for one or more short periods of time, would be reinforced (Green, in press) if the environment were an interglacial one, a possibility now raised by Currant's analysis of fauna from the Buff Intermediate layer (p.179).

The tool-kit itself is suggestive of hunting (Mousterian point and Levallois points as spear-tips), butchery (handaxes, Levallois flakes and blades) and hide-processing (scrapers) for the preparation of skins for clothing and perhaps also for mobile shelters. Unfortunately the condition of the bones has not so far offered any chance of recognising traces of actual butchery and thereby discovering which species were certainly used for food. We can see a faunal range from which game may have been – and almost certainly was – selected; but there is highly likely to be some mixing at the site of carnivore (principally bear) accumulations and the bones discarded by the hominids who used the site as a temporary hunting camp.

Some guide to the possible duration of the human occupation is given by the volume of raw materials (Table VIII.4) where Richard Bevins has listed several dozen different rock-types. Among these, the heavier groups, in terms of simple weight, are the ignimbrites (3654 grammes) and the feldspar-phyric lavas (3712 grammes). Even in total, these add up to no more than the weight of many single pebbles from the cave and less than half that of others.

We may take a minimum view and argue that there need have been no more than a few dozen knapping events. Such a volume of activity does not imply a long occupation when one consideres the figures produced by Peter Jones (1981, 195), who suggested that the production of nearly 150 hard-rock handaxes and cleavers at the WK site at Olduvai might have involved no more than three tool-makers working for a day! We would clearly require a considerable increase in the frequency of artefacts at the site in order to justify a revision of this interpretation.

The Age of the Industry

Several dozen dates are now available for Pontnewydd. The interpretation of these has been well described by Schwarcz (Chapter IV). A minimum age is given by dates from *in situ* stalagmite found on the Lower Breccia. These (Chapters IV. A–C) suggest a *terminus ante quem* of *c*.225 ka. In addition, Joan Huxtable's thermoluminescence (TL) determination of 200 ± 25 ka (ka = 1,000's of years ago) is our best estimate of the age of the hominid activity at the cave since the event dated is the burning, presumably in a domestic fire, of a globular flint core. This age is not at variance with the Uranium-Thorium (U-Th) and TL determinations on stalagmite.

The standard practice with any age-determination expressed as a probability, is to accept it only within a range of two standard deviations (2σ). A date of 200 ± 25 ka would thus yield a potential bracket of 250–150 ka. A true age within 175–150 ka is rendered unlikely both for climatic reasons (Green *et al,* 1981, 6) and by the age-distribution of dates obtained from the *in situ* stalagmite which overlies the Lower Breccia. Indeed, the latter consideration would make an age in the range 250-225 ka the most likely and, for the time being, it seems best to think of the human settlement at Pontnewydd as most likely to have occurred during this period (see Green, pp.208–216).

The Archaeological Context

The starting point for this discussion lies with our overall picture of the British Lower Palaeolithic, which has three aspects – geographical, chronological and cultural.

Geography

The apparent isolation of Pontnewydd Cave from other British earlier Palaeolithic sites is shown by Fig. I.2. This map shows the remoteness of Pontnewydd both from contemporary settlement sites and from readily available supplies of flint. A preference by later Pleistocene hominids for flint as a raw material is evidenced at La Cotte de Saint-Brelade on the island of Jersey (Callow, 1981) but – given the early mastery of hard rock technology in many parts of the world – it is difficult to believe that the availability of flint would have acted as an important constraint against colonisation of the north and west of Britain, had demographic or economic circumstances dictated otherwise. The problem which confronts us is the evaluation of the extent to which successive glaciations have destroyed the evidence for human activity in these areas. Some of the evidence is necessarily circumstantial. For instance, the density of settlement falls off markedly as one moves from the south-east of England into the unglaciated south-western peninsula of Devon and Cornwall, suggesting that the latter area was not sought out for settlement. The model of earlier Palaeolithic settlement as restricted largely to the south and east of Britain is reinforced by study of the comparable distribution of Late Glacial settlement in Britain (Jacobi, 1980, 42–3) just before the end of the Devensian complex but after its maximum cold phase. We may see also that such a distribution makes sense when viewed upon a European scale (Collins, 1976). It seems reasonable then to regard Pontnewydd as one of the relatively small number of sites visited by hominids in what were the nearest and most readily accessible areas of the highland zone of Britain. Such sites are likely, then, to have been only occasionally and temporarily occupied by relatively small numbers of people. British caves, in any case, tend to be small in size and the evidence from them points generally to transitory use only (*cf.* Roe, 1981, 280, 283 fn. 3). If this is so, any occupation-sites must have been open-air ones. What we do not know - and cannot tell from the progress of the Pontnewydd research programme to date - is the location of any other site in the region likely to have been contemporaneously occupied by the same band of people. Roe (1981, 279) has even suggested that all or many of the British earlier Palaeolithic sites may merely be seasonal summer encampments with the corresponding winter base-camps located in what is now Continental Europe.

We can, however, reasonably suppose that Pontnewydd Cave formed part of a complex hunting strategy in north-east Wales. The cave must, on the one hand, have provided an admirable vantage point for monitoring and intercepting game moving along the Elwy Valley but, on the other hand, it could well have been a kill-site also, where animals driven over the cliff above the cave-entrance might be despatched and butchered in the same way as has been suggested for La Cotte de Saint-Brelade in Jersey (Scott, 1980). It is possible that the occupation may have taken place in Spring or Autumn when animals might be intercepted *en route* to or from the summer grazing of Mynydd Hiraethog (Fig. V.26).

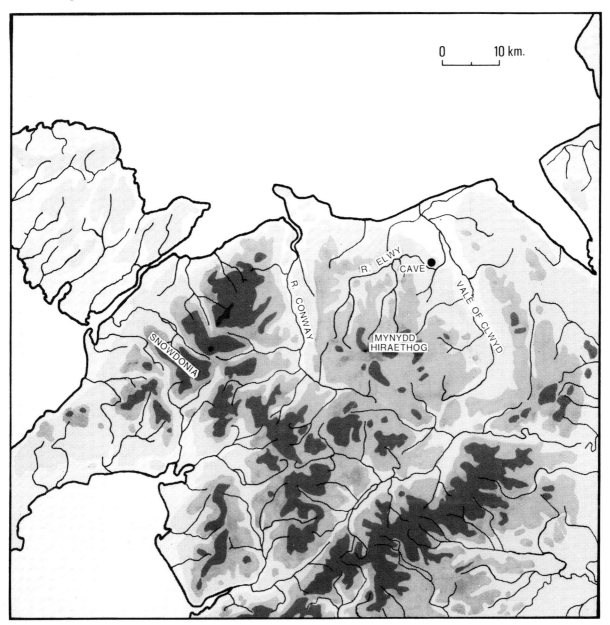

Fig. V.26 Pontnewydd Cave in relation to the physical geography of North Wales.

Chronology

Only a few other absolute age determinations have been made on samples from earlier Palaeolithic sites in Britain. Some U-Th dates on bone from certain interglacial sites have been published (Szabo and Collins, 1975) but it is fair to say that uncertainty still exists in the scientific world about the validity of Uranium series dates on bones because bone, like shell, behaves as an open system which takes up Uranium *post mortem*. However, it is now believed that this *post mortem* period of Uranium uptake is often short and so the method may indeed possess a general validity within certain limits (Schwarcz, 1982, 318 quoting Szabo). It is worth noting that in their 1975 paper Szabo and Collins produced two relevant dates from British archaeological sites with Acheulian indistries, viz.

Swanscombe > 272 ka (sample a few cm below the skull horizon – base of Upper Middle Gravel).
Brundon 174 ± 30 ka (exact context unclear)

The date from Swanscombe is no more than a minimum age but one recent review of the chronology of the Swanscombe sequence by Hubbard (1982) would suggest a true age for the Middle Gravels within the temperate Oxygen Isotope Stage 9 (between *c.* 347 and 297 ka), with the Upper Middle Gravels belonging late in this stage.

The Brundon artefacts include both fresh and derived material and the fauna may be similarly mixed (Moir and Hopwood, 1939; Roe, 1981, 220–2); for do we not know whether the bone was genuinely associated with the human occupation. If it was, then we could say that the determination probably dates the use of Levallois technique at the site, products of which were present among both the fresh and the derived material. Such a finding would not be at variance with the evidence from Pontnewydd but would add little to it.

The Cultural Background

We may take as our starting point Derek Roe's comment on the Pontnewydd industry – published in a review article of Green (1981a) and Green *et al* (1981) in the *Quarterly Review of Archaeology* for June 1981 – that "there is in fact nothing else quite like it in Britain". The full evaluation of the industry will remain a task for the future, but, for the present, we can at least indulge in a brief and speculative consideration of the artefacts in the context both of Britain and north–western Europe in order to assess their possible position among the industries of the later Middle Pleistocene. It is important to remember here that the artefacts are not in primary context and that, whilst I have argued for this, the integrity of the assemblage as an industry cannot be assured.

Our first difficulty is the fact that the Pontnewydd artefacts are principally made of local hard rocks, whereas those of England and N.W. Europe are far more commonly made of flint, a fact with implications both for technology and typology. Nevertheless, it is clear that the industry is an Acheulian one, rich in handaxes and in the use of Levallois technique, and with a very low proportion of such tools as end-scrapers and truncated blades. Viewed from a north-western French standpoint (*cf.* Tuffreau, 1976a), the industry would be regarded as a form of Upper Acheulian, but it is unfortunate that neither of the potentially comparable sites of Vimy or the *série jaune* of Beaumetz-les-Loges in the immediately adjacent areas of the continent has been the subject of modern controlled excavation, and thus the possibility is always present that these particular industries had been artificially "enriched" with handaxes by selective collection (Tuffreau, 1981). Taking the relevant north-western French industries described by Tuffreau as a whole (see also Tuffreau, 1976 b–c) we may note, however, certain parallels at a general level in the main components of the industries – handaxes, Levallois technique, scrapers – and also amongst some of the other implement types which occur. The latter would apply for example, at Bapaume (Tuffreau, 1976d) where in two Upper Acheulian industries (but with only low percentages of handaxes) Mousterian points, naturally backed knives and truncated flakes are all present. It is also instructive here to look at two other relevant sites, one likely to be broadly contemporary (Biache) and the other very probably earlier (Mesvin IV): both have been the subject of modern excavation. Mesvin IV (Cahen, 1981), a Belgian site, probably belongs to the first half of the Saalian cold stage and has been dated by the Uranium-Thorium method to between 300,000 and 250,000 years ago. The industry is quite unlike that of Pontnewydd, lacking both genuine handaxes and tools of "Upper Palaeolithic" type (end-scrapers, burins, awls), among which end-scrapers only are present at Pontnewydd. Certain other types are present at Mesvin but absent at Pontnewydd. What we do see at Mesvin, however, is an industry characterised by the strong presence of Levallois technique, which was used to produce large oval flakes with centripetal preparation, flake-blades and rare points. There are also numerous naturally backed knives and a few retouched backed knives. The latter are, of course, absent at Pontnewydd but this apparent *lacuna* may be no more than an effect of sample size. The site of Biache-Saint-Vaast (Tuffreau, 1978) in the Pas de Calais, which belongs to an interstadial of the Saalian, is of particular interest because it has produced a skull fragment of early Neanderthal affinities (Vandermeersch, 1978). The industry is without handaxes and, but for its age, could almost have been regarded as a typical Mousterian. What is relevant from the point of view of our consideration of Pontnewydd is the great importance of Levallois technique at Biache and the appearance there of Mousterian points, pseudo-Levallois points and a low component of Upper Palaeolithic-type tools. Tuffreau further makes the point that Saalian industries in northern France, with or without handaxes, tend to display important components both of blades and of unretouched Levallois flakes. The latter is certainly true at Pontnewydd, only a few retouched artefacts being made on Levallois blanks, but we have seen that blades, by contrast, are unimportant at Pontnewydd, forming only around 7% of the total number of measurable pieces.

One discordant note is perhaps struck at Pontnewydd by the presence here on a British site of a flake cleaver, and of a chopper and chopping tools. In Europe, these are more characteristically found in Continental assemblages, for example from the southern half of France. But that is of course just where there is a high incidence of the use of non-flint rocks similar to the situation at Pontnewydd. This would be in keeping with the view that flake-cleavers tend to be made in regions where flint is little used for tool manufacture (*cf.* Monnier and Texier, 1977, 627) a fact which may reflect both the general unsuitability of flint for this class of artefact and, conversely, the favourable properties of hard rocks (Villa, 1981, 26–7).

If we turn now from Europe at large to the more local context of our site, we find that, in Britain, there is an absence of well excavated comparable assemblages and we can point to only a handful of sites of potentially similar age which can, in some way, be compared. The only British site to be claimed as a possible "Acheulian industry of Levallois facies" is Caddington (Roe, 1981, 191) but the material attributed to this place-name is known to come from a series of separate sites which need not be of the same age (*cf.* Sampson, 1978). But we may certainly note among the Caddington artefacts a whole series of Levallois cores, including examples of the "reduced Levallois" technique (Roe, 1981, fig. 5–42, pp.194–5) which are distinctly reminiscent of some of the Pontnewydd cores, particularly those of flint (Fig. V.5). In an as yet unpublished paper Roger Jacobi has suggested that a Lower Palaeolithic industry with handaxes and the use of Levallois technique exists at Shide on the Isle of Wight but this is unsupported by clear stratigraphic evidence. We may note in this context, too, Wymer's designation (1982b, 121) of the finds from the Crayford brickearth pits as Levalloiso-Acheulian. But even if these finds genuinely constitute a single industry – a matter which is open to question – the assemblage is one of wholly different character from

Pontnewydd, being typified by Levallois flake-blade production with only a few handaxes and one chopping tool (Wymer, 1968, 322–6; Roe, 1981, 86–8). The age of this industry would seem to be Last Interglacial.

The nearest assemblage, in a purely geographical sense, to Pontnewydd comes from the gravels of the Trent Valley around the contiguous Derbyshire villages of Hilton and Willington (Posnansky, 1963). This area, though on the northern margin of the distribution of earlier Palaeolithic finds in Britain, lies within the lowland Midlands plain and cannot be regarded as a true upland site, like Pontnewydd. The age of the Hilton/Willington material is not clear and nor is it certain how many separate occurrences may be represented there. The existing collections appear to contain a roughly equal proportion of amygdaloid and ovate handaxes, almost all of flint although a few quartzite examples do occur. Some of the handaxes, like some from Pontnewydd, are of plano-convex cross-section, a circumstance which Posnansky (1963, 391) attributes to the use of tabular flint. Overall, there is no direct point of comparison between these Trent gravel sites and Pontnewydd.

Much the same may be said of. the small assemblage, conventionally – and probably correctly – regarded as Mousterian, from Robin Hood's Cave, Creswell Crags (Dawkins, 1876 and 1877; Mello, 1877). Here a range of artefacts, of quartzite and ironstone, is present and includes chopping tools, discoidal cores, side-scrapers (one with thinned back and base), denticulates, a naturally backed knife, and six handaxes among which are two cordiforms, one amygdaloid and three ovates (one a diminutive limande). This group of artefacts, if genuinely an industry, has individual points of comparison with Pontnewydd but the typology of the handaxes would argue for a Mousterian date.

The absence of close British parallels to the Pontnewydd assemblage – if correctly diagnosed as the products of one or more brief occupations of the site – may be no more than a reflection of the fact that the originally comparable industries are now mixed in with much larger assemblages as the result either of multiple long-term occupation of particular sites by the same group or of cyclic re-occupation by different human groups at widely separated periods of time. It is, indeed, possible then that future research may locate elsewhere in Britain a pattern of assemblage composition similar to that found at Pontnewydd. For the present, however, it must be said that the quality of evidence for most other British sites of potential relevance is depressingly inadequate.

PART B
FLAKING EXPERIMENTS WITH PONTNEWYDD RAW MATERIALS
by
M.H. Newcomer

The flaking experiments presented in this paper have two main aims: firstly, to see how the tough igneous rocks used as raw material by the Acheulian inhabitants of Pontnewydd Cave influenced the technology and typology of the stone tool assemblages, and secondly, to gain some idea of how much of the flaking waste produced by working these materials would be recognisable as artefacts.

MATERIALS AND PROCEDURES

All the experimental work presented here was done by the author, who has some fifteen years' experience in making tools of the types found at Pontnewydd, although most of this experience has been with more tractable materials like flint and obsidian. The rocks used came from the archaeological and geological layers at Pontnewydd and were collected during the excavations. The blocks knapped are all igneous rocks (Table V.7).

Flaking hammers were pebbles of quartzite and a red deer antler soft hammer, which were used to flake cores and handaxes and to retouch flake tools, all by direct percussion; examination of the archaeological material indicated that no other flaking techniques were necessary to produce the Pontnewydd artefacts. The quartzite hammers were rather heavier than those which might be used to strike flakes of the same size from material like flint, weighing about 500 g. each. Convincing hammerstones have not been found in the archaeological deposits, but it is quite possible that small pieces of the same igneous rocks were used as hammers and then flaked as cores if they broke. Flaking strategy was to some extent influenced by the shape of the block of material, with thinner pieces chosen for handaxes and thicker blocks made into discoidal or Levallois cores. All waste flakes, dust and debris were carefully collected after each block was flaked, and some of the larger flakes retouched into tools like side-scrapers.

RESULTS

The flaking properties of the fifteen pieces of Pontnewydd material tested were somewhat different, but no piece was easy to flake and some were extremely tough. Every piece tested had cleavage planes and some blocks split into several slabs along these planes. Several blocks had deeply weathered outer surfaces and repeated blows with the quartzite hammers were needed to detach the first few flakes. Five hammerstones were broken during these experiments, and this contrasts sharply with a life expectancy of several weeks' constant use for similar hammers used on flint, which are normally discarded when worn but unbroken. None of the ancient artefacts showed unequivocal signs of soft hammer flaking on retouch, and the occasional flake with a lipped butt was also produced experimentally with hard hammer percussion.

Flaking accidents of the type known as 'Siret's burin' (Bordes, 1961, 23), where the flake splits in two or more or less equal halves down the axis of percussion, were quite common with all the materials tested, and similar split flakes were observed in the archaeological collections (Pl.XVII). It is perhaps worth remarking here that the alleged burins in Beds I

154

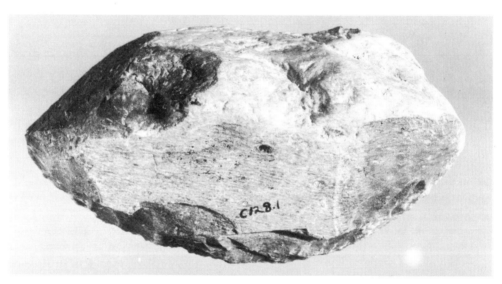

Plate XVIII Pontnewydd Cave. (a) Handaxes, Upper row: modern replicas (left to right: B404 A.3; B404 C.1; B404 C.2; B403 E.1; B404 B.1.) Lower row: Palaeolithic examples (left to right: D601, D714, D481, A68/1, D639). (b) Quina-style scraper, Modern replica: C128.1. Maximum dimension 107mm.

cm. 0   5   **a**

cm. 0   5   10   15   **b**

Plate XIX   Pontnewydd Cave. (a)   Scrapers with Demi-Quina retouch. Left: Palaeolithic (B5). Right: Modern replica (B403 D.1). (b)   Scrapers. Modern replicas. Top row (left to right): D928.2; B415.1; D928.1. Bottom row (left to right): B404.2; B403 A.1; B403 D.2.

Petrology	Dimensions (cm)	Code	Type	Hammer
Shardic tuff	16×10×4	B403 A.1	Side-scraper	Red deer antler
		B403 A.2	Handaxe (failed)	Quartzite pebble
		B403 A.3	Handaxe	Quartzite pebble
Crystal tuff	22×17×6	D928.1	Side-scraper	Red deer antler
		D928.2	Side-scraper	Quartzite pebble
		D928.3	'Siret' pseudo-burins (×3)	Quartzite pebble
		D928.4	Handaxe	Quartzite pebble
Silicic tuff	12×11×7	B404 C.1	Handaxe	Quartzite pebble
		B404 C.2	Handaxe	Quartzite pebble
Crystal tuff	20×13×7	B415.1	Side-scraper	Red deer antler
		B415.2	Side-scraper	Quartzite pebble
Ignimbrite	12×11×7	C128.1	Side-scraper (Quina)	Red deer antler
Ignimbrite	18×16×10	B403 D.1	Side-scraper	Red deer antler
		B403 D.2	Side-scraper	Quartzite pebble
Interbedded sandstone and crystal tuff	16×11×8	C279.1	'Siret' pseudo-burin	Quartzite pebble
		C279.2	Proto-Levallois flake	Quartzite pebble
		C279.3	Side-scraper	Red deer antler
Crystal vitric tuff	16×13×6	B403 E.1	Handaxe	Quartzite pebble and Red deer antler
Feldspar-phyric lava	12×14×5	B404 B.1	Handaxe	Quartzite pebble and Red deer antler

TABLE V.7 Pontnewydd Flaking Experiments. Schedule of Finished Artefects

Notes:
1. The code is composed of the site reference number (e.g. B403), which may denote a series of pebbles from one context, plus a capital letter, used to refer to a particular pebble within that bulk number (e.g. B403 A), and a numeral which refers to an individual artefact made from a particular pebble thus (B403 A.1).
2. 'D916' (13 × 11 × 5 cm.) split in two halves after a few blows and was abandoned.
3. 'B403' (15 × 13 × 9 cm.) was a block which proved too hard to flake.
4. Two blocks labelled 'PN 81 B404D' (11 × 8 × 8 cm.) and 'B404E' (16 × 11 × 7 cm.) and the flint control (15 × 12 × 10 cm.) were used to test proportions of recognisable artefacts. The raw material types, respectively, are B404D (feldspar-phyric lava) and B404E (shardic tuff).

and II of Olduvai Gorge (Leakey, 1971) are probably the result of the same flaking accident occurring in the similarly tough raw materials used at Olduvai.

Seven handaxes were made, five with hard hammer only and two with a combination of hard and soft hammers (Pl. XVIIIa). The soft hammer was not effective in producing long, invasive thinning flakes, since the raw materials were so tough and unpredictable. Only one of the ancient Pontnewydd handaxes shows signs of having been made on a large flake, but three of the experimentally flaked blocks split down cleavage planes into several slices, each of which could be used to make a handaxe. Handaxes on struck flakes tend to have plano-convex cross-sections, the domed face being the old dorsal surface and the flat face the ventral, and blocks split down cleavage planes would encourage a similar effect (Green, 1981a, 190). As expected, it proved difficult to detach long thinning flakes from the handaxes, and all the axes made would be classed as 'thick' by Bordes (1961, 65; width: thickness ratio of less than 2.35:1), although it was possible to make pointed or ovate forms at will. Refinements like twisted edges and tranchet tips were also difficult to make, and these features are not surprisingly lacking on the archaeological·specimens.

Problems in controlling the flaking of these materials also showed up in the experimental cores, and only one block was good enough to attempt a Levallois core, although a cleavage plane which appeared in the final stages of preparation prevented the striking of a good Levallois flake. Facetting of striking platforms was possible with some pieces, but the improvement of flaking angle achieved by facetting was offset by problems caused by the facetting spreading the hammer's impact and making flake removal more difficult. Flakes with facetted butts certainly exist in the archaeological assemblages, but tend to be found on flakes of finer-grained material. A few direct percussion blades were made, but came from opportunistic use of a long ridge on a core's corner rather than any special blade core preparation. There are no blade cores in the archaeological material.

Flake tools like side-scrapers were on the contrary quite easy to make, using direct percussion with hard or soft hammer, though the edges of some of the coarser flakes tended to crumble rather than flake neatly (Pl.XIX). Stepped and scaled 'Quina' type retouch was possible on flakes from two of the finer-grained blocks, and I would infer that the rarity of Quina retouch in the archaeological sample is due to cultural choice and not constraints imposed by raw material (Pl.XVIIIb).

Examination of the waste flakes and chips produced by flaking each block revealed that some of the coarser materials yielded very few flakes exhibiting conchoidal fracture, even when the hard hammer alone had been used. An attempt to quantify this observation was made by flaking three blocks of material, one fine-grained, one much coarser and a flint control, using the alternate flaking method, where one flake scar forms the striking platform for the next removal. The same quartzite hammer was used and the resulting flakes, chips and dust from each block were separated into two piles: flakes with clear signs of having been deliberately struck (that is, obvious butt and bulb of percussion or at least clear bulbar surface) and, second, all other pieces lacking these features (Table V.8).

	Total Weight of Block	Weight of Recognisable Flakes and Core	Weight of Undiagnostic Material	Ratio of Diagnostic to Undiagnostic	Weight of Particles < 1 mm.	Ratio of Particles < 1mm. to Original Block Weight
COARSE BLOCK	1782.2	255.6	1526.6	14.3%	7.3	.4%
FINE-GRAINED BLOCK	1355.5	1141.7	213.8	84.2%	7.2	.5%
FLINT CONTROL	2507.2	2477.8	29.4	98.8%	1.8	.07%

TABLE V.8 Diagnostic and undiagnostic material made by flaking three blocks of material. Particles less than 1 mm. across were separated by passing all the material through a 1 mm. mesh sieve. All weights in grams. The 'coarse block' was a shardic tuff and the 'fine-grained block' a feldspar-phyric lava.

This table illustrates the contrast between the block of East Anglian flint used as a control, where 98.8% of the products are recognisable as humanly struck, and the coarser piece of Pontnewydd material, where only 14.3% by weight of the products are diagnostic. It is also interesting that the coarse material, which seemed quite dusty to knap, in fact yielded a relatively small proportion of particles less than 1 mm. across.

The main lesson to be learned from this last experiment is that excavated samples of debitage from sites like Pontnewydd, where coarse igneous rocks are being worked, will not reflect anything like the quantity of flaked material, simply because so much of the debitage will be unrecognisable as artefacts. This experiment also suggests that it may be worthwhile to examine the sediment samples from the different archaeological layers to see whether they contain high concentrations of angular igneous rock debris which would indicate flaking on the spot. Fine flint particles have been successfully isolated in sediment samples by Fladmark (1982) and used as indicators of flint flaking areas but, of course, such tiny particles of siliceous rock would be very vulnerable to chemical attack in an alkaline environment like the Pontnewydd cave sediments (see Collcutt, p.76).

DISCUSSION

A main aim of these experiments was the evaluation of the effect of the difficult-to-flake raw materials on the Pontnewydd assemblages. If the inhabitants of the site had moved on to an area where good chalk flint was available for tool making, how would their tools have differed? Examination of Lower and Middle Palaeolithic tools from different parts of the world in different raw materials shows that handaxe-makers continued to make handaxes and Levallois-flakers continued to practice Levallois flaking whatever the raw material available, and therefore the concentration of the Pontnewydd knappers on handaxes, side-scrapers and Levallois flakes probably would not change if they had access to better raw materials. Details of the industry might change however, with handaxes perhaps being thinner, having more flake scars on each face and incorporating refinements like twisted edges and tranchet finish. Side-scrapers might be better retouched but otherwise un-changed, while Levallois flakes might be clearer and perhaps more numerous. If the Pontnewydd tool makers had used finer-grained materials probably the biggest difference we would see is in the size of the assemblages which increase enormously as more of the waste flakes and chips become identifiable as artefacts.

Future experimental work with the Pontnewydd raw materials will concentrate on using copies of the Acheulian tools and reporting on their functional efficiency.

Chapter VI

THE HOMINID FINDS
by
C.B. Stringer

The non-specialist reader should first turn to Fig. VI.1 which gives the standard nomenclature applied to the upper and lower human dentitions. Figure VI.2 gives the average ages of tooth eruption and loss in a sample of recent humans. The nomenclature used in the description of the molar teeth is illustrated in plates XX and XXII.

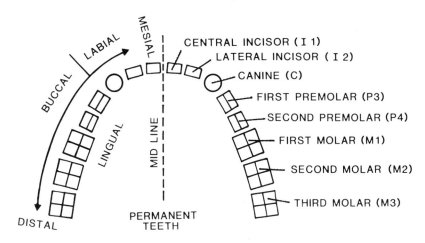

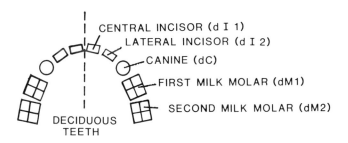

Fig. VI.1   Standard nomenclature for upper and lower teeth, based on Day (1977) with modifications. *NB* Upper and lower teeth may be distinguished one from the other by the use of superscript and subscript notation: e.g. M^2 denotes an *upper* second molar and M_2 denotes a *lower* second molar.

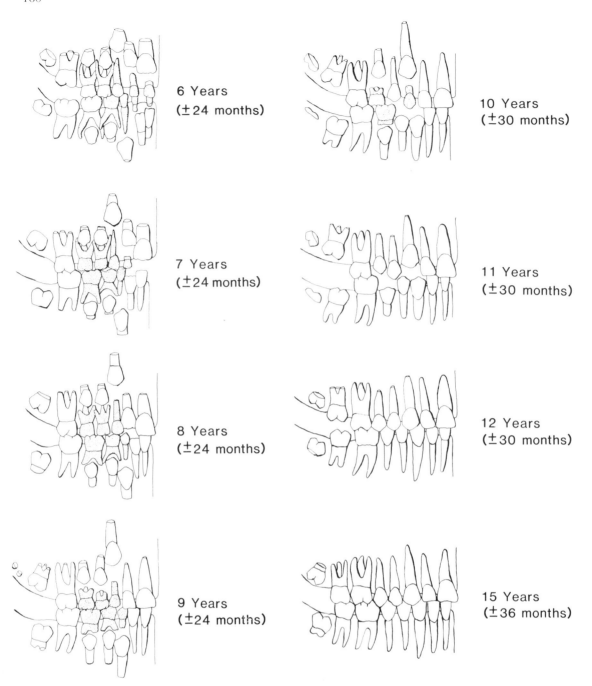

6 Years
(±24 months)

10 Years
(±30 months)

7 Years
(±24 months)

11 Years
(±30 months)

8 Years
(±24 months)

12 Years
(±30 months)

9 Years
(±24 months)

15 Years
(±36 months)

Fig. VI.2   The sequence of formation and eruption of teeth among American Indians. Redrawn from D. H. Ubelaker (1978). Deciduous teeth are shown stippled.

The hominid specimens PN1–3 (Table VI.1) have already received preliminary descriptions, while the upper molar (Pontnewydd 1) was described and illustrated in more detail (Stringer in Green *et al* 1981). However some additional comments can now be made about the specimens, following further study together with comment on finds from the 1982–3 seasons.

Pontnewydd 1

As already reported, the molar in question is probably a left upper second (M^2) which displays taurodontism (Fig. VI.3). Its roots are robust and are undivided over most of their length (Plate XX). A limited examination of published and unpublished original

Hominid Reference No.	Site Ref. No.	Context	Grid Square (and depth)	Description
PN1	PN80 D415	Junction of Buff & Orange Intermediate. East Passage	H9 (98.92)	left M^2
PN2	PN80 A80	World War II Dump. Site A	-	Immature mandible fragment with crown of unerupted molar (M_3?)
PN3	PN78 C5	Dump of modern spoil in East Passage	-	Fragment of adult vertebra
PN4	PN82 D1740–1	Lower Breccia	I8 (98.95)	Fragment of right maxilla with M^1 and dM^2 in place
PN5	PN83 D2212	Lower Breccia	J7NW (99.18–08)	Left lower premolar
PN6	PN83 D2261	Lower Breccia	J7SW/K7NW (99.66–33)	Lower premolar (unworn)

TABLE VI.1.   Hominid finds from Pontnewydd.

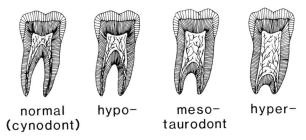

normal (cynodont)   hypo-   meso-taurodont   hyper-

Fig. VI.3   Diagrammatic representation of normal (cynodontic) tooth and three subclasses of taurodontic teeth proposed by Shaw (1928).

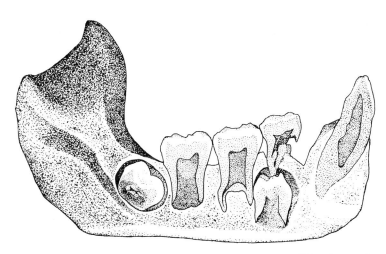

Fig. VI.4   Drawing of radiograph of lateral view of the Krapina C mandible. Approximate dental age 11–12 years. Note taurodontism of M_1 and M_2, and relatively delayed loss of dM_2 and eruption of P_4 (see discussion in Wolpoff, 1979).

specimens and casts of Middle and early Upper Pleistocene molars from French sites such as Biache, Abri Suard and Bourgeois-Delaunay demonstrates that it is possible to match closely the morphology and the size of the crown, but not the root, of the Pontnewydd fossil. However radiographs of several specimens where the root morphology cannot be observed are not available, so further data are required for a fuller comparison. Comparison with Upper Pleistocene Neanderthal molars demonstrates that the degree of taurodontism exhibited by Pontnewydd 1 does not match that of the more extreme examples from sites such as Krapina (Fig. VI.4) and La Cotte de St Brelade, but corresponds with the meso-taurodont condition and Kallay's category of supraradicular taurodontism (the most common form in the Krapina molars at 49% frequency), rather than the more extreme radicular taurodontism, as originally reported (Green et al.,1981).

Pontnewydd 2

Further comparisons of the right mandibular fragment (Plates XXI–XXIII) with other Middle and Upper Pleistocene immature specimens suggest that the degree of posterior narrowing of the unerupted molar favours the identification of the molar as a lower third (M_3), giving an age estimate from modern developmental patterns of greater than eleven years (Fig. VI.2). Such an age is also more consistent with the morphology of the coronoid and mandibular foramen areas (N. Minugh and T. Bromage, pers. comm.). It is certainly possible to match the size of the molar with the smallest Neanderthal examples and even with a supposed Middle Pleistocene specimen such as Atapuerca 1 but none that I have seen so far matches the Pontnewydd specimen closely in both size and morphology, while the contrast seems even greater with earlier European specimens. However, the tooth can be matched much more readily among recent examples.

In the size of the ascending ramus (minimum breadth = 31.5 mm), the specimen is well within the range of variation for a comparative sample chosen from Romano-British and Saxon mandibles aged dentally at c.11–13 years (28.35 ± 1.91 mm, n = 50) and even for those aged c.8–10 years (27.92 ± 2.04 mm, n= 58). Such a narrow ascending ramus breadth could still be matched in early Neanderthal specimens, since a cast of the Krapina C mandible, aged c.11–12 years (Fig. VI.4) has a value of 30.5 mm, although the value for the slightly older Ehringsdorf 7 (G) specimen, aged c.12 years, is considerably larger at 36.5 mm; but neither of these specimens bears molars comparable in size or morphology with that of Pontnewydd 2.

From the preserved parts there seem, therefore, to be insufficient data to exclude Pontnewydd 2 from the morphological and metrical range of comparable samples of anatomically modern humans. Recovery of further parts of the mandible (e.g. the symphysial area and anterior dentition) may allow more definite conclusions as to its affinities.

Pontnewydd 3

The preserved part of the body of this thoracic vertebra is quite large (transverse breadth immediately anterior to inferior demi-facets = 35.2 mm; maximum superior-inferior thickness, measured on the posterior surface of the body = 24.5 mm), but it can be closely matched in recent large adult specimens (Plates XXIV–XXV). The lack of well-preserved human vertebrae from the Middle and early Upper Pleistocene precludes any useful morphological comparisons with thoracic vertebrae from non-"modern" hominids.

Pontnewydd 4

The 1982 excavations recovered a hominid specimen from the base of the Lower Breccia, in the East Passage, close to the 1980 find of the upper molar, Pontnewydd 1, (see above) from the Intermediate complex. A deciduous and permanent molar, with the surrounding

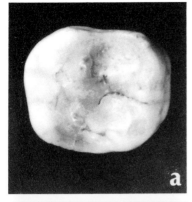

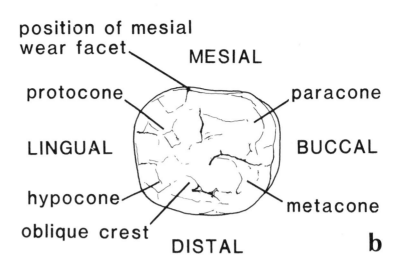

position of mesial
wear facet

MESIAL

protocone

paracone

LINGUAL

BUCCAL

hypocone

metacone

oblique crest

DISTAL

b

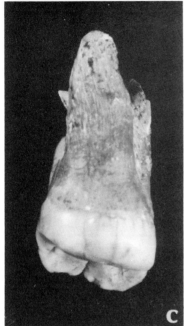

1   0   1 cm.

Plate XX a–c   Molar tooth (PN1). (a) Occlusal view (distal side at bottom); (b) labelled drawing of view a; (c) Lingual view.

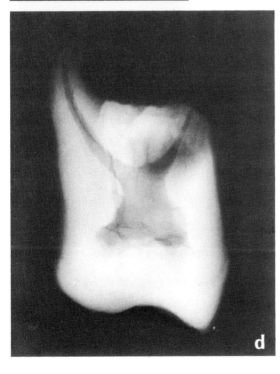

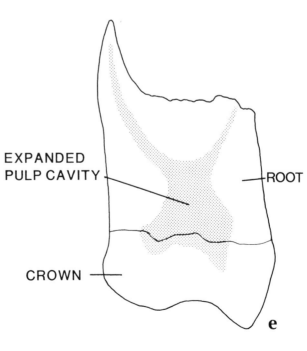

EXPANDED
PULP CAVITY

ROOT

CROWN

e

Plate XX d–e Molar tooth (PN1). (d) Mesial radiograph. (e) Labelled drawing of features shown in the radiograph. *N.B.* The scale applies only to a–c.

164

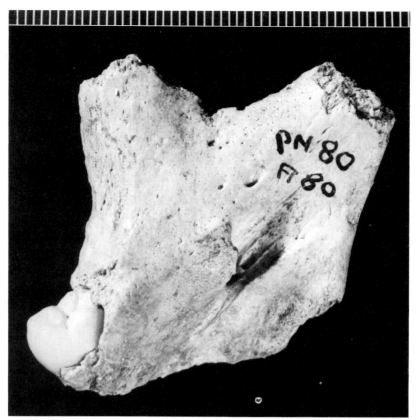

Plate XXI   Immature mandible fragment (PN2). Internal view.

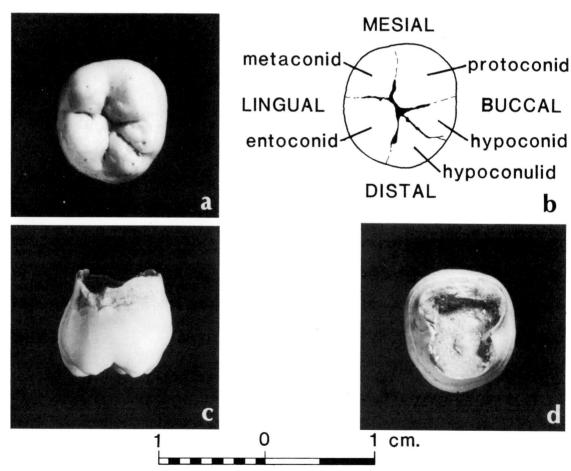

MESIAL

metaconid — — protoconid

LINGUAL   BUCCAL

entoconid — — hypoconid

hypoconulid

DISTAL

a

b

c

d

1   0   1 cm.

Plate XXII   Tooth from immature mandible fragment (PN2). (a) Occlusal view (mesial side at top); (b) Labelled drawing of a; (c) Mesial view; (d) Inferior view of tooth (mesial side at top).

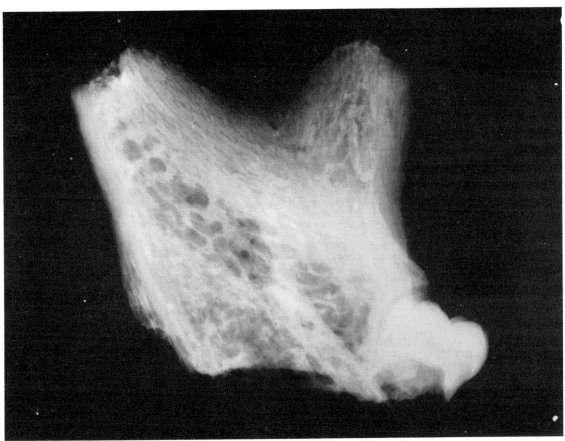

Plate XXIII   Immature mandible fragment (PN2). Radiograph of lateral view.

alveolar bone, were reconstructed from fragments by A. P. Currant (Plates XXVI–XXVIII). The specimen can be positively identified as a right maxillary fragment from an individual aged according to modern developmental patterns at about 8–9 years (Fig. VI.2). The M^1 crown (Pl. XXVI) is unworn, large and rhombic (mesio-distal length 12.25 mm; bucco-lingual breadth 12.35 mm). These dimensions are slightly smaller than the Krapina mean dimensions for M^1 (Wolpoff 1979), but slightly larger than the means of a European last glaciation Neanderthal sample (data from Frayer, 1978). There is no distal contact facet for M^2. The tooth has a fully developed robust, prismatic, but waisted root, and the single buccal root has an unusual lobed apex (Plates XXIX–XXX, XXXII). Radiographs (Plate XXXIII) reveal a degree of taurodontism as marked as in PN1, again resembling that reported for the Krapina molars (Kallay, 1963; Skinner and Sperber, 1982). Recent work has further supported the suggestion that the development of taurodontism may have a genetic basis (Jaspers and Witkop, 1980), and the recovery at Pontnewydd of molars from two different individuals, both displaying the condition, suggests that it was a population characteristic. As discussed previously (Green et al., 1981), taurodontism is not a trait found in all Neanderthals, nor is it exclusive to them (Jaspers and Witkop, 1980), but in overall morphology, the closest fossil matches to the Pontnewydd molars are to be found in the probably early Upper Pleistocene Neanderthal sample from Krapina (Fig. VI.4), despite a time difference between these specimens of perhaps 100,000 years. As far as I know, no other Middle Pleistocene molars are yet reported to show this type of morphology.

The dM^2 crown (Plate XXVI) is rhomboidal, with a high degree of occlusal and mesial wear (length 9.2 mm, approximately 9.8 mm allowing for mesial wear; breadth 10.25 mm). These dimensions are at the lower end of the Krapina range for dM^2 (Wolpoff, 1979), and are close to mean values for Neanderthals generally (data from Frayer, 1978). Even though

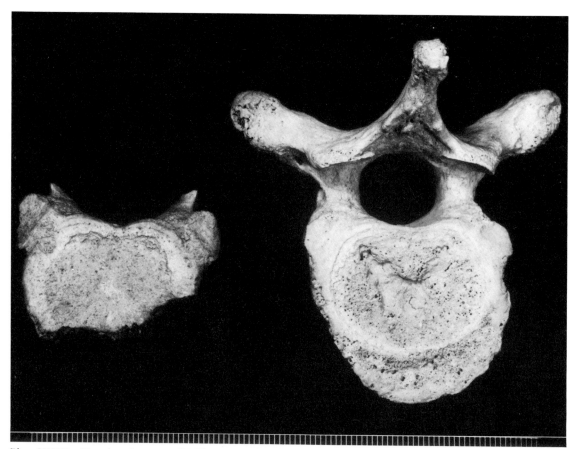

Plate XXIV   Vertebra fragment (PN3) compared with recent 8th thoracic vertebra from Poundbury, Dorset.
Inferior view.

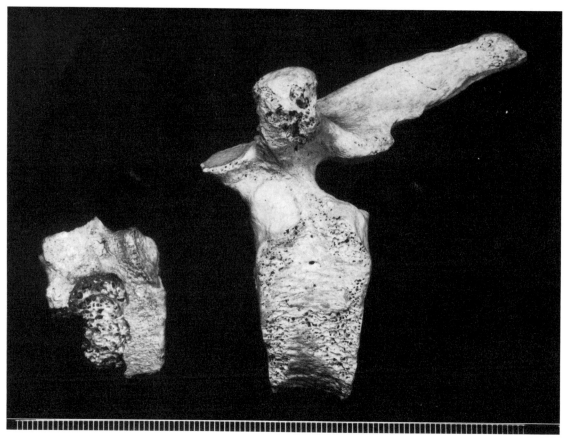

Plate XXV   Vertebra fragment (PN3) compared with recent 8th thoracic vertebra from Poundbury (Dorset).
Left lateral view.

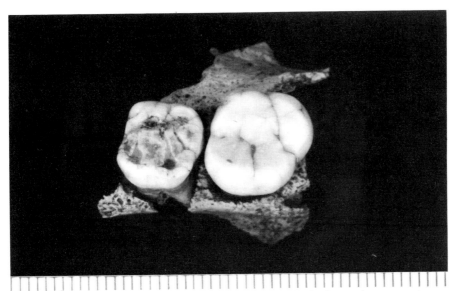

Plate XXVI   Occlusal view of maxillary fragment (PN4). Although the teeth are not in contact in this reconstruction, there are, in fact, clear contact facets.

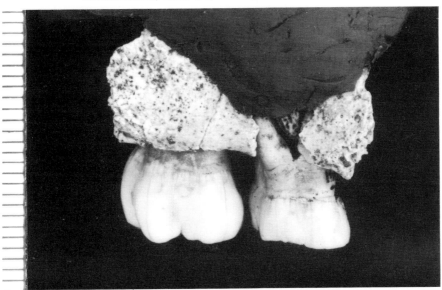

Plate XXVII   Buccal view of maxillary fragment (PN4).

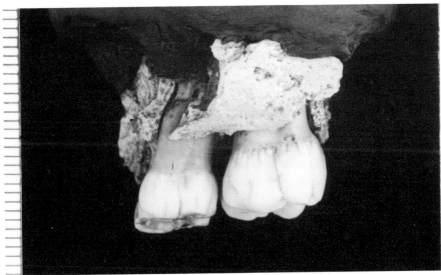

Plate XXVIII   Lingual view of maxillary fragment (PN4).

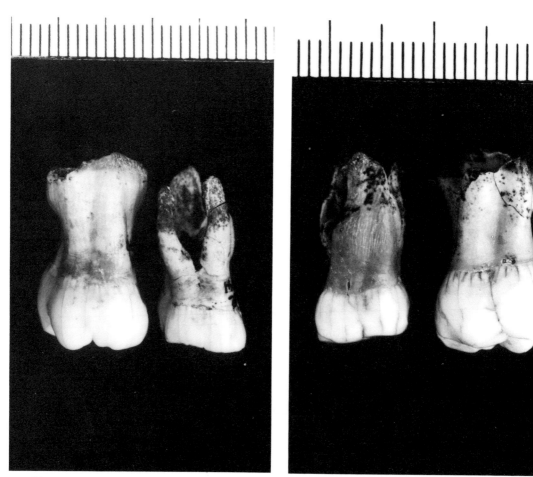

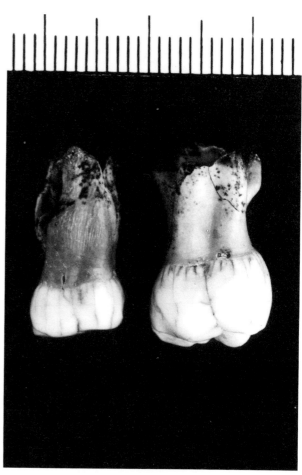

Plate XXIX   Buccal view of teeth (PN4).   Plate XXX   Lingual view of teeth (PN4).

the roots for the M^1 are completely formed in Pontnewydd 4, implying a dental age of perhaps 9 years, the lack of wear on the crown would suggest a slightly younger age. The roots of the dM^2 are not yet resorbed and unlike the roots of M^1, they are not prismatic (Plates XXIX–XXX, XXXII). A probable explanation for the relative lack of resorption in the dM^2 roots is given by the lingual occurrence of what is probably the crypt for P^4 (Plates XXXI–XXXII). This apparently anomalous position for the P^4 crypt might have led to medial replacement of dM^2, rather than from above, or it might even have led to retention of dM^2 alongside P^4, as is known from a few modern examples (e.g. Brothwell, 1981, p.113). Probably because of this unusual situation, the alveolar bone just anterior to M^1 is unusually broad bucco-lingually.

Given a dental age of $c.8$–9 years, there is the possibility that PN4 is of the same dental age as the unstratified mandibular fragment PN2, if the molar crown contained in the latter specimen is assumed to be an M_2 (but see earlier discussion). The fragmentary nature of the upper and lower jaw fragments and doubt about the dental age and stratigraphical position of PN2 make it impossible to associate the fragments at present.

Pontnewydd 5 and 6

The 1983 excavations of the Lower Breccia in the East Passage produced two further hominid teeth. Preliminary study suggests that they both may represent left lower first premolars. Even if this is not certain, they appear to represent two different individuals. One may be from a child aged, from modern developmental patterns, at between 8–12 years (PN 6); the other from a somewhat older, perhaps even adolescent individual (PN 5). Both

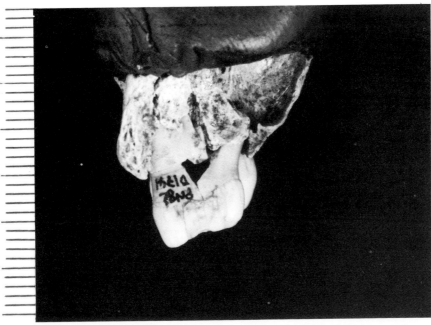

Plate XXXI   Mesial view of jaw (PN4). Note the position, top right of the assumed crypt for P⁴.

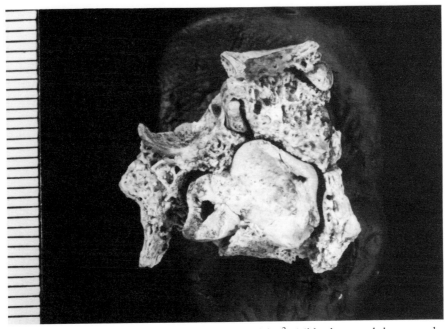

Plate XXXII   Superior view of jaw (PN4). Note the roots of dM² visible above and the unusual root form of M¹ seen below. The position of the assumed crypt for P⁴ is shown top left, lingual to dM².

are large-crowned compared with the modern average for P₃ but compare well in size with Neanderthal specimens. If these preliminary identifications are correct, PN5 might be from the same individual as PN2, while PN6 might belong with PN4.

CONCLUSION

Comparison of the specimens from Pontnewydd with other European fossil hominids confirms the recognition of Neanderthal-like features in the stratified upper molars. However on present evidence, the unstratified mandibular and vertebral fragments cannot be positively aligned with archaic rather than anatomically modern hominids. It seems that

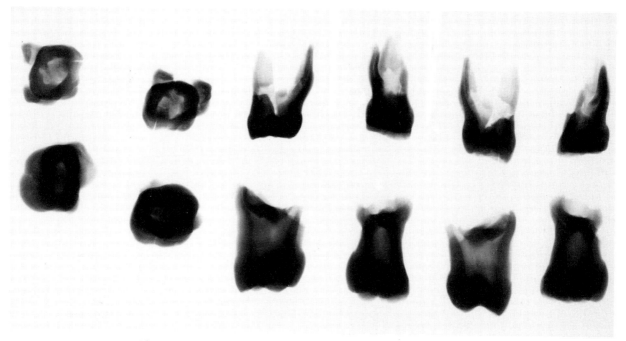

Plate XXXIII   Radiographs of dM² above and M¹ below (PN4).

only further fieldwork or the recovery of additional skeletal or dental material can satisfactorily resolve the question of the affinities of these specimens.

ACKNOWLEDGEMENTS

I would like to acknowledge L. Martin, A.M. Tillier, A. Boyde, J.J. Hublin, J. Musgrave, B. Berkovitz and B. Moxham for providing helpful discussion about the Pontnewydd specimens, and B. Vandermeersch, Y. Coppens, J. L. Heim and B. Senut for allowing access to fossil hominid material. R. Eames provided comparative data for this study. Funds for my recent work on Pleistocene hominids have been provided by the British Museum (Natural History), L.S.B. Leakey Foundation, and the Cambrian Archaeological Association. Photographs were provided by the British Museum (Natural History) studio except for Plate XXII (National Museum of Wales). Radiographs were taken by T. Molleson, Figures VI.1–4 and the illustrations in Plates XX and XXII were drawn by Paul Hughes, National Museum of Wales.

CHAPTER VII

THE MAMMALIAN REMAINS
by
A. P. Currant

INTRODUCTION

Study of the mammal remains from Pontnewydd Cave has progressed considerably since the announcement of the preliminary results of the present excavations (Green *et al.*,1981). Material from the 1981 field season has improved our understanding of the site's faunal history: three assemblages of different ages can now be at least partially differentiated. This would not have been possible without the multidisciplinary approach that has been adopted, and I would like to acknowledge the great benefit derived from collaboration with other members of the project.

The fragmentary nature of nearly all finds makes identification very difficult, and approximately 90% of the collected material is not determinable. All previous determinations have been critically reviewed and the resultant additions and alterations to the species lists should be noted.

At the present stage of collecting several taxa are represented by only one or two specimens, and even collections of the commoner forms are not sufficiently large to yield samples of any one skeletal element that would be statistically viable in metrical comparisons with material from other sites. It is hoped that further collecting will improve this position.

Fauna from the nineteenth century excavations

The precise date of the earliest work at Pontnewydd is uncertain. At the time of his visit to the excavations in nearby Cefn Caves in February 1832 the Rev. E. Stanley referred to the site as a cave "never yet opened" (Stanley, 1832), and it is possible that small scale digging could have taken place at any time between then and 1869/1870 when Dawkins (1871) indicated that a major phase of excavations was under way. In 1874, Professor T. McKenny Hughes and the Rev. D. R. Thomas reported that the site had been examined by the owner, Mr. Williams Wynn "some years ago", and mentioned that the upper (fossiliferous) deposits had been almost entirely removed for about 25 yards (*c.* 23m) into the cave. This approximates quite closely to the position of the standing face of *in situ* material until the present excavations. Subsequent activity at Pontnewydd (prior to the present work) appears to have been largely confined to recovering quantities of animal remains and implements from the accumulations of spoil left outside the cave.

Material from the spoil heap, identified by Professor G. Busk, is listed by Hughes and Thomas (1874) as:

Hyaena spelaea	= *Crocuta crocuta*
Ursus spelaeus	
Ursus ferox	= *Ursus arctos* (a large form)
Equus caballus	= *Equus ferus*
Rhinoceros hemitoechus	= *Dicerorhinus hemitoechus*
Cervus elaphus	
Cervus capreolus	= *Capreolus capreolus*
Canis lupus	
Canis vulpes	= *Vulpes vulpes*
Meles taxus	= *Meles meles*
Homo sapiens	

(The modern nomenclature is included on the right to facilitate comparison with the new faunal lists).

With the exception of the lost 'human molar', all of Busk's determinations can be verified from surviving specimens in the National Museum of Wales collections. It should be noted that Hughes, who maintained a long-term interest in Pontnewydd, quoted the same list without alteration in 1887.

Considerable and lasting confusion has arisen from accounts of the Pontnewydd fauna published by Dawkins (1871, 1874, 1880), whose accuracy must here be open to question, for there are internal inconsistencies in his references to Pontnewydd as indeed to several other sites with which he is known to have been involved. His first observations on the site appear as an aside in an account of the finding of remains of the glutton (*Gulo gulo*) at Plas Heaton (Dawkins, 1871), in which the cave is referred to as "Cefn no.2" and the fauna is listed as:

Ursus spelaeus	
Ursus ferox	= *Ursus arctos* (a large form)
Canis vulpes	= *Vulpes vulpes*
Canis lupus	
Hyaena spelaea	= *Crocuta crocuta*
Cervus tarandus	= *Rangifer tarandus*
Cervus elaphus	
Bison priscus	
Hippopotamus major	= *Hippopotamus amphibius*
Equus caballus	= *Equus ferus*
Rhinoceros hemitoechus	= *Dicerorhinus hemitoechus*
Elephas antiquus	= *Palaeoloxodon antiquus*

In 'Cave Hunting' (1874, 286–7) Dawkins made further reference to Pontnewydd. He first gave a partial list of the Cefn Cave mammals (for full list see Falconer, 1868, Vol.II.p.542) in which he included "Cave bear, Spotted hyaena, Reindeer, Hippopotamus, *Elephas antiquus* and *Rhinoceros hemitoechus*" and then went on to say:

"The same group of animals has been obtained by Mrs. Williams Wynn, the Rev. D. R. Thomas, and myself out of a horizontal cave at the head of the defile leading down from Cefn to Pont Newydd, in which the remains are embedded in a stiff clay, consisting of rearranged boulder clay, and are in the condition of waterworn pebbles. From it I have identified brown, grizzly and cave bear. A further examination by the Rev. D. R. Thomas and Professor Hughes has recently resulted in the discovery of rude implements of felstone and a tooth which has been identified by Professor Busk as a human molar of unusual size."

Later in the same work, Dawkins included Plas-newydd *(sic)* in a table of British sites (pp.360–1) listing the following species:

Homo palaeolithicus	= *Homo sapiens*
Ursus ferox	= *Ursus arctos* (a large form)
Ursus spelaeus	
Canis lupus	
Canis vulpes	= *Vulpes vulpes*
Equus caballus	= *Equus ferus*
Bos bison	= ? error; *Bos/Bison* sp.
Cervus elaphus	
Cervus megaceros	= *Megaceros giganteus*
Cervus tarandus	= *Rangifer tarandus*
Hippopotamus amphibius var. *major*	

In this instance *"Hyaena spelaea"*, *"Rhinocerous hemitoechus"* and *"Elephas antiquus"* are omitted, as is the typical form of brown bear *(Ursus arctos)* even though Dawkins mentioned it specifically in the text quoted above. *Cervus megaceros* is, on the other hand, completely new.

Three of the species mentioned by Dawkins at various times cannot be confirmed from remaining nineteenth century material, *"Elephas antiquus"* (= *Palaeoloxodon antiquus*), *"Cervus megaceros"* (= *Megaceros giganteus*) and *"Hippopotamus amphibius"*, nor are they mentioned by any other contemporary author. It is unlikely that Dawkins was personally involved in the original excavations to any great extent for, if so, Hughes and Thomas (1874) would have acknowledged his contribution in some way. If his experience of the finds was limited to examination of the material in the Williams Wynn Collection then confusion between material from Pontnewydd and Cefn is a definite possibility. It is worth noting that the occurrence of *Hippopotamus* is particularly unlikely, for this animal is only known from a few cave faunas in Britain, and then only as a rare element of otherwise rich Ipswichian assemblages dominated by hyaena (*Crocuta crocuta*). Nothing approaching an Ipswichian faunal assemblage (see Sutcliffe, 1960) has been found at Pontnewydd; and although it could be argued that there may once have been a deposit of Ipswichian age close to the cave entrance, of such limited extent that it has been completely removed by excavation, the nature of the Pontnewydd deposits is such that one would expect some material derived from it to be present in the area of the current excavations. Without independent means of corroboration, the extra species recorded by Dawkins are best ignored at present. Oakley (1971, 36) suggested an Ipswichian age for the Pontnewydd vertebrate fauna as a whole, but this opinion rested partly on the erroneous assumption that *Dicerorhinus hemitoechus* was restricted to this period, whereas the species ranges in Europe from the Middle well into the Late Pleistocene.

Recording and reference to specimens

From 1978 onwards, finds from each site within the cave have been individually recorded on a standard horizontal grid system with X and Y coordinates and their depth measured as an absolute height above Ordnance Datum. Each find has been numbered, the numbers for each site starting with 1 and continuing sequentially irrespective of year (see pp.21–22). The only major exceptions to this system are microfauna samples taken for myself, and the material recovered from sediment samples by S.N. Collcutt. Individual specimens are referred to here by year, site and number (e.g. PN80 D553, a rhinoceros tooth fragment found in 1980 in Area D).

Fossiliferous lithostratigraphic units

Organic remains are limited to the upper part of the Pontnewydd sequence, the Calcareous member of the Pontnewydd Cave formation as defined by Collcutt (p.49). The following table of unit names, in stratigraphic order, covers all of the deposits containing Pleistocene fauna referred to in this report:

Red Cave Earth bed (Area B only)
Upper Breccia bed
Silt beds (Area D only)
Stalagmite lithozone
Lower Breccia bed
Intermediate complex

In the following text the informal terms bed and lithozone are omitted.

The Intermediate complex, Lower Breccia, Silt and Upper Breccia have been systematically excavated, but the Red Cave Earth, which was represented by a small wedge of sediment in Area B, has produced only a small sample of material. All of the above listed units (other than the stalagmite) have yielded animal remains – the Intermediate complex, Lower and Upper Breccia in some abundance.

With the exception of a small number of specimens from the Silt of Area D, all of the vertebrate material from Pontnewydd appears to have been redeposited at least once since its original introduction into the cave. In the first instance, it is more instructive to regard the animal remains not as teeth and bone but as sediment particles; it is certainly very clear that any attempt to interpret their present position, condition and relationships is heavily reliant on a clear understanding of the lithogenesis of the Pontnewydd sequence. If one were to accept the lithostratigraphic subdivisions at face value, listing the species present in each, the result would be a muddle of conflicting information that becomes more confounded upwards in the succession. The principal mode of emplacement inferred for the Intermediate complex, Lower Breccia and Upper Breccia is that of debris flow (Collcutt, *supra*) in which each successive phase of activity would involve large scale reworking of pre-existing deposits within the zone of the cave currently under examination. Under such conditions a considerable and increasingly derived faunal component could be expected to be incorporated into ever younger debris flows, limited only by the capacity of the skeletal elements concerned to survive the mechanical pressures involved in this kind of mass movement. Examination of the collections recently obtained show that this is in fact the case.

Type I.	10YR 7/6 yellow to 7.5YR reddish brown, with dark brown to black staining and speckling. Dense bone, often with a crazed and friable appearance but actually quite solid. Most observed breaks are obviously secondary.
Type II.	10YR 7/4 very pale brown to 10YR 7/6 yellow, with sparse black speckling. Light, very friable bone that is easily broken and crushed, with very fine surface detail. Original breakage patterns difficult to assess; most appears to be secondary.
Type III.	7.5YR 6/2 pinkish grey to 7.5YR 4/2 brown to dark brown, with no obvious staining. Dense bone, with slight edge rounding and some degree of polish to exposed edges. Much of this material was broken when the bone was still green (i.e. more or less fresh); gnawing marks common.

TABLE VII.1   Pontnewydd Cave. Preservation types. Preliminary definitions.

At present, the single factor which allows subdivision of the total assemblage into more or less coherent groups is preservation type. Assignment to a particular group is based upon such factors as colour, secondary staining, surface texture and the character of broken surfaces (Table VII.1) By taking account of the nature of bone preservation in combination with the lithostratigraphy, it is possible to distinguish at least three phases of faunal input, forming assemblages that are ecologically plausible and yield useful biostratigraphic information which integrates well with the results of the various age-dating methods that have been applied to the Pontnewydd sequence (Debenham *et al.*; Schwarcz, Ch.IV). It is hoped that the preliminary results of analyses of trace element uptake reported by Molleson, (p.108) may lead to the establishment of a chemical signature for each preservation type, reducing the subjectivity in distinguishing between them – particularly in the case of the mixed material in the Lower Breccia. The derivation series as represented in Area D is illustrated diagramatically in Fig. VII.1.

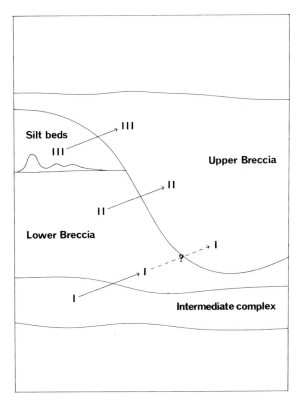

Fig. VII.1 Pontnewydd Cave. Schematic section of Area D (East Passage) showing principal lithostratigraphic units and the derivation series of faunal preservation types I, II and III (See Table VII.1).

THE FAUNA

Intermediate complex/Preservation type I

The following animals have been recovered from the Intermediate complex or are identified from characteristic preservation type I material in the Lower Breccia.

Homo sapiens	man
Canis lupus	wolf
Ursus sp.	a bear with spelaeoid characters
Panthera aff. *pardus*	a leopard-like felid
Equus sp.	a horse
Dicerorhinus hemitoechus	narrow-nosed rhinoceros
Capreolus capreolus	roe deer

Castor fiber	beaver
Arvicola cantiana	a water vole
Microtus gregalis	narrow-skulled vole
Apodemus cf. *sylvaticus*	wood mouse

Of the three principal faunal groupings, this is the most likely to be increased by further excavation. At the present stage of collection, no one species from preservation type I can be said to be common, but more specimens referable to *Ursus* sp. have been found than any other form. The presence of deciduous canines strongly suggests that the cave was being used as a bear den. In common with those from the Lower Breccia (preservation type II), the isolated bear teeth found in the Intermediate complex show many characters traditionally taken as spelaeoid, but the value of these features alone in establishing specific identity would appear to be small (Erdbrink, 1953; Kurten, 1955). Remains of *Canis lupus* make up most of the rest of the group, all other species being represented by only one or two specimens. Little can be said about how the environment in which this apparent assemblage may have lived other than to observe that there would have been some trees close to running water for the beaver, and sufficient vegetation cover to accommodate roe deer. An open woodland habitat would not exclude any of the forms represented. *Microtus gregalis,* although a common element of high latitude tundra faunas, is a wide ranging species also characteristic of wooded steppe environments.

Lower Breccia/Preservation type II

The Lower Breccia has been extensively collected in areas B, C and D and its fauna is accordingly well known. There is relatively little difficulty in distinguishing between preservation types I and II when dealing with the megafauna from this unit, but the same is not true for the microfauna. All of the Microtinae recovered from the Lower Breccia are included in the following list, but it should be noted that some or all of them may have been derived from the underlying Intermediate complex. For the present,the absence of such forms as *Lemmus* and *Microtus oeconomus* from the older unit is taken as indicating a true difference between the assemblages.

Canis lupus	wolf
Ursus sp.	a bear, with spelaeoid characters
cf. *Crocuta crocuta*	spotted hyena
Panthera aff. *pardus*	a leopard-like felid
Equus sp.	a horse
Dicerorhinus hemitoechus	narrow-nosed rhinoceros
D. cf. *kirchbergensis*	Merck's rhinoceros
Cervus elaphus	red deer
Bovini *(Bos* or *Bison* sp.)	a bovine
Lemmus lemmus	Norway lemming
Arvicola sp.	a water vole
Microtus gregalis	narrow-skulled vole
M. oeconomus	northern vole
Ochotona sp.	a pika

The larger mammal fauna is very similar to that from the Intermediate complex but for the absence of obligate woodland/scrubland forms *(Capreolus* and *Castor).* In terms of abundance, the assemblage is dominated by three species, *Ursus* sp., *Equus* sp. and *Dicerorhinus hemitoechus,* though it is accepted that this may only reflect the relative durability and the comparatively easy recognition of quite small tooth fragments of each of these forms. Both the red deer and bovine are very rare. If the small mammals really do belong to the preservation type II group then there is a marked increase in what many would regard as "cold climate" indicators, but such a change could be caused by a shift to a more continental climatic regime rather than being due to an overall climatic deterioration. The more truly characteristic cold elements such as *Rangifer* and *Dicrostonyx* are absent. An open steppe environment would accommodate all of the recorded species, with a small "rocky upland" component in the form of *Ochotona*.

Dicerorhinus cf. *kirchbergensis* appears in the faunal list for the Lower Breccia on the basis of a single fragment, a large piece of the lingual border of an upper M1 or M2, PN80 C286, which has the shelving profile normally characteristic of this species.

Silt beds and Upper Breccia/Preservation type III

This preservation type is known principally from its derived component in the Upper Breccia of area D. A few specimens are known from the extreme outer margin of the South Fissure excavation (area B); these were collected in 1978 before the establishment of the present lithostratigraphic units, but they appear to be attributable to the Upper Breccia. *Rangifer* is certainly represented by two specimens (PN78 B1; B2) of which B1 is unstratified; most other fragments are indeterminate. In spite of extensive excavation, no further type III material has been found in this part of the cave.

Once again, there are problems with the original provenance of the microfauna. To date, only *Dicrostonyx torquatus* has been found *in situ* in undisturbed Silt beds. *Lemmus lemmus, Microtus gregalis, Arvicola terrestris* and *Ochotona pusilla* have been recorded from the Upper Breccia, but these could have been reworked from older deposits during emplacement of the Upper Breccia. The list of species from the type III assemblage excludes these dubious records.

Bulk processing of the Silt beds took place during the 1982 season and this material is now in course of study.

Canis lupus	wolf
Vulpes vulpes	red fox
Ursus cf. *arctos*	brown bear
Equus ferus	horse
Rangifer tarandus	reindeer
Ovibos moschatus	musk ox
Dictostonyx torquatus	collared lemming
Lepus cf. *timidus*	arctic hare

There is a marked difference between this group and the type I and II assemblages. This is a classic cold fauna which, with the exception of horse, can still be found in the arctic tundra today. As will be seen, the type III assemblage has important biostratigraphic implications and is the most readily placed of the three faunal groupings. Prevailing conditions would probably have been harsh, with open treeless vegetation and extensive seasonal snow cover.

TAPHONOMY

Preservation types I and II

The extreme fragmentation of this material has already been commented on. There is some evidence to suggest that many of the specimens concerned were very much more complete at the time of their initial burial, particularly in the case of the preservation type I remains, and that subsequent comminution has taken place, under pressure, when the bone was in a weakened condition as a result of loss of much or all of its organic component. The process is best seen in areas of the cave where mass movement of the sediments has been in some way restricted, so that specimens show various stages of the disintegration process without being spread over too wide an area. This is well illustrated by the almost entire maxillary dentition of a bear (PN80 B296) from the Upper Breccia of the South Fissure, which in this area contains a considerable number of derived type II specimens. The maxilla and teeth have been heavily crushed, distorted and recemented – the teeth are still quite recognisable, but the bone has been reduced to fine spicules. Against this sort of destructive process only the most robust materials such as tooth enamel and the dense bone of carnivore foot elements has survived in any quantity. The degree of destruction caused by these phases of debris flow makes it impossible to comment on processes that may have affected this material prior to its final stage of deposition, but the faunal composition of both assemblages strongly suggests that these were, in their original state, primary cave accumulations and not derived from outside.

Preservation type III

The small collection of material from the Silt beds and Upper Breccia of Area D forms a tight group at once separable from the rest of the Pontnewydd animal remains. By comparison with other sites this assemblage is most readily interpreted as the food debris of denning wolves, for several bone fragments show the kind of terminal gnawing patterns shown to be the work of foxes and young wolves in recent taphonomic studies (Haynes, 1982). Cub-raising female wolves often use natural shelters such as caves, and such an interpretation is supported by the find of a shed lower left DP4 of *Canis lupus* in sieving samples taken from the Upper Breccia (PN 79 Area D, 99.60 to 99.72). Most fragments show slight surface abrasion, even those few from the Silt beds. The reworked component in the Upper Breccia seems to have survived the derivation process very well indeed and was probably in quite fresh condition at the time that the Silt beds were partly incorporated into the Upper Breccia debris flow. The pond-like feature in which the Silt beds and the preservation type III material accumulated must have been quite localised, if judged by the restricted spread of this particular assemblage.

An unusual feature of the type III fauna is the occurrence of *Ovibos moschatus*, believed to be the first record of this animal from a British cave. It almost certainly found its way in as part of the diet of a carnivore, and again, wolves are likely agents.

FAUNAL DATING

Before considering the biostratigraphic implications of the Pontnewydd assemblages a few words of qualification are necessary. Existing means of Quaternary subdivision are currently under critical review from many quarters, arising largely from the realisation that the cycles of climatic change which characterise the period are more complex and certainly more numerous than previously suspected. For the present, the marine oxygen isotope record is being widely used as a yardstick against which to measure the timing and duration of Quaternary events, but the problems of correlation between the marine and terrestrial environments are considerable, being heavily reliant on absolute dating techniques. Certain parts of the terrestrial vertebrate record have been successfully tied in with the oxygen isotope record, for instance the Ipswichian *(sensu stricto)* "hippopotamus fauna" which has been dated by the ^{230}Th/^{234}U method to around 120 ± 6 ka at Victoria Cave, N. Yorkshire (Gascoyne, Currant and Lord, 1981), placing it in Substage 5e of the oxygen isotope system (Shackleton and Opdyke, 1973). Sadly, the fortuitous occurrence of a highly characteristic mammal fauna embedded in a datable stalagmite is not a piece of luck often encountered in the British sequence.

The standard British Quaternary framework of Mitchell, Penny, Shotton and West (1973) allows for four Middle and Late Pleistocene interglacial periods, including the Flandrian. Vertebrate assemblages have been attributed to each of these stages (Stuart, 1975, 1976; Sutcliffe, 1960, 1964; Sutcliffe and Kowalski, 1976) with varying degrees of confidence, and in essence the mammal faunas of the Cromerian, Hoxnian, Ipswichian and Flandrian interglacials are reasonably well defined – though there are various faunas from particular sites that are contentious with respect to their dating, principally those assigned to the later part of the Ipswichian by Stuart (1976). There is growing evidence for at least one extra warm phase between the Hoxnian and Ipswichian interglacials (Briggs *et al.*, in preparation) to which at least some of these supposed late Ipswichian faunas may really belong.

In the preservation type I assemblage of the Intermediate complex (plus its derived component in the Lower Breccia), the presence of *Arvicola cantiana,* a water vole with a dental morphology intermediate between that of the Cromerian *Mimomys savini* and the Late Pleistocene to Recent *Arvicola terrestris* (Koenigswald, 1973), is taken to be indicative of a post-Cromerian date, following Bishop (1982) in his argument on the likelihood of the Ostend *Arvicola cantiana* assemblage post-dating the Cromerian *sensu stricto (contra* Stuart and West, 1976). *A. cantiana* morphotypes survive into the Ipswichian, but such a late date can be ruled out on the basis of differences in the species composition of the associated megafauna. Comparison of the type I fauna with that from the Hoxnian type site is suggested (Gladfelter, 1975) other than for the presence of *Microtus gregalis,* but this could be due to local geographical and environmental factors. No well-described cave faunas have been assigned to the Hoxnian, and it is difficult to estimate the effect of the inevitable bias caused by differences in the mode of accumulation between open and cave sites. While there is no aspect of the fauna which militates against the type I assemblage being Hoxnian in age, there is sufficient uncertainty in the British biostratigraphic framework to allow for its assignment to a later, pre-Ipswichian, phase. An earlier date is most unlikely; the remains of *Canis lupus,* though fragmentary, do not fall within the size range of pre-Hoxnian/ Holsteinian "inter-Mindel" *Canis lupus mosbachensis,* a small form of the wolf found in the mid to early Middle Pleistocene.

The type II assemblage appears to be close in age to the type I fauna, with comparatively minor changes in species composition. As the excavation proceeds further into the cave, it seems likely that better preserved material will be recovered from the Lower Breccia, and this will allow a more detailed evaluation of its biostratigraphic value.

Material from the preservation type III assemblage is readily assigned to the Late Devensian. This faunal grouping, entirely lacking extinct forms, is known from numerous well dated British Cave sites (Stuart, 1974, 1977; Collcutt, Currant and Hawkes, 1981) at around 10 ka B.P.

POST-PLEISTOCENE FAUNA

In 1982, a prepared section of the UCS in the East Passage was examined and sampled for microfauna. The upper 25 cm of this bed, a gritty gravel with clay matrix, contains an abundance of anuran bones and mollusca which were clearly visible *in situ*. The material recovered includes the following animals (the mollusca have yet to be studied):

Sorex sp.	a shrew
Apodemus sylvaticus	wood mouse
Clethrionomys glareolus	bank vole
Meles meles	badger
Anguis fragilis	slow worm
Anura	frog/toad

This assemblage is indicative of a well established temperate woodland environment and is almost certainly Holocene. Similar faunas, dominated by anuran remains, are found in the upper levels of many British caves, often associated with Holocene speleothems.

CHAPTER VIII

MINERALOGY AND PETROLOGY

PART A
SAND AND CLAY MINERALOGY
by
David A. Jenkins

Pontnewydd Cave is sited close to the junction of Lower Palaeozoic mudstones and sandstones to the south-west and Carboniferous-Triassic limestones and sandstones to the north and east. It is also in an area where there has been a succession of complex glacial events including invasion by Irish Sea Ice from the north (Embleton, 1970 and above p.000) leading to the possibility of a variety of superficial deposits of diverse origins. Such diversity might be reflected in the mineralogical composition of the derived cave sediments. Preliminary mineralogical analyses have therefore been made of the "heavy" (S.G. > 2.95) fine sand (200–63μm) fractions and of the clay fractions (2<μm), separate by wet-sieving and sedimentation respectively, from the five cave sediment samples listed in Table VIII.1a. The mineralogy of the former fraction is a product of the various geological sources that have contributed to the sediment, as modified by the selective depletions of less stable species by weathering. The mineralogy of the latter fraction again reflects sediment provenance but tends to be less diagnostic: it is, however, more sensitive to modification, depletion, and even addition, by weathering as determined by environment.

HEAVY MINERAL ANALYSES

Heavy minerals were separated from the fine sand fraction by centrifugation in tetra-bromoethane, preceded by removal, where necessary (e.g. sample 3), of ferric oxides with dithionite/citrate. In this preliminary study the samples were examined under methyl salicylate and the relative abundance of the mineral species recognised assessed visually. The results are presented in Table VIII.1b together with an analysis of a sample of present alluvium from the River Elwy at Bont Newydd.

Various assemblages can be recognised and related to particular sources. Present in all 5 samples is an abundant pale grey-green chlorite, together with minor zircon and tourmaline, characteristic of the local Lower Palaeozoic mudstones: subordinate mafic material is represented by clinopyroxenes, clinozoisite, amphiboles and apatite. Sample 2 is comprised almost exclusively of minerals from these two sources. In sample 1 and, to a greater extent, sample 4, there are higher levels of detrital zircon and tourmaline, together with traces of rutile, garnet, anatase and brookite, all of which are resistate minerals, probably from a sandstone source. In sample 5 there are additional traces of staurolite, andalusite, hypersthene, pink/blue tourmaline and glauconite, etc., which indicate a more heterogeneous geological source. The remaining sample 3 also carries rare staurolite but is particularly

Sample No.	Sample Description	Stratigraphic Context
6	Present Day Alluvium from River Elwy, Bont Newydd	–
5	Laminated reddish clay	Upper Clays and Sands. East Passage.
4	Laminated clay	Silt beds. East Passage
3	Orange brown loamy deposit	Orange Intermediate. East Passage
2	Sand lens	Upper Sands and Gravels. Deep Sounding.
1	Sand lens	Lower Sands and Gravels. Deep Sounding.

TABLE VIII.1a   Details of the Samples

	1	2	3	4	5	6
% heavy mins.	0.74	0.65	0.13	0.78	0.82	1.5
clinozoisite	4	4	5	3	1	3
clinopyroxenes	4	4	4	3	3	3
amphiboles	3	3	3	3	3	2
chlorite-dark	–	–	2	–	–	–
chlorite-pale	6	7	4	6	6	7
apatite	2	1	3	1	2	2
tourmaline	4	2	4	3	4	3
zircon	3	1	3	1	5	4
rutile	2	–	2	2	3	2
anatase	1	–	1	–	1	–
brookite	1	–	–	–	–	–
epidote	–	–	2	–	1	2
garnet	2	–	2	–	3	3
staurolite	–	–	1	–	2	1
andalusite	–	–	–	–	1	–
orthopyroxenes	–	–	–	–	1	1
glauconite	–	–	–	–	1	–

(Abundances assessed visually on the scale 7 – dominant; 5 – common; 3 – occasional; 1 – rare; – not detected)

TABLE VIII.1b: Non-opaque heavy mineralogies (SG>2.95) of the fine sand fractions (63–200μm)

samples	1	2	3	4	5	6
felspars	1	1	2	1	1	1
quartz	3	3	4	3	3	3
hydrous mica	4	4	3	4	4	3
chlorite	3	2	–	4	3	3
vermiculite	2	2	–	–	2	2
kaolinite	2	1	2	1	1	(n.d.)
1.2nm I/S	1	2	–	–	1	1

(Relative peak heights: 4 – dominant; 3 – major; 2 – minor; 1 – trace; – not detected; n.d. – not determined)

TABLE VIII.1c: Mineralogies of the clay (<2μm e.s.d.) fractions

distinguished by the markedly lower level of pale chlorite and higher levels of clinozoisite, epidote and apatite. This suggests intense chemical weathering to which the relatively unstable chlorite would be most susceptible, an interpretation supported both by the very ragged nature of the chlorite flakes and also by the significantly lower heavy mineral %. Such chemical weathering is also evident in the deeply etched nature of the clinopyroxene grains in this sample and also, to a lesser extent, in samples 2 and 4.

CLAY MINERAL ANALYSES

Clay fractions were analysed by XRDA (Ni-filtered CuK_α: 40kV/20mA using Philips equipment) following the usual pretreatments (i.e. K^+/20°C; K^+/550°C; Mg^{2+}; Mg^{2+}/Eth. glycol). Relative abundances, as assessed from peak heights, are given in Table VIII.1c.

The results indicate that samples 1, 2, 4, and 5 have generally similar mineralogies, dominated by quartz and hydrous mica, with major chlorite and – except in sample 4 – subordinate vermiculite. There are traces of K-felspar and of kaolinite (1.12 nm on DMSO treatment: Lim *et al.* 1981) together with some irregularly interstratified material (1.20 nm – K^+/550°C only) as yet not fully characterised: no expanding minerals were detected on treatment with ethylene glycol. Traces of haematite are possibly present in the pinkish clay sample (No. 5). Sample 3 differed markedly in producing a weak trace and requiring dithionite/citrate pretreatment (Mehra and Jackson, 1960) to obtain decipherable peaks: surprisingly, however, no iron oxide minerals were detectable in the untreated sample. The treated sample showed a clear dominance by quartz, accompanied in this instance by significant Na as well as K felspars, with major amounts of hydrous mica and traces of kaolinite: however no chlorite or vermiculite (or expanding minerals) were detectable. Traces of an irregular interstratified mineral (A1-interlayers?) are suggested by a low angle tail to the 1.00 nm peak.

The clay mineral assemblages of samples 1, 2, 4 and 5 all suggest a provenance dominated by Lower Palaeozoic mudstones (i.e. hydrous mica and chlorite, with derived vermiculite (Rezk, 1976)), but the traces of kaolinite imply a small contribution from Carboniferous or Triassic material throughout. Minor differences in proportions and crystallinities appear to exist between these four samples, for example the absence of vermiculite and 1.20 nm interstratified minerals from sample 4. However, their significance could be established only by more detailed analyses, preferably involving size fractionation which would allow characterisation of the kaolinite (2.0 – 0.6μm) and interstratified material (<0.2μm). Sample 3, however, is again clearly different due to its enhanced quartz and felspar contents and absence of chlorite and vermiculite in particular. This could imply derivation from a

184

different geological source omitting Lower Palaeozoic mudstones, but it is more likely that it represents material from the same source as the other samples, albeit one which has been modified by the selective destruction of the relatively unstable chlorite and vermiculite by the intense and/or prolonged chemical weathering typical of warm climate conditions.

CONCLUSIONS

The combined results of these preliminary sand and clay fraction analyses thus present a reasonably consistent picture in terms of the provenance of the sediments and their weathering history. The sand and clay mineralogies of all the samples show similarities, and are relatively simple. Not surprisingly, they are typically North Welsh in composition in that they are dominated by material from the Lower Palaeozoic mudstones which occupy most of the present catchment of the Elwy on the Denbigh moors to the west. Heavy mineralogy also indicates minor additions to all five samples of material from mafic sources (e.g. dolerites); these could lie to the west in Snowdonia or, more likely, to the south-west or south in the Arenig or Berwyn mountains respectively whence it is suggested glaciers fed into the Vale of Clwyd (Smith and George, 1961; Embleton, 1970). A further minor contribution of both certain resistate heavy minerals and also the traces of kaolinite in samples 1, 4, and 5 could derive from either Triassic or Upper Carboniferous rocks which outcrop to the north and east. The rare grains of other heavy minerals which add to the diversity of composition in sample 3 and, in particular, sample 5 indicate a more heterogeneous source of sediments. The particular species involved (i.e. staurolite, andalusite, hypersthene, glauconite) are usually associated in North Wales with the "Red Northern Drift" of late Devensian age (Smithson, 1953). However, the influence of such material is apparently of minor significance within the mineralogy of the fine sand fraction, despite the distinctive pinkish tinge to the clay sample No.5 (Munsell colour 7.5YR6/4 – "light brown") usually associated with Triassic influence in the Irish Sea tills; unfortunately additions from such a source are not readily distinguishable in the mineralogy of the clay fraction. It is not surprising to find the most diverse mineralogical assemblage in the latest sample (i.e. No. 5), for presumably successive phases of glacial, fluvial and also aeolian transportation produced increasingly mixed deposits. There are suggestions of small differences between these otherwise similar sample assemblages but it would require more detailed and quantitative data to establish their significance.

The possible presence of a Northern Drift component in samples 3 and 5 deserves some further comment. It can be stated with reasonable certainty that such minerals as andalusite, staurolite and glauconite originated in glacial deposits of northern origin; likewise, therefore, would a small proportion of the other less distinguishable minerals. However, it is not yet possible to say how such material arrived at Pontnewydd. It could have been directly by glacial intrusion into the area from which these materials were subsequently washed into the cave and deposited. Alternatively, such material could have been dispersed by wind as periglacial loess over large areas peripheral to Northern glacial deposits and so might ultimately arrive in the cave indirectly. This is a possibility whose significance is of importance in relation to soil parentage in North Wales and studies (Younis, 1983) in Anglesey suggest that there has indeed been detectable aeolian dispersion over distances of the order of ten kilometres. Nevertheless, by whatever means this material was incorporated into samples 3 and 5, its presence still distinguishes them from samples 1, 2 and 4.

The analyses also provide an indication of the severity of the weathering to which the deposits had been subjected. Such weathering could have occurred either externally, prior to deposition, or within the cave after deposition, although the latter seems unlikely to have been significant in view of environmental pH, leaching intensity and variations in detectable weathering within the cave sediments examined. In early stages of weathering, derivative clay minerals such as vermiculite and interstratified material could be produced, as in samples 1, 2 and 5. Under more severe and/or protracted conditions of weathering, there might be a selective depletion and/or etching of such relatively unstable minerals as chlorites and pyroxenes: this is clearly evident in sample 3, both in its sand mineralogy and in the absence of vermiculite, chlorite and the 1.20 nm interstratified material from its clay fractions. It can therefore be concluded that the severity of weathering was least in sample 4, moderate in samples 1, 2 and 5 and most pronounced in sample 3. This would be consistent with the interpretation of the brownish yellow (10YR6/6) sample 3 as relating to a "cave-earth" which accumulated during a protracted period of chemical weathering. Further relevant evidence could be obtained from analyses of the amorphous components and the various forms of iron oxides present, and by textural and fabric analysis.

In terms of provenance, it can therefore be concluded that all the sediments are dominated by the local Lower Palaeozoic mudstones, with minor amounts of dolerite of uncertain origin. There are, however, small differences detectable indicating the influence of sandstones (in 1, 3 and 5 – Carboniferous?) and of "Northern Drift" (3 and 5). In terms of weathering sample 3 stands out as having been subjected to a far more intense and/or prolonged episode than the other samples.

186

PART B
THE FLINTS
by
Chris Clayton

INTRODUCTION

Flints and cherts are an important component of the rock types recovered from Pontnewydd, comprising about 10% of the artefacts found to date. As the source rocks for most of these materials do not outcrop in the vicinity of the cave, it is important to assess whether the materials recovered from the cave were originally collected from the local drift, or imported from elsewhere. A total of 42 finds of 'flinty' appearance have been studied microscopically at the time of writing (May, 1982), of which two were non-Cretaceous cherts, probably of Carboniferous age, and the remainder were flints derived from Upper Cretaceous chalks. This study will concentrate on the flints but the others are included in Tables VIII.2 and 3 for documentation purposes.

GEOLOGICAL BACKGROUND

Much confusion exists as to the terminology of the siliceous sedimentary rocks but, for the benefit of this work, the following definitions are adopted:

CHERT   is a siliceous rock consisting predominantly of microcrystalline or cryptocrystalline non-clastic silica occurring as beds, nodular masses or veins in sedimentary rocks (Smith, 1960). This definition includes flint, agate, silexite, hornstone, jasper etc. but does not refer to colloidal or opaline rocks or vein quartz.

FLINT   is a variety of chert originating in the Upper Cretaceous Chalk. It is characteristically homogeneous black and breaks with a conchoidal fracture, but may also be partly or wholly white to grey with a flat fracture or weather white, grey, red, orange, yellow or brown. An outer chalky 'crust' of incompletely silicified chalk is present on fresh specimens but is rapidly lost on reworking. It is also common to find a weathered zone inside the crust termed a 'cortex' and this forms by the same process as the 'patina' on flint artefacts.

The usual method of petrographic investigation of rocks is of 30 μ thick (1 mm = 1000 μ) thin-sections. In cherts however, the very fine grained nature of the rock (<5 μ) makes this method of only limited use. The most useful alternative approach has proved to be reflected light microscopy of acid etched specimens (Clayton, 1982). Etching periods of 1–2 minutes in 40% HF (Hydrofluoric acid) are sufficient to pick out most structures which are then easily visible in the binocular microscope or scanning electron-microscope (SEM).

In etched cherts, six main silica phases (= morphologies or generations) are commonly found in varying proportions:

1. *Silicified Skeletal (Fossil) Fragments*
   These represent the first stage of chert growth and occur on all scales of size and packing density. Sometimes, characteristic forms, particularly foraminifera or sponge spicules, may be of some use in source-typing.

2. *Lepispheres*
   Lepispheres are inorganically precipitated spherical aggregates of quartz crystals, generally between 5 and 20 μ across. They are one of the main silica phases precipitated at the site of chert formation and with the silicified skeletal fragments comprise the framework of one of the two major groups of cherts, the 'lepispheric cherts' (Clayton, in prep.). Lepispheres show a wide range of packing density ranging from an 'open lepispheric' structure where the lepispheres are only just in contact (pl.XXXVA) to a

completely 'coalesced-lepispheric' form (e.g. Pl.XXXVB) in which the true nature is only visible when the lepispheres protrude into rare voids in the material.

3. *Type 1 Chalcedony*
This in an extremely fine grained fibrous silica which acts as an interstitial 'cement' to the framework of lepispheres and silicified skeletal fragments. In reflected light it is a pale blue colour due to light scattering effects associated with a high structural disorder and associated bound-water.

4. *Type 2 Chalcedony*
Type 2 chalcedonly is a recrystallised variety of type 1 and is responsible for the white colour of some cherts. It is highly susceptible to etching and frequently dissolves altogether during acid treatment.

5. *Quartz Druse*
This is a much coarser grained late-stage void filling phase. It shows all variations from a fine blocky fibrous quartz (type 3 chalcedony or 'chalcedonic quartz') to large well formed quartz crystals.

6. *Type 4 Chalcedony*
Structurally, this is intermediate between type 1 and type 3 chalcedony, but in occurrence it is very distinct. Type 4 chalcedony occurs as 1–5 mm radiating bundles and sheaths of silica fibres and, where it is present, it usually comprises the bulk of the chert with varying amounts of skeletal fragments and druse/chalcedonic quartz (e.g. see Pl.XXXIVC and D).
  It is very rare to find type 4 chalcedony in association with lepispheres so that cherts of this kind can be referred to as 'chalcedonic cherts'.

Cherts can therefore be conveniently split into two main groups: the lepispheric cherts which comprise most nodular cherts such as the flints (e.g. Pl.XXXIVA) and carboniferous limestone cherts (Pl. XXXVD); and the chalcedonic cherts, which are characteristic of more extensive replacement such as the Greensand cherts of Southern England and the Tertiary 'Meulière' of Southern France. Further classification is then possible based on the relative abundance of the various phases so that one may refer to an 'open-lepispheric' chert (Pl.XXXVA), a 'coalesced-lepispheric' chert (Pl.XXXVB) or a 'skeletal chalcedonic' chert (Pl.XXXVE). In all cases, the name follows the geologic convention of listing the most common component last in the sequence.

THE FLINTS FROM PONTNEWYDD

The structural type of the Pontnewydd flints, based on acid etched specimens, is given in Table VIII.2 according to location and in Table VIII.3 according to type. The bulk of the specimens (40) fall into two groups: a main group of coalesced-lepispheric flints with a few open-lepispheric forms (total of 33 specimens), and a smaller group of 7 lepispheric and chalcedonic forms dominated by skeletal fragments. Many of the specimens were collected from the Boyd Dawkins and World War II excavation dumps and are therefore unstratified. Of the securely stratified flints, there are single examples only from the Upper Breccia and Intermediate and eight from the Lower Breccia; the higher number from the latter context reflects the greater density of all artefact-types in the Lower Breccia (Table V.2, p.114).

The coalesced-lepispheric type is characteristic of flint which has grown in a fairly porous soft white chalk, such as that of southern England, by replacement of the host carbonate. The skeletal rich variety, however, is a replacement of bioclastic (i.e. shell fragment) rich chalk such as typically formed in shallower water than the normal white chalks, often

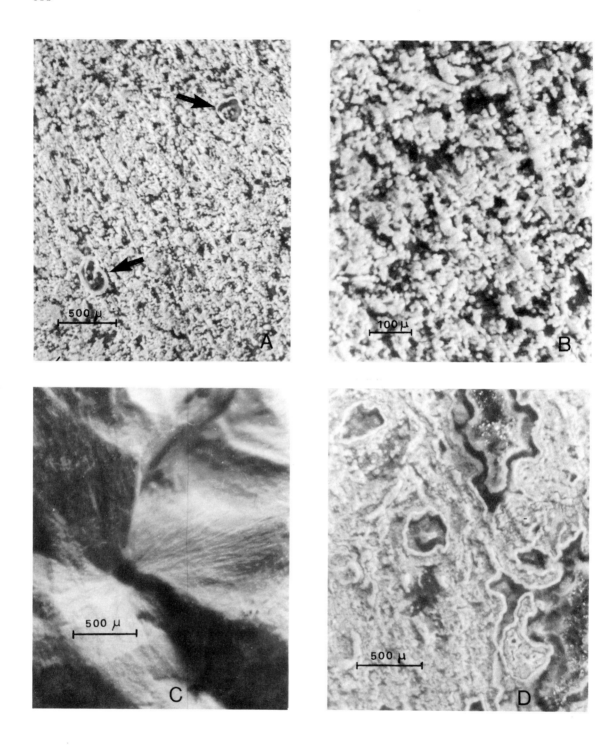

Plate XXXIV Basic Flint Types (a & b) Typical open structured lepispheric flint (Brandon, Norfolk) showing framework of lepispheres and skeletal fragments (e.g. foraminifera, arrowed) and interstitial dark chalcedony cement. (c) Pure chalcedonic–chert, composed entirely of type 4 chalcedony. Tertiary, Perigord, France. (d) More complex skeletal chalcedonic chert with isolated fragments encased in numerous generations of chalcedony (types 3 and 4).

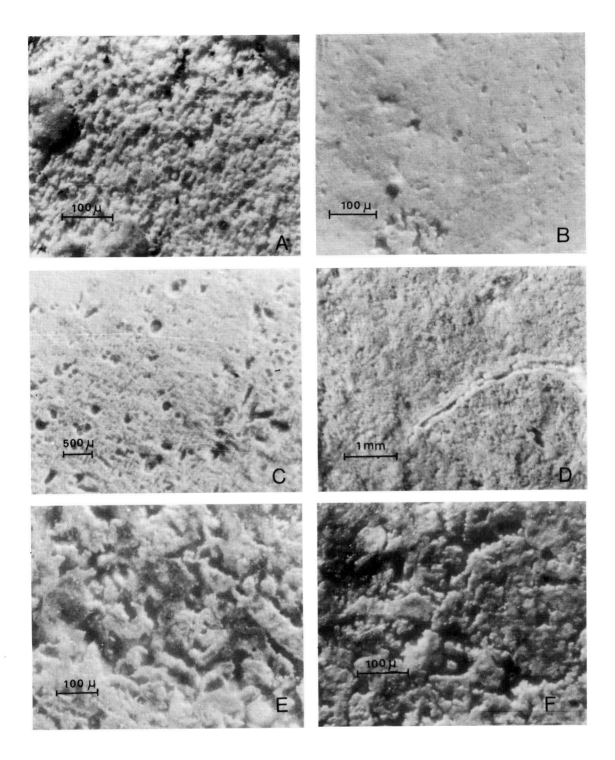

Plate XXXV   Flint types from Pontnewydd. (a)   Open lepispheric type. A86/5. (b)   Coalesced lepispheric type. Note clear lepispheres protruding into void in relic foraminifera but not visible in main body of flint. A68/20. (c)   Skeletal lepispheric type. Coalesced lepispheres around a number of abraded skeletal fragments (now etched out to form voids). A57. (d)   Carboniferous semi-coalesced lepispheric chert, with large silicified shell fragment. A66/60. (e)   Skeletal chert with numerous irregular silicified skeletal fragments in type 1 chalcedony matrix. B420. (f)   Skeletal lepispheric form. A99/6.

around the margins of the Cretaceous sea. It is therefore uncommon to find these flint types together in any number, and the Pontnewydd material probably represents derivation from at least two outcrops, widely separated either stratigraphically or geographically. However, this is only the ultimate source, and the two types may well have been collected together as reworked material from local drift deposits.

AVAILABLE SOURCES OF FLINT

Chalk flints and other cherts are a well known component of the drift deposits of North Wales (Embleton, 1970), but their detailed distribution, both stratigraphically and geographically, is little known in detail. In order to determine the extent of any transportation of such cherts to Pontnewydd by human agency, it is necessary first to characterise the cherts found naturally in the area and then to compare the archaeologically recovered material with these. In addition, it is necessary to know the chronology of emplacement of the drift deposits in order to determine whether or not they were available at the time of cave occupation.

The drift deposits of the region are the result of a complex interplay between the ice sheets from the North Wales mountains ('the Welsh Ice') bearing erratics dominated by Lower Palaeozoic igneous rocks, and the flint and red sandstone bearing Irish Sea Ice. Although the Irish Sea Ice is believed to have penetrated 20 km up the vale of Clwyd, the relative timing of this event is not yet clear; if indeed of early Devensian age (see Embleton, p.28) then it's drift would not have been available when the cave was occupied; but if it is pre-Ipswichian, it may well have provided a suitable source of flint. It must be stated, nevertheless, that my preliminary investigation has failed to locate any flint at all in the drift deposits of the Elwy valley; and although there is a possibility that such drift may have been removed subsequent to the cave occupation, the absence of flint here and in natural form in the cave breccias also, probably suggests that it was not available locally at the time.

Alternative sources of raw material are the North Wales coast or the Irish Sea Drift deposits of the Shropshire-Cheshire Plain, both of which would be compatible with the interpretation of the cave as a temporary rock shelter seasonally occupied by a mobile hunting party. It has not yet been possible to study material from these areas to test if it matches the variety and composition of the Pontnewydd flint but a possible complication here is the selection by ancient man of specific flint types which would imbalance the overall composition of the cave flints.

The ultimate source of the flint is unfortunately uncertain. Based on the abundance of Cretaceous flint in association with marine shells and sediment of undoubted Triassic age in the drift deposits of the Irish Sea Ice, Greenly (1919) postulated the reworking of an outcrop of Upper Cretaceous age in the Irish Sea between the Isle of Man and Cheshire. More recent work however has failed to confirm this, either by boreholes near the proposed outcrop (IGS holes 73/32 and 73/54: IGS, 1974), or as a geochemical anomaly in superficial sediments over the area (Cronan, 1970). In addition, the absence of Tertiary basalt in the drift would exclude Northern Ireland as a possible source, as it is unlikely that extensive reworking of the Irish Chalk could occur without affecting the overlying basalt. Flints are however known from Western Scotland (Wickham-Jones and Collins 1978), and although now predominantly present in reworked deposits, the existence of numerous small remnants of Cretaceous age over much of Western Scotland (e.g. Mull, Morvern, Eigg, Skye, Arran etc.), attests to a much more extensive cover of this area in the past. Such an outcrop, or even residual deposits from it, would have provided a source of flint for southward flowing glaciers. That the source for the Irish Sea Ice is northerly is supported by the presence of erratics from the Firth of Clyde, Galloway, and the Lake District in the Irish Sea Drift (Greenly, 1919).

DUMP

A57	c.l.
A61	o.l.s.
A66/29	c.l./s.
A66/60	c.l. (carb)
A66/66	c.l.
A66/67	?rhyolite
A67/73	fine o.l.
A66/96	c.l.
A68/15	c.l.
A68/20	c.l.
A71/2	c.l.
A79/4	c.l.
A84	c.l./o.l.
A86/3	c.l.
A86/4	c.l. + dr.
A86/5	o.l.
A99	fine c.l.
A99/3	c.l./30%s.
A99/4	c.l.
A99/6	o.s.l.
A122	c.l.

S. FISSURE

B10	Breccia	l.s. + dr.
B61	Breccia	c.l.
B117	Breccia	c.l.
B167	Breccia/INT	c.l.
B215	Breccia	c.l.
B227	Breccia	c.l.
B240	Breccia	s.
B244	Breccia	s.ch.
B261	Breccia/INT	c.l.
B333	Breccia	c.l.
B337	Breccia	c.l.
B385	Breccia	c.l.

S. PASSAGE

C204	L.B.	c.l.(carb)

E. PASSAGE

D119	L.B.	c.l.
D231	L.B.	c.l.
D233★	L.B.	?c.l.
D330	L.B.	c.l.
D617	L.B.	o/c.l.
D687	INT	c.l.
D710	L.B.	c.l.
D775★	L.B.	c.l.
D927	U.B./S.	c.l.

KEY

o:	open	L.B.: Lower Breccia
c:	coalesced	U.B.: Upper Breccia
s:	skeletal	INT: Intermediate
ch:	chalcedonic	S: Silt
l:	lepispheric	(carb): Carboniferous in age
dr:	druse	

★sample not etched

TABLE VIII.2 Structural type of Pontnewydd flints (excavated 1978–81) arranged according to location in cave.

CONCLUSIONS

Upper Cretaceous flints were introduced into North Wales by the Irish Sea Ice and were probably derived ultimately from sources in Western Scotland. Although Irish Sea Drift deposits are quite extensive in the area, and at one time were deposited as much as 20 km up the vale of Clwyd, the absence of naturally deposited flints in the Elwy Valley, in general, and particularly in the Upper and Lower Sands and Gravels in the cave suggests that such deposits may not have been available at the time of cave occupation. This would raise the possibility of human transportation of the flint as raw material to the site from some distance away. The nearest alternative sources of flint may have been the North Wales Coast or the Shropshire-Cheshire Plain, either of which would be compatible with interpretation of the cave as a temporary shelter.

True lepispheric forms			Skeletal rich forms			Others		
A57	–	c.l.	A61	–	o.l.s.	A66/60	–	c.l.(carb)
A66/66	–	c.l.	A66/29	–	c.l./s.	C204	L.B.	c.l.(carb)
A66/73	–	fine o.l.	A99/3	–	c.l/30%s.			
A66/96	–	c.l.	A99/6	–	o.s.l.			
A68/15	–	c.l.	B10	Breccia	l.s.+dr.			
A68/20	–	c.l.	B240	Breccia	s.			
A71/2	–	c.l.	B244	Breccia	s.ch			
A79/4	–	c.l.						
A84	–	c.l./o.l.						
A86/3	–	c.l.						
A86/4	–	c.l.+dr.						
A86/5	–	o.l.						
A99	–	fine c.l.						
A99/4	–	c.l.						
A122	–	c.l.						
B61	Breccia	c.l.						
B117	Breccia	c.l.						
B167	Breccia/INT	c.l.						
B215	Breccia	c.l.						
B227	Breccia	c.l.						
B261	Breccia	c.l.						
B333	Breccia	c.l.						
B337	Breccia	c.l.						
B385	Breccia	c.l.						
D199	L.B.	c.l.						
D231	L.B.	c.l.						
D233★	L.B.	?c.l.						
D330	L.B.	c.l.						
D617	L.B.	o/c.l.						
D687	INT	c.l.						
D710	L.B.	c.l.						
D775★	L.B.	?c.l.						
D927	U.B./S.	c.l.						

Table VIII.3
Collation of flint types from Pontnewydd.
Finds 1978–81. Key as in Table VIII.2.

PART C
PETROLOGICAL INVESTIGATIONS
by
Richard E. Bevins

INTRODUCTION

Petrological investigations of material from Pontnewydd Cave have been undertaken on both artefacts and erratics★. The results presented here are preliminary, as a full petrographic examination programme has not yet been possible. Artefacts collected during seasons 1978 to 1981, and erratics collected during seasons 1978–1982 were used in this study.

ARTEFACT LITHOLOGY

The principal aims of the investigation into artefact petrology were twofold; firstly to identify the range of lithologies used in artefact manufacture in order to determine whether the raw materials were of local origin (that is whether they were naturally present within the vicinity of the cave), or if they were brought into the area by man or by some other process; and secondly to determine the influence of lithology on typological groupings.

(a) *Lithological variation:* Artefacts were examined from the Upper Breccia, Lower Breccia and the Intermediate complex (see Collcutt, this volume, for stratigraphic details). No particular petrological characteristics appeared to typify any individual stratigraphic unit, but high frequencies of artefacts occur only in the Lower and Upper Breccias (Table VIII.4).

Approximately 90% of the worked stones are of altered igneous, pyroclastic and volcaniclastic rocks (feldspar-phyric lavas, crystal tuffs, ignimbrites and fine silicic tuffs are the most common, although a number of the fine silicic tuffs may in fact be highly silicic mudstones). The remaining 10% are of flint and chert, which is discussed elsewhere (Clayton, p.186) and so will not be described in any detail here.

The igneous, pyroclastic and volcaniclastic rocks are almost entirely silicic in character, hence their relatively tough aspect and suitability for knapping purposes. However, many possess an inherent weakness caused by the presence of a pervasive fabric in the form of a spaced cleavage. This, coupled with the evidence of secondary alteration (low-grade metamorphism), suggests that these rocks are of at least Lower Palaeozoic age, and possibly older.

The range of rock types utilised in artefact manufacture is presented in Table VIII.4. None is exposed in the vicinity of Pontnewydd Cave, which is situated on the east side of the Elwy Valley (Fig. VIII.1), and opens off a steep, westward-facing Carboniferous Limestone scarp, on the dip slope of which are exposed younger Coal Measures micaceous sandstones. On the western slopes of the valley Silurian mudstones with thin sandstones crop out, strata which underlie most of the Denbigh Moors area to the west, and extend as far as the Conwy Valley. Clearly, therefore, the raw materials utilised in artefact manufacture were imported into the area. The lithologies bear a close resemblance to Lower Palaeozoic (in particular Ordovician) rocks which crop out in Snowdonia and the Arenig Mountains of Gwynedd, although another possible source to be considered is the English Lake District.

★erratic is here used in its widest sense meaning a relatively large rock fragment lithologically different from the bedrock on which it lies, either free or as part of a sediment.

	Weight in grammes	Int.	LB	UB
PYROCLASTIC/VOLCANICASTIC ROCKS				
TUFF	278	–	–	–
Fine silicic tuff	3977	–	+	+
Shardic tuff	62	–	–	+
Crystal pumice tuff	500	–	–	–
Vitric tuff	21	+	–	–
Crystal tuff	2753	–	+	+
Crystal lithic tuff	1495	–	+	+
Pumice-crystal-lithic tuff	149	–	–	+
IGNIMBRITE	3654	–	+	+
SEDIMENTARY ROCKS				
FLINT AND CHERT	635	+	+	+
SANDSTONE	90	–	+	–
Siliceous sandstone	289	–	–	–
Sandstone with fine siltstone	99	–	–	–
Fine sandstone	80	–	–	–
QUARTZITE	28	–	–	+
SILTSTONE	33	+	+	–
MUDSTONE	50	+	+	–
IGNEOUS ROCKS				
FELDSPAR-PHYRIC LAVA	3712	–	+	+
Phenocrystic lava	97	–	–	+
Feldspar-porphyry	655	–	+	+
RHYOLITE	2144	–	+	+
Flow-banded perlitic rhyolite	356	–	–	–
Quartz-phyric lava	45	–	–	–
DIORITE	190	–	+	+
Microdiorite	167	–	–	–
FINE GRAINED BASIC LAVA	130	–	–	–
OTHERS				
Rhyolite or ignimbrite	285	–	–	–
Rhyolite or fine silicic tuff	94	–	–	–
Rhyolite or fine crystal tuff	125	–	–	–
Silica vein	42	–	–	–

TABLE VIII.4   Pontnewydd Cave. Excavations 1978–81. Provisional analysis of raw materials used for artefact manufacture. Where the finds are securely stratified in the Intermediate complex, Lower or Upper Breccia beds, this information is tabulated (Int., LB or UB respectively)

Of particular importance, however, is the fact that the rock types from which the artefacts are made are very similar to the unworked specimens in the various stratigraphic units of the cave deposits (discussed below), the implication being that the source of raw materials was either the cave deposits themselves or contemporary deposits, probably from the valley outside the cave.

(b) *Lithological control on typological groupings:* Typological grouping of artefacts is generally undertaken on flint specimens. In the present case flint and chert form only about 10% of the recovered artefacts, the remainder being igneous, pyroclastic and volcaniclastic rocks, of probable Lower Palaeozoic age. The latter generally contain a spaced-cleavage, which influenced the final form of the worked material. An understanding of the lithological variation is important for knapping experiments, which is an essential precursor to the final typological ordering of the artefacts (see Green and Newcomer, Chapter V).

ERRATIC LITHOLOGY

The lithology of erratics (Table VIII.5) now contained in the mass flow deposits of the cave was examined in order to

(a) ascertain whether the petrological types used in artefact manufacture were present in the erratic content of the mass flow deposits and therefore whether this was the possible source of raw materials and

(b) to determine what information the erratic lithologies reveal about the Pleistocene history of this area.

A wide variety of igneous, pyroclastic and volcaniclastic rocks were recovered as erratics from the various stratigraphic units within the cave. A number of the rock types was similar to those which were utilised in artefact manufacture, whilst a high proportion of those not used would have been of a totally unsuitable nature. These include locally derived rock types (see above), as well as some of the other rock types in which the spaced cleavage has hampered knapping. In addition others, such as the granites, which were weathered and accordingly weak, and rocks of intermediate or basic composition, such as the dolerites, were similarly avoided.

Rock type	Upper Sands and Gravels	Intermediate complex	Lower Breccia	Upper Breccia
Sandstone	+	+	+	+
Vein quartz	+	+	+	+
Vein quartz with haematite				+
Silicic tuff		+	+	
Feldspar-phyric lava	+	+	+	+
Quartzite		+	+	
Crystal tuff	+	+	+	+
Pumice crystal tuff	+		+	
Granodiorite/tonalite			+	
Granodiorite	+			
Crystal lithic tuff	+		+	+
Siltstone			+	+
Rhyolitic autobreccia	+		+	
Rhyolite	+		+	
Ignimbrite	+		+	+
Mudstone	+		+	
Diorite			+	+
Shardic tuff				+
Flow-banded rhyolite		+		
Nodular rhyolite	+			
Dolerite	+			
Granite	+			
Microgranite	+			

TABLE VIII.5 Pontnewydd Cave. Erratic lithologies. Excavations 1978–82.

The majority of the igneous, pyroclastic and volcaniclastic rocks are silicic in character and are very similar in many aspects to rocks exposed in Snowdonia. Although it is not possible to match individual erratics with a specific source, in one or two cases approximate source locations can be suggested with moderate confidence. For example, although actinolite-bearing meta-dolerites are relatively common over central Snowdonia, those with compositionally zoned epidotes (as in an erratic collected from the Upper Sands and Gravels) are rare. Such meta-dolerites crop out along the western side of the Conwy Valley. A further example is an erratic of rhyolite tuff from the Upper Breccia. Thin section examination reveals that this tuff is composed of delicately preserved glass shards, now replaced by a recrystallization aggregate of quartz and feldspar. Such perfect preservation of texture is not common, but identical features are present in certain tuffs of the Crafnant Volcanic Formation exposed near Betws-y-Coed (Howells *et al.*,1973).

As mentioned previously, another possible source for the igneous, pyroclastic and volcaniclastic erratics might be the English Lake District. A considerable thickness of such strata comprise the Borrowdale Volcanic and Eycott Volcanic Formations of Ordovician age (for a review see Millward *et al.,* 1978) which are associated with contemporaneous granitic and granophyric intrusions. Rocks from this area possess many of the characteristics exhibited by the samples examined during this study (e.g. the presence of a well-developed spaced cleavage and low-grade metamorphic recrystallisation). There are, however, important differences in a number of cases. For example, in the various altered basic to intermediate lavas and dolerites collected from the site area, actinolitic amphibole is sometimes an important mineral phase. Actinolite develops as a result of metamorphic recrystallisation within the greenschist facies, and is common in rocks of the right composition from the Snowdonia region (Bevins and Rowbotham, 1983), whilst in contrast rocks of a similar composition from the Lake District are devoid of actinolite, where they appear to have suffered a lower grade of metamorphism, within the prehnite-pumpellyite facies (author's own observations; R.J. Suthren, pers. comm.). However, the fact that actinolite is not present in all specimens examined indicates no more than the possibility of a 'mixed' origin for the erratics, since actinolite is not present in all rocks of the appropriate composition exposed today in Snowdonia. This absence results from incomplete reactions during metamorphic recrystallisation, and/or variations in metamorphic grade across Snowdonia (for example, varying from prehnite-pumpellyite facies on the Llŷn peninsula and along the north coast around Penmaenmawr and Conwy, to greenschist facies in central Snowdonia). However, a number of erratics bear a strong resemblance to rocks of the Borrowdale Volcanic Group (e.g. certain epidote-rich, feldspar-phyric lavas with altered feldspar phenocrysts which show the former presence of compositional zoning are very similar to rocks of the Thirlmere Andesites). Although suggesting a 'mixed' origin adds complications to the picture, it must remain a possibility for the present time at least.

In this context, it is also relevant to discuss the heavy mineral separates from five cave samples (Jenkins, p.181). Dominant heavy minerals include clinozoisite, epidote, clinopyroxene, amphibole, chlorite, apatite, zircon, rutile, anatase and brookite, all of which are constituent mineral phases of the Lower Palaeozoic igneous, pyroclastic and volcaniclastic rocks of the Snowdonia area (many in fact being found in the altered dolerites). Of particular interest is the presence of brookite and anatase. The former is particularly well developed in certain meta-dolerites from the Tremadog area, the latter in an altered intrusion at Manod, near Blaenau Ffestiniog. However, the rare amounts of staurolite, andalusite and tourmaline etc. cannot be matched to sources in North Wales.

More problematical than the origin of the erratic lithologies described above is that of the muscovite and biotite granites and biotite granodiorites, which so far have only been recovered from the Upper Sands and Gravels. A number of large granodiorite intrusions invade Lower Palaeozoic strata along the North Wales coast from Llŷn to Penmaenmawr, and though the particular petrographic varieties could not be matched exactly, this is a possible source area.

The granites are considerably weathered and oxidised, particularly the biotite-bearing varieties. Muscovite-bearing granites of late Precambrian age crop out on Anglesey and the Llŷn peninsula, and preliminary thin section examination suggests a resemblance to the Pontnewydd material, not only in mineralogy, but also in terms of states of alteration and deformation. Present in both is evidence for low temperature dislocation deformation, resulting in undulose extinction and fracturing of quartz crystals, and the bending and fracturing of feldspar laths. However, granitic and granodioritic rocks of a broadly similar character occur in the English Lake District (e.g. the Eskdale Granite and the Ennerdale Granophyre).

The restriction of granite and granodiorite erratics to the Upper Sands and Gravels may merely be a function of the limited number of such rocks collected so far. If it proves to be real, then it might imply a compound source for the materials of the various debris flows.

Flints and cherts, both artefactual and natural, were recovered in small numbers only from the breccia horizons. Clayton (p.190) describes the problems of provenance, and discusses possible ways for their incorporation into the deposits at the site. The evidence presented here concerning the provenance of other erratics, the lack of source area for the Upper Cretaceous flints in North Wales or in the seabed area to the north of the North Wales coast, their limited number and their restriction to stratigraphic units which also show clear evidence of human occupation, all lend support to the idea that the flints and cherts were introduced into the immediate area by man.

SIGNIFICANCE OF ERRATIC LITHOLOGIES IN TERMS OF QUATERNARY HISTORY

On the basis of surface textures identified during scanning electron microscope studies of quartz grains from various horizons at Pontnewydd Cave, Bull (p.84) suggests that the materials comprising the cave deposits were derived from a mixed provenance, by a variety of processes. The mixed provenance has been mentioned above, and the physical character of the erratics themselves supports derivation by a number of different processes; some of the clasts are well-rounded suggesting a fluvial episode in at least a part of their history, whilst others are angular and fractured and are probably of direct glacial origin. Clearly this complex history reduces the chances of gaining a clear understanding of Pleistocene events since material brought into the cave by the debris flows may have been derived from a number of different ice sheets from a number of different sources and subsequently reworked by a number of different processes. However, the fact that no significant lithological differences exist between reworked erratics and artefactual material suggests that the various deposits outside the cave (prior to reworking in the debris flows) served as the source of raw materials for working.

If the various deposits outside the cave were the source of raw materials for working, then clearly they were brought to the cave by one process or another not only before man's occupation of the cave (i.e. before c.225 ka) but also before emplacement of the first mass flow deposits into the cave, which underlie the layers producing evidence of human occupation of the site. Unfortunately, however, we cannot be certain of the date of this earlier glacial event and there is little present sign that other deposits dating from it in the immediate area outside the cave still survive. Therefore, the chance of placing these deposits into a Pleistocene stratigraphy related to other sequences in North Wales is limited. The period around 225 ka, during Oxygen Isotope Stage 7 (Shackleton and Opdyke, 1973) was one of a temperate climate. It is therefore tempting to suggest that the deposits were related to ice sheets of the previous cold period, during Oxygen Isotope Stage 8 (approximately 300 to 250 ka). It is also possible, however, that no ice from this period reached the Pontnewydd area, and that the ice responsible was related to a still earlier cold period (Oxygen Isotope Stage 10, or 12, etc.). Whichever is the case, the ice appears to have been derived from the west, from central Snowdonia, even possibly as far afield as Anglesey and the Llŷn peninsula and may be also from the English Lake District. The former source compares with that for the later 'Welsh Ice', which similarly contains erratics of various igneous rocks derived from Snowdonia and the Arenig Mountains, along with abundant debris from the Silurian sedimentary rocks of the Denbigh Moors area, whilst the latter source compares with that for the later 'Northern Ice'.

Emplacement of the mass flow deposit responsible for the Lower Breccia is considered to have occurred by 225 ka (i.e. the middle of Oxygen Isotope Stage 7). The similarity of erratic lithology to that in the Upper Sands and Gravels suggests that this second mass flow may merely represent further reworking of the various deposits from outside the cave. The Lower Breccia does, however, contain artefacts and testifies to man's presence in the area at this time.

Dating evidence, combined with faunal identifications, suggests emplacement of the Upper Breccia at a much younger time, probably in the range 10–15 ka. Again, the erratic content shows identical lithological varieties to the earlier deposits in the cave which, along with artefacts similar to those from the Lower Breccia, suggests reworking of the same material preserved, presumably, within the cave and thereby escaping removal by later glacial action.

It is hoped that further petrological investigation will help to clarify the Middle Pleistocene glacial and human history of this area of North Wales, and add support to knapping experiments and typological groupings.

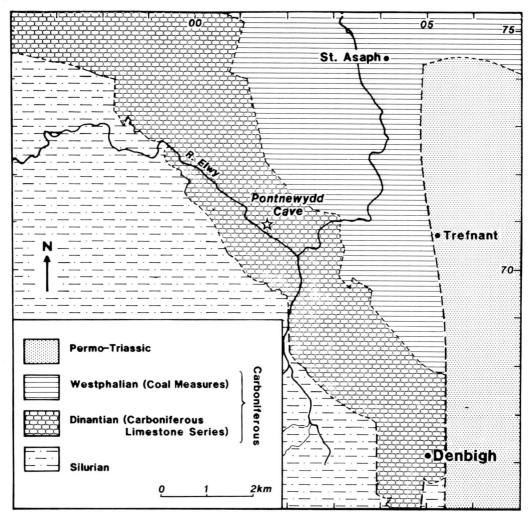

Fig. VIII.1 Pontnewydd Cave. The local solid geology.

CHAPTER IX

SUMMARY AND DISCUSSION

by

H. Stephen Green

This chapter summarises and updates with results from the 1982 and 1983 field seasons, the work of 1978–81. The modern history of the cave has been described in detail in Chapter I and will not here be repeated. One purpose of the present chapter is to make an interpretative statement, necessarily from an archaeologist's viewpoint, of the project as a whole.

THE STRATIGRAPHIC SEQUENCE

The sequence of layers in the cave (Fig.IX.1) is of the greatest interest, for almost all the deposits have been introduced into the cave by the various agencies of fluvial deposition or mass movement and all of the archaeological and most of the faunal remains discovered have been emplaced by debris flows. Whilst this process has totally destroyed any living-floors that might have existed inside or immediately outside of the cave, it has nonetheless been the agency which has preserved the evidence of human habitation in a region which has suffered, in all probability, several subsequent episodes of glaciation. This circumstance of cave-infill holds out the distinct possibility of the discovery of cave-habitation sites in areas similarly glaciated and far beyond the known distribution of settlement (Fig.I.2).

The overall sequence is divided into two main elements, a basal Siliceous member and an overlying Calcareous member. The layers which appear in these two members are detailed in Table IX.1 (see also Figs.IX.1–2) but it is important to note that the full succession is not present in any one area of the cave and so correlation between areas is important. The Siliceous member deposits contain neither artefacts nor fauna. These are almost entirely restricted to the two early debris flows (?250–225 ka) of the Calcareous member which form, on the one hand, the Intermediate complex and the Lower Breccia bed and, on the other hand, the Upper Breccia bed which contains equally early artefacts and some early fauna but whose emplacement probably dates to 15–10 ka.

The fullest sequence of cave-deposits is to be found in the Area B (Deep Sounding and South Fissure) sequence (Fig. IX.1). Unfortunately, the important archaeological and faunal deposits of the Intermediate layers and the Upper and Lower Breccias are here represented only by sediment-films on the cave-walls or by the deposits present in the narrow South Fissure; however, the South Fissure sequence was the first to be studied and it is here that the type-sequence of deposits was defined.

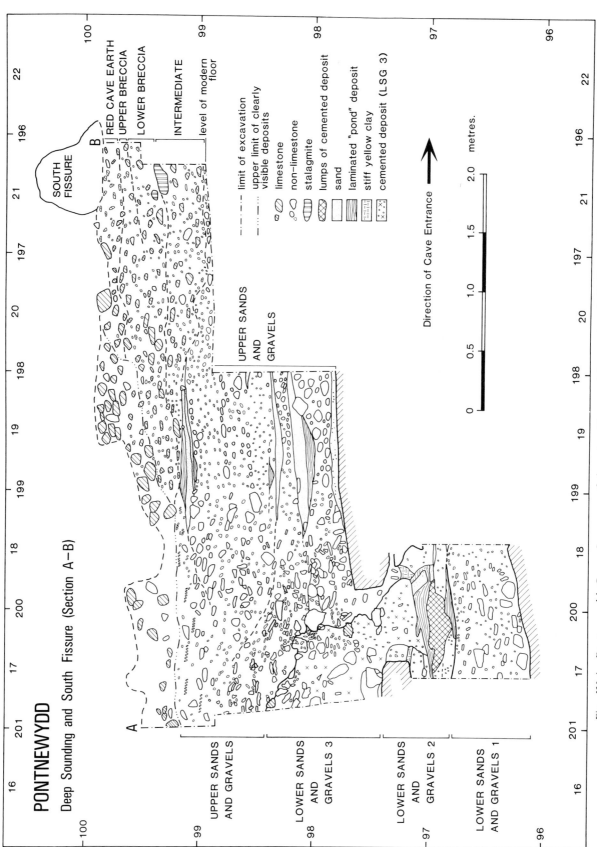

Fig. IX.1 Pontnewydd Cave. Sequence of deposits, illustrated by section A–B (South Fissure and Deep Sounding). Composite of sections drawn 1978–9, 1982. See fig.I.7 for location of section.

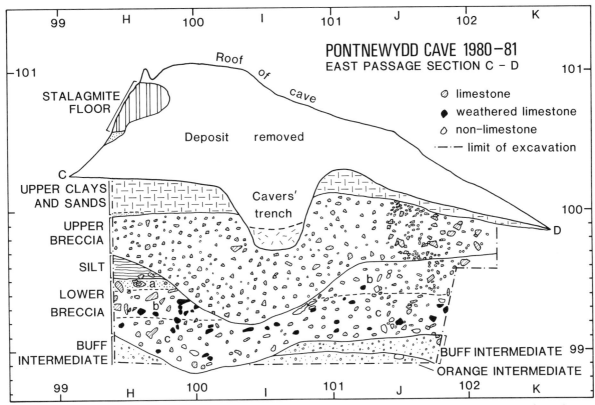

Fig. IX.2 Pontnewydd Cave. Section CD. The East Passage. (See Plate XXXVIII). 1980. The a–b–c subdivisions of the Lower Breccia, shown here, are not believed to be significant. See Fig. I.7 for location of section.

	Layer		Layer Abbreviation	Whether present in South Fissure (B) and/or East Passage (D)	Principal mode of emplacement	Probable age	Archaeological and faunal remains
Calcareous member	XII.	Laminated Travertine	LT	BD	*in situ*	Post-glacial	fauna
	XI.	Upper Clays and Sands	UCS	BD	fluvial	Late-and Post-glacial	fauna, including mollusca
	X.	Red Cave Earth	RCE	B	debris flow	10–15ka	some fauna
	IX.	Upper Breccia	UB	BD	debris flow	10–15ka	fauna & artefacts
	VIII.	Silt	–	D	fluvial	10–15ka	fauna
	VII.	Stalagmite	–	D	*in situ*	225–80ka	absent
	VI.	Lower Breccia	LB	BD	debris flow	>225ka	fauna, artefacts. human maxilla fragment & premolars
	V.	Intermediate	–	BD	debris flow	>225ka	fauna, artefacts & human molar
Siliceous member	IV.	Upper Sands and Gravels	USG	B+?D	debris flow	>225ka	absent
	III.	Lower Sands and Gravels 3	LSG3	B+?D	debris flow	?>300ka	absent
	II.	Lower Sands and Gravels 2	LSG2	B	fluvial	>250ka	absent
	I.	Lower sands and Gravels 1	LSG1	B	debris flow	>250ka	absent

TABLE IX.1.   Pontnewydd Cave. Simplified stratigraphic sequence with suggested dates.

> *N.B.* (1) UCS and LT do not appear on Fig. IX.1 but are present deeper within the South Fissure.
> (2) In the South Fissure area only one Intermediate layer is recognized. In the East Passage however, a "Buff Intermediate" overlies an "Orange Intermediate".

On the north side of the cave, bedrock is at the level of the floor laid by the army in 1940, but it steps down into a channel running on the East–West axis of the cave, cutting (or cut by) a deep Fissure running North–South which can be seen to continue northwards under the rock floor of the main cave (Pl. XXXVIa). The bottom of the deep Fissure was reached in 1982 but no certain demonstration can yet be offered that the rock 'floor' discovered there is *in situ* bedrock (Pl. XXXVIb).

The sequence of deposits located may be described as follows:

Siliceous Member

Lower Sands and Gravels (LSG). This unit, not completely exposed until 1983, may be divided provisionally into three subunits (see p.30).

I. *Lower Sands and Gravels 1* is best interpreted as a debris-flow because the rock fragments (or clasts) which it contains are supported by sediment ("matrix-supported clasts"). Such "matrix-support" is characteristic of flows of debris which, by definition, contain stones, mud and other materials: in true fluvial deposits the stones are not normally surrounded by sediment but touch one another. In a debris flow, the clasts "float" in a clay-water fluid whose properties of finite cohesion and buoyancy act as a support mechanism for these clasts, up to a given weight (Middleton and Hampton, 1973). We may note, however, that LSG 1 exhibits a crude grading with larger pebbles distributed in the basal area of the flow. This phenomenon may result simply from these pebbles sinking through the flow, as a consequence of their weight relative to the fluid strength buoyancy of the flow, or could equally reflect incorporation within the flow of previously underlying clasts "picked up" by the base of the flow. At the top of LSG 1 the pebbles overlap and a study of this imbrication, depending upon our diagnosis of its mode of emplacement, may show the direction of flow since pebbles tend to overlie one another broadly in the direction of the flow, like slates on a roof. No sample has yet been systematically measured but study of the imbrication in section is suggestive of a northwards flow.

II. *Lower Sands and Gravels 2* This is a complex fluvial episode in which both gullying of the underlying LSG1 and undercutting of the overlying LSG3 have taken place. Clasts of LSG3 are present in LSG2. It is not clear, however, whether the very large lump of cemented deposit (LSG3) shown within LSG2 (Fig.IX.1) is a derived clast or is a tongue of *in situ* LSG3.

III. *Lower Sands and Gravels 3* The main feature of the LSG is a debris-flow deposit (S. Collcutt's layer DPS 14 (p.37)) which has been cemented by calcite after its deposition (pl.XXXVII). The hardness of this layer was sufficient to necessitate the use of a pneumatic drill to excavate it. That this hard layer pre-dates the overlying Upper Sands and Gravels (USG) is clearly seen by the way in which the USG has ridden over LSG3 (Fig. IX.1). On the other hand, on the basis of work done in 1982–3, we may note that, whilst LSG2 must post-date LSG3, no clear chronological relationship can be determined for LSG1 and LSG3.

IV. *Upper Sands and Gravels (USG)* This unit contains layers deposited by a variety of processes including debris flow, deposition from running water (the sand layers) and settling out in still water (the finely laminated clay "pond" deposits). Pebble orientation indicates flow into the cave.

Calcareous Member

The lower units have been described on the basis of sediments exposed in the Deep Sounding and South Fissure. One upper deposit of the Calcareous member – Red Cave Earth – has been identified only in the South Fissure area but the clearest sequence of the

Plate XXXVI a   Pontnewydd Cave. Deep Sounding and deep Fissure, 1981. View taken from Grid Square J20. The roof of the deep Fissure is behind the left-hand scale. Looking East.

Plate XXXVI b   Pontnewydd Cave. The Deep Sounding and deep Fissure. View taken from grid square J20 looking East, 1982.

Plate XXXVII   Pontnewydd Cave. Deep Sounding from West. Nicholas Debenham is shown drilling into the heavily cemented deposit (Lower Sands and Gravels 3) to insert a dosimeter which will record the soil radiation dose, necessary for thermoluminescence dating.

upper deposits is to be found in Area D (the East Passage (Fig.IX.2 and Pl.XXXVIII)) and description of these layers is best based on the East Passage sequence. It may be noted first that deposits possibly equivalent to the Upper Sands and Gravels and to the cemented Lower Sands and Gravels 3 have been located, in 1982, in the East Passage and there is every hope that future excavations may reveal a full sequence of stratigraphic units which may enable the East Passage deposits – which have yielded an important series of absolute dates, artefacts, faunal and hominid finds – to finish a clearer and better type-sequence for the site.

V. *Intermediate* We turn next to the emplacement of the deposits termed 'Intermediate' because they are lithologically intermediate between the underlying and overlying layers. Their characteristic is the presence of siliceous pebbles, quartz and a highly altered limestone. Only one Intermediate layer is recognised in the South Fissure, but in the East Passage a Buff Intermediate overlies an Orange Intermediate layer. The "Buff Intermediate" Deposit in the East Passage is the richest of all the "Intermediate" layers and contains not only artefacts and fauna but also a human molar tooth. Like the overlying Breccias, it was introduced into the cave by debris flow.

VI–IX. *The Lower and Upper Breccias and intervening Stalagmite and Silt layers* The Lower Breccia (LB), like the Upper Breccia (UB), is composed of cemented angular coarse particles, chiefly of limestone. In other ways, however, the composition of the two layers is quite different: the Lower Breccia contains many non-limestone pebbles of sedimentary rocks, more siliceous pebbles and fewer (and more severely altered) limestone fragments. The Lower and Upper Breccias are stratigraphically separated in the East Passage by pond formation (Silt) and in the E. and S. Passages by local stalagmite growth, dating of which has provided an important *terminus ante quem* for the Lower Breccia and Intermediate deposits. Both Breccias also contain derived stalagmite and stalactite reflecting earlier flowstone formation. Such derived fragments are much commoner, however, in the Upper Breccia and must be derived, in part, from the long phase of calcite formation which followed emplacement of the Lower Breccia. There is some evidence that a plug of Lower Breccia had substantially blocked the mouth of the cave from the time of its emplacement until after the Devensian glacial maximum when fauna of Late Glacial age became incorporated in the Silt beds. The overlying Upper Breccia is clearly composed in part of redeposited Lower Breccia and added limestone fragments, whose accumulation is typical of cave entrances. There is no evidence for occupation by man during the interval between emplacement of the Breccias, when the cave was sealed for at least part of the time (p.93), and I believe the artefactual and much of the faunal component of the Upper Breccia to be redeposited from the Lower Breccia entrance-plug. A younger fauna is present in the Silt deposit and in the Upper Breccia and this is, fortunately, easily recognisable both in the condition of the bones in question and by the presence among them of distinct species.

Stalagmite growth, discontinuous but locally substantial, is present at the interface of the Silt and Lower Breccia. Before 1982 only isolated stalagmite bosses had been located on the LB and the *in situ* growth of some of these could not be demonstrated with certainty. The 1982 season, however, produced an area of *in situ* stalagmitic floor (Pl.XXXIXa) stratigraphically underlying the Silt deposit and immediately overlying a localised roof-fall (Pl.XXXIXb) upon the Lower Breccia. The limestone of the roof-fall had suffered some post-depositional rounding, and was cemented by the same phase of stalagmite growth as the flow.

X.*Red Cave Earth* This deposit immediately overlies the Upper Breccia in the South Fissure area and is present nowhere else in the cave. It represents, despite its name, a minor debris flow.

XI–XII.*Upper Clays and Sands and Laminated Travertine* Overlying the Red Cave Earth in the South Fissure or, in the East Passage, the Upper Breccia is a continuous but complex water-laid deposit – the Upper Clays and Sands – introduced from higher up within the cave–system. Holocene fauna within the top of Upper Clays and Sands and the overlying Laminated Travertine clearly indicate a Post-glacial age for part of the UCS and for the overlying LT.

Plate XXXVIII   Pontnewydd Cave. The East Passage, from the West. Section CD is shown. (See Fig. IX.2).

THE HISTORY AND SOURCE OF THE DEPOSITS
WITH REFERENCE TO THE HUMAN OCCUPATION
AT THE CAVE

Some general observations may be made on the layers of the Siliceous member, taken together and on the question of the raw materials present in the cave. Neither the LSG nor the USG contains artefacts, fauna or organic matter and they must have been laid down when surface vegetation was absent locally. Scanning Electron Microscope study of the quartz grains by Peter Bull, of the petrology by Richard Bevins and of the sand and clay mineralogy by David Jenkins, have shown that these basal layers contain, in all probability, elements of redeposited glacial till including erratic pebbles of igneous, pyroclastic and volcaniclastic rocks derived certainly from North-West Wales but possibly also from the English Lake District. It was pebbles of such rocks which were later made into tools by the Acheulian hunters. Flint has not been identified from the Siliceous member deposits but David Jenkins' analysis of the sand and clay mineralogy of the overlying Orange Intermediate layer of the East Passage evidences the local presence of Irish Sea Drift, likely to have contained flint, perhaps only 5–10 kilometres from the cave (p.184). Study of the flint used for some 10% of the artefacts by Chris Clayton, indicates that it is Upper Cretaceous in age, and two sources may be involved. The possible location of these sources cannot be assessed as yet, but the geological evidence from the bed of the Irish Sea would seem to rule out the likelihood of derivation from such a source. A more distant place of origin, in Scotland, seems possible, but one would have to invoke glacial transport in the Irish Sea Drift to account for its presence in North Wales.

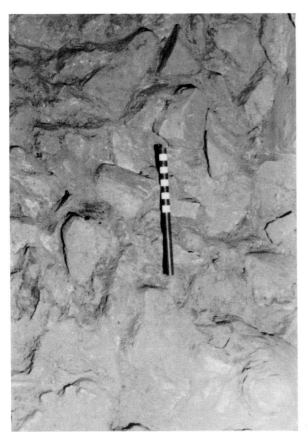

a

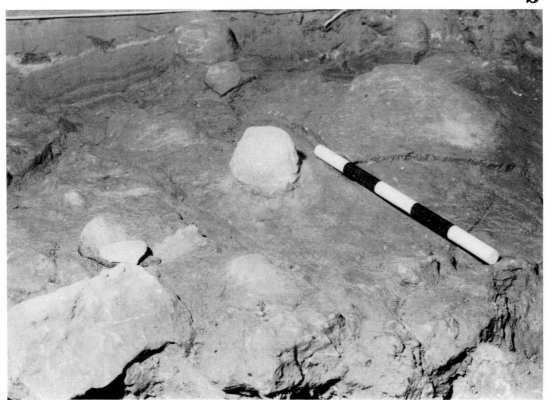

b

Plate XXXIX a   Pontnewydd Cave, 1981. Roof fall deposit on Lower Breccia and underlying *in situ* growth of calcite. Near vertical view, East at top.

Plate XXXIX b   Pontnewydd Cave. East Passage. The *in situ* stalagmite floor discovered in 1982. The overlying Silt deposit is shown to the rear. Square J7. View from WNW. (The stalagmitic boss shown disappearing (rear centre left) into the section may be seen in Plate XXXIX a, just above the bottom right corner).

The evidence suggests that the environment in which the basal deposits, the Upper and Lower Sands and Gravels, were emplaced was one of extreme bleakness. It was one from which typical cave debris – limestone fragments – was almost completely absent. The cementing of LSG3 is likely, however, to reflect a milder climatic event before deposition of LSG2 and the USG.

The interpretation of the immediate source and the significance of the archaeological layers (Intermediate, Lower and Upper Breccias) is much less problematic. Andrew Currant (p.178) has indicated that the composition of the fauna included in these layers is consistent with its recognition as a cave–assemblage in which an archaeologist would expect to find a component of human food-bones. The presence of limestone in all these layers reflects the inclusion of the typical products of cave-entrance weathering as does the presence of stalagmite which can only be derived from within the cave itself, albeit perhaps in part from an area of the cave of unknown size, now destroyed by erosion of the valley-sides, west of the modern entrance. The source of both the fauna and the artefacts is necessarily a matter of inference. It would be quite unreasonable, however, to suggest that the latter are derived from anywhere but an occupation site in or near the original cave-entrance. Most archaeologists would regard this as no more than a commonsense statement but it may be worthwhile to give some indication of the basis of this view:

(1) the artefacts are not rolled (p.115) and it is, therefore, implausible to suggest that they were a component of a pre-existing river terrace which had become incorporated in the debris flows.

(2) in terms of typology and technology, the artefacts present a coherent archaeological assemblage with no hint of the mixing of industries of different ages.

(3) knowledge of the actual distribution of earlier Palaeolithic settlement in Britain gives no support to any notion that the Elwy Valley was strewn with palaeoliths available for incorporation into any passing debris flow.

(4) Peter Bull's study of quartz grains shows no evidence of the sort of edge-abrasion which would result from long distance transport in far-travelled debris flows. Rather, he would regard the debris flow layers as derived very locally from a source close to the cave entrance (pers. comm., January 1983).

(5) furthermore, it would be equally implausible to suggest that the artefacts represent, even in part, a human occupation which predated the emplacement of the Upper and Lower Sands and Gravels. This follows from (2) above, but also and principally because one would then have to invoke the existence of a totally protected stratum at the cave entrance which survived the incoming of the basal Sands and Gravels but from which not one bone or artefact was incorporated into those flows.

In sum, I have not the least doubt but that the human occupation took place after the deposition of the Upper Sands and Gravels but before the emplacement of the Lower Breccia.

THE DATING EVIDENCE

The chronology of the cave-deposits is based on determination of both derived and *in situ* stalagmite made by the Uranium-Thorium (U-Th) and Thermoluminescence (TL) methods of dating (Chapter IV). The U-Th method is based, like the familiar Carbon-14, on the measurement of radioactive isotopes. In the case of U-Th, uranium decays into a series of daughter isotopes of which the important radioisotopes for us are Uranium-234 and

209

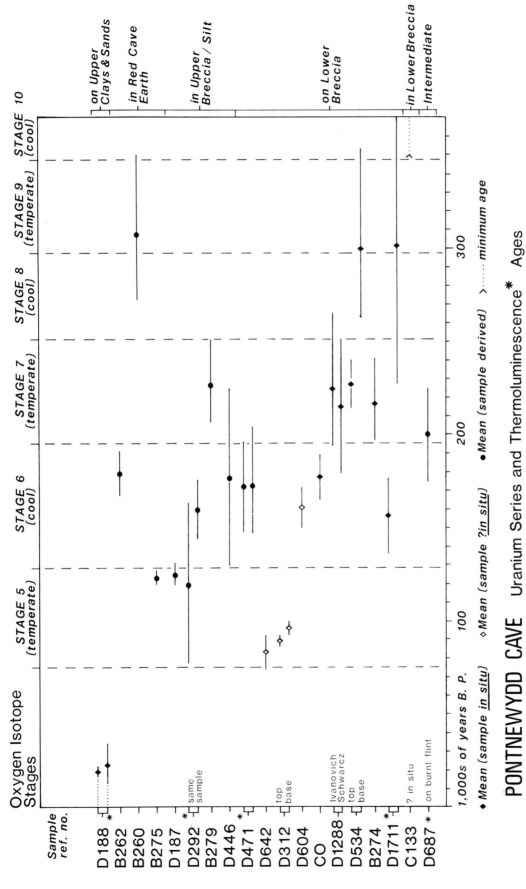

PONTNEWYDD CAVE Uranium Series and Thermoluminescence* Ages

Fig. IX.3 Uranium series (U–Th) and Thermoluminescence (TL) age determinations from Pontnewydd Cave. The horizontal bars represent one standard deviation (1σ). The South Fissure samples B0a, B0b, B111, B148, B162 and B396 are omitted (cf. p.30) as is sample B409 from LSG 3 (Tables IV.2A, 4–6). D1693, replicate dates by Debenham on Schwarcz's sample D642, is also not shown.

Thorium-230 (or [234]U and [230]Th in normal scientific notation). [234]U is quite soluble in ground water and thus is precipitated with dissolved limestone to become sealed in stalagmite. [230]Th, however, is not soluble and is not deposited with [234]U. It is, therefore, possible to use to ratio of [230]Th to [234]U to calculate the lapse of time since formation of the stalagmite.

The TL method is well known for its dating of pottery and burnt flint but its application to the dating of stalagmite is relatively new. The method dates the crystallisation (or re-crystallisation) of the stalagmite by measuring the quantity of radiation energy produced by radioactive decay within the substance since its formation. This energy is released by heating and is measured as a visible light signal (hence the name, thermo-luminescence).

In addition to dates on stalagmite, Joan Huxtable has made a single TL determination of 200 ± 25 ka (ka = 1000's of years ago) on a burnt flint core found in close proximity to the human molar in the Buff Intermediate layer in the East Passage. It is reasonable to suppose that the core was burnt in a domestic fire, and it offers thus our best estimate of the date of human habitation at the cave. A series of U-Th and TL dates has been determined by Henry Schwarcz, Nicholas Debenham and Miro Ivanovich from stalagmites certainly or probably *in situ* on the surface of the Lower Breccia in both the East and the South Passages. These dates fall into two groups: first in the range 225,000–160,000 years ago showing that the Lower Breccia was in place by this period; and second, in the range 95,000–80,000 showing that renewed growth was taking place. It seems clear that a long interval separated the emplacement of the Lower and Upper Breccias, and that the Lower Breccia – and therefore its contained fauna, artefacts and hominid specimens – was emplaced by around or soon after 225,000 years ago. A combination of U-Th and TL determinations on the one hand and faunal evidence on the other suggest that the stalagmitic floor which overlies the Upper Clays and Sands began forming in the Post-glacial period after about 10,000 years ago.

In all, over three dozen absolute dates have been produced on samples from Pontnewydd Cave, some of them on fragments of stalagmite or stalactite which had become incorporated in the debris flows. All are published in this volume and the resulting pattern of age-determinations is depicted in Fig.IX.3. The U-Th and TL methods are described in Chapter IV where the comparability of the age-determinations produced by the different techniques can be judged. Something must, however, be said about the reproducibility of the U-Th technique, for the dates produced by Miro Ivanovich (pp.98-99) show clearly that U-Th dates are no more than statistical expressions of probable age. Indeed, of his nine determinations, no fewer than four lie outside the range of one standard deviation (σ) of his grand average of 224 + 41/–31 ka, although all lie within 1.5σ. This is just the sort of variability one would expect in what is, in statistical terms, a small sample. It is important to remember here that a standard deviation is no more than an expression of probability, there being roughly two chances out of three that the true age lies within a range of one standard deviation either side of the mean (± 1σ), and nineteen chances out of twenty that the result lies within ± 2σ. It would be quite unwise, therefore, to infer a true age for any sample more closely than within a range of two standard deviations either side of the mean. In Fig.IX.3 the horizontal bars represent only one standard deviation and so the reader must mentally double this length to form an accurate impression of the possible range within which the true age is likely to lie.

The reader should note certain differences from the diagram published at an earlier stage of the excavations (Green, 1981a, Table 2). These differences result from a stratigraphic re-allocation of certain samples (*cf.* p.30), arising from the complete study, made in the 1982–3 season, of the South Fissure stratigraphy. The effect of these changes is to remove from consideration a number of dates which were thought to have come from around the interface of Lower Breccia and Intermediate but which can now be seen as almost certainly derived instead from the interface of Upper Breccia and Intermediate (*cf.* Tables IV.2a and

IV.4–6). These determinations, all producing dates closer to 100 ka than 200 ka, were clearly inconsistent with the *terminus ante quem* of 225 ka here proposed for emplacement of the Lower Breccia and would only have been explicable through invoking some such mechanism as recrystallization of the stalagmites concerned. That some such factor was at work in the South Fissure area of the cave is shown, however, both by the two statistically distinguishable U-Th determinations of 130 ± 7 ka and 204 ± 20 ka for the same block (B0b) found at the base of the Breccia and by Debenham's two dates, of 154 ± 19 ka (TL) and 243 + 91/–48 ka (U–Th), on sample B409 from Lower Sands and Gravels 3. The TL age from LSG3 is far too young (*cf.*Table IX.1) and probably results from recrystallization leading to a re-zeroing of the TL signal at *c.*154 ka. However, it cannot be too strongly emphasised that the East Passage has a particularly clear and well dated stratigraphic sequence which means that the age of the hominid remains, and of the associated industry, is in no way dependent either on sediment correlation or on the dates obtained on samples from the South Fissure. The discrepant determinations, noted by Debenham (p.105) from the South Fissure/Deep Sounding area of the cave, do not recur in the East Passage.

THE CLIMATIC CONTEXT

The dates (Fig.IX.3) demonstrate a patterning which shows some correspondence with the climatic conditions which would have limited the formation of stalagmite (p.54). The earliest certain growth of stalagmite in the cave seems to belong to the warm Oxygen Isotope Stage 7c, roughly 250–230 ka, (Fig.IX.4). Pending further evidence, I would regard the two early dates with means around 300 ka (B260 and D534), together with sample C133 with an age of > 350 ka, as being no more than statistical aberrations of the kind just discussed. It is unfortunate that no confidence can be placed in the two dates (Tables IV.5–6) from the calcite cementation of Lower Sands and Gravels 3.

It would seem that the Lower Breccia was emplaced in Stage 7, perhaps in the cooler conditions of stadial phase 7b dated to around 230 ka (Ninkovich and Shackleton, 1975). Phase 7b is now recognised as perhaps a "short ice age", a perfect context for such a mass-flow event (Andrews, 1983). In this case, the archaeological, hominid and faunal remains would date to stages 7c–b and, indeed, the successively warm and cool faunas of the Intermediate Complex and the Lower Breccia may belong within this warm-cool climatic succession. The hominid and archaeological finds could belong in part to Stage 7c, but we cannot say whether any belong to the succeeding cool stadial. The human occupation of the site may then be roughly bracketed as possibly lying some time between 250 and 230 ka, the former being a rough figure for the beginning of Stage 7. There is general agreement on the age of Stage 7. Shackleton and Opdyke (1973) give a date of 251 ka for the start of Stage 7, whilst Kukla (1977) suggests an age of 240 – 20/+10 ka and Kominz *et al.* (1979) quote 259 ka. Ninkovich and Shackleton (1975, 32) suggest that the true age of substage 7b lies within the range of 240–220 ka with *c.*230 ka as the most likely age.

Stalagmite growth continued in the cool conditions of the first part of stage 6 but had ceased altogether before the intensely cold conditions attested world-wide at the end of this stage. Renewed growth is attested during Stage 5e, (regarded by many as the classic Ipswichian interglacial, 128–116 ka), but it continued also during at least one of the succeeding interstadial phases (sample D312, see p.93). Calcite formation certainly ceased by 75 ka at the end of the last Stage 5 interstadial (5a). No new stalagmite growth is recorded in the cave until the growth of the recent stalagmitic floor whose true age is Post-glacial. The absence of growth during the Devensian cold stage is perhaps surprising, but this *lacuna* may perhaps be filled by future discoveries.

Direct climatic evidence has been obtained by the analysis of the ratio of oxygen isotopes 18 and 16 contained within single growth layers of stalagmite sample D312. This analysis

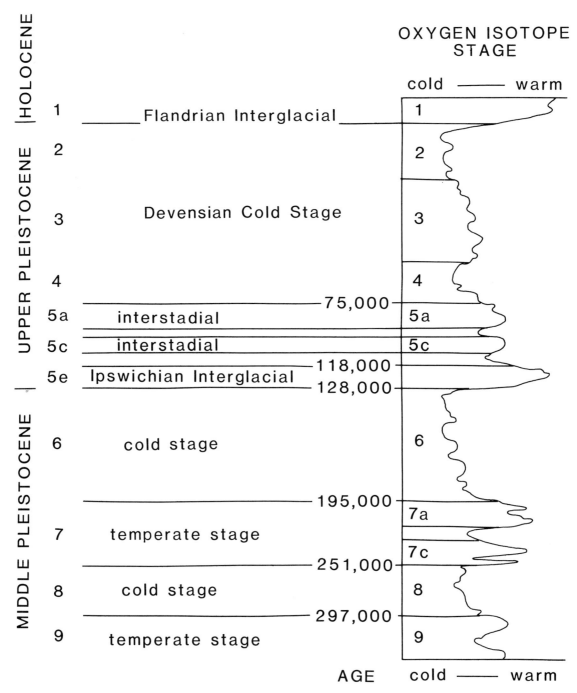

Fig. IX.4 The climatic history of the later Pleistocene (after Ninkovich and Shackleton, 1975).

shows that the calcite formed in isotopic equilibrium with the water from which it was deposited, and indicates that the cave was sealed at the time when this stalagmite was growing, namely around 90,000 years ago. We can further report that comparison of the ^{18}O composition profile of this fossil stalagmite with the ^{18}O composition of modern drip water and young 'soda-straw' stalactites in the cave indicates that, over the period when this sample was growing from 96,000 to 89,000 years ago, the temperature was falling from a peak warmer than that of the present day to a level which was appreciable colder. What we seem to see in this small stalagmitic boss is a terrestrial record of the temperature decline, defined on the basis of deep-sea deposits (Fig.IX.4), from warm stage 5c to cold stage 5b.

GEOMORPHOLOGY

We can only understand the cave deposits and their emplacement in the context of the local geomorphology. The course which the River Elwy follows past Pontnewydd Cave is believed to result from diversion by Irish Sea Ice at some glacial stage of the Pleistocene (p.26). A length of 3.5 kilometres of the Elwy was involved in this diversion, which is likely to be more recent than the beginning of the Middle Pleistocene 700,000 years ago because glacial activity is not certainly attested at an earlier date in Britain. We cannot be absolutely sure whether one or both of the distinct mechanisms of valley incision or river capture was involved in this process. Our model for the emplacement of the successive deposits of the cave relates to the alternate effects of infilling of the valley with glacial drift, followed by renewed down-cutting by the River Elwy. The height of the cave corresponds to the terrace system along the valley and – as the stable isotope analysis actually shows – it is likely that the cave was blocked with drift on more than one occasion. Peter Bull's study (Chapter IIIB) is important here for he presents persuasive evidence, based on rounding of some quartz grains as a result of fluvial transportation, that a river had indeed flowed at about the height of the cave on more than one occasion; clearly such a topographical situation may have proved the context in which entrance deposits became saturated and, thus lubricated, slumped into the cave (pp.29 and 80).

POLLEN ANALYSIS

Systematic analysis, by Philip Gibbard, of soil samples from the cave has produced no pollen evidence whatsoever. Analysis, by Josette Renault-Miskovsky, of a sample (D1288) of the *in situ* stalagmitic floor discovered, in 1982, on the surface of the Lower Brecccia and dated to *c*.225 ka (Ch.IV) again yielded no pollen or plant remains. In the latter case, the result is in harmony with the hypothesis that the cave-entrance was blocked following the emplacement of the Lower Breccia.

THE FAUNA

The fauna from the cave is being studied by Andrew Currant (Chapter VII) and he believes that three discrete Pleistocene assemblages may be identified both stratigraphically and, even when disturbed into upper layers by later debris flows, by the different states of preservation of the bones. The first of these comes from the Buff Intermediate layer in the East Passage. Certain species occur only in this Intermediate layer – roe deer *(Capreolus capreolus)*, beaver *(Castor fiber)* and wood-mouse *(Apodemus)* – which, taken with the other species present, are indicative of interglacial conditions. The fauna could indicate an open woodland environment.

The assemblage from the Lower Breccia is perhaps best termed a 'cool-temperate' one, very cold species seeming to be absent. The presence here of animals such as lemming, and the narrow-skulled and northern voles, indicates a climate which, although continental, need not have been particularly cold. An open steppe environment is possible. The frequency of deciduous bear canines in the Intermediate and perhaps in the Lower Breccia also suggests use as a bear den. It is not clear what component of the fauna may represent human food-bones.

Study of the condition of the fauna shows a definite hiatus at the top of the Lower Breccia. The Upper Breccia certainly contains an important element derived from the Lower Breccia but present there also and in the intercalated Silt deposit, is a fauna differentiated by its state of preservation. The species recognised to date in this youngest preservation type include reindeer *(Rangifer tarandus)* and Musk ox *(Ovibos moschatus)* which, taken in conjunction with the other species present, suggest conditions of marked coldness with a treeless tundra environment. The species form a typical late Devensian fauna. There is evidence to suggest that denning wolves used the cave at this time.

THE HOMINID REMAINS

Seven human fragments have been found in the cave. The first, that of a molar tooth, was made during last century and is now lost. Its description as being of larger than usual size may suggest a Pleistocene age. Finds from the present excavations have been studied by Christopher Stringer (Chapter VI) and include the molar tooth of an adult (Pl.XX) stratified in the Buff Intermediate deposit in the East Passage in close proximity to the burnt flint core already mentioned, which yielded a TL date of 200 ± 25 ka. Near this find, but in the overlying Lower Breccia, was a fragment of upper jaw containing two contiguous teeth from a juvenile individual. These finds, probably from a child aged 8–9 years, comprise an upper right first molar and a deciduous tooth (Pls.XXVI–XXXIII). Also from the cave have come fragments of a child's mandible (Pl.XXI–XXIII) and of an adult vertebra (Pls.XXIV–XXV). These last two finds are from unstratified contexts but relative dating, by Theya Molleson, has shown them to be old, possibly of Pleistocene age, and study of their state of preservation may eventually allow them to be assigned with confidence to one of the preservation-types provisionally defined by Andrew Currant (p.174). From the 1983 season came two lower premolars, one probably from an 8–12 year old and the second from an older, possibly adolescent, individual. Both were stratified in the Lower Breccia.

The two permanent upper molars are of great interest since both metrically and morphologically they resemble early Neanderthal teeth. The presence of a marked degree of taurodontism in both (a condition in which there is an enlargement of the pulp cavity extending sometimes, as in this case, well into the unseparated roots) makes them particularly comparable with the series of human teeth from the early Upper Pleistocene occupation site of Krapina in Yugoslavia.

The vertebral fragment is part of a middle thoracic vertebra. It lacks a distinctly archaic morphology, although this does not preclude it from being of Middle Pleistocene age.

The juvenile mandible is of some interest. The fragment represents part of a right ascending ramus, having in place the crown of a molar tooth whose roots had not developed. The size of the jaw-bone rules out any possibility that the tooth is a first molar for in that case the individual would then have been only 3 years or less in age. Radiography shows that a more posterior molar is absent and so the tooth must either be a third molar, which would imply an age of greater than 11 years, or a second molar, implying an age of perhaps 8–9 years. In this latter case one would suppose, as is quite possible, that neither the third molar nor its crypt had yet developed. It is, unfortunately, impossible without more material to be sure whether a second or third molar is involved, but the molar has a simple crown morphology, without accessory cusps, and is small in size. The overall morphology of the specimen cannot readily be distinguished from that of modern humans, but it favours the older of the two proposed ages.

The hominid fragments from Pontnewydd are at present tantalisingly few in number, but we have only to think of such middle Pleistocene sites as Caune de l'Arago or La Chaise to realise that where hominid fragments are present at all, they often occur in profusion. The potential of the site for further discoveries is, therefore, considerable.

The importance of the human finds may as yet be assessed only tentatively but the presence of a marked degree of taurodontism does invite comparison with early Neanderthal remains and the fact that taurodontism is present in two individuals does suggest it to be a population characteristic. The occurrence at Pontnewydd of such hominid finds is not surprising given the Neanderthal features seen in the later Middle Pleistocene skull from Biache in the Pas-de-Calais (Vandermeersch, 1978) and also the possible Neanderthal characteristics noted on the Swanscombe skull itself (Stringer *et al.*,1979, 246).

The recognition of some possible Neanderthal features on the Pontnewydd fossils, some 150,000 years before the appearance of the 'classic' last glacial Neanderthals, lends some small support to an evolutionary model in which long periods of stability were followed by rapid periods of change. However, more material representing cranial or mandibular parts will be needed before we can be more definite about the affinities of the Pontnewydd hominids.

THE ARCHAEOLOGICAL FINDS

We turn finally to the archaeological industry, or industries, present in the cave. I believe, at the present time, that the occupation was short-lived, even if perhaps over several seasons, and that the artefacts in the Upper Breccia were a part of this same early assemblage, naturally incorporated in the incoming Upper Breccia. Such an interpretation is supported by the typology of the artefacts and, indeed, also by Richard Bevins' study of the petrology, where he suggests that the erratic pebbles in the Upper Breccia are derived from reworking of earlier deposits.

If we turn first to see what artefacts are actually present in the Intermediate deposits and Lower Breccia of the East Passage, we find the key elements of the assemblage – handaxes, the use of Levallois technique and the presence of smaller implements – already present. The raw materials seem to show no variation; in particular, flint is present throughout the archaeological layers. The artefacts have been detailed by context in Chapter V but, for the present summary, I will treat the assemblage as a whole.

The tool and debitage-types which make up the assemblage may be listed as follows: handaxes, a flake-cleaver; a chopper; several chopping tools; Levallois cores and debitage; one Mousterian point; discoidal and other cores; naturally backed knives; transverse and side and end-scrapers; notches and denticulates and one truncated blade. About 30 handaxes have been discovered in all among which pointed types predominate. They are generally crudely made, using hard-hammer techniques. Typological study is rendered difficult by the fact that the non-flint rocks present frequently do not show the clean conchoidal fracture characteristic of flint but may exhibit a laminar fracture along natural cleavage planes in the rock. We may note, however, that the amygdaloid and sub-triangular forms characteristic of the Continental Upper Acheulian industries predominate. Several handaxes are plano-convex in cross-section but none compare closely with handaxes of Roe's Wolvercote type. One flint handaxe only is present (found in 1983) and two probable handaxe trimming flakes have been noted in this raw material. The presence of the flake-cleaver, chopper and several chopping tools is probably a reflection of the raw materials used for artefact production.

It has sometimes been claimed that the use of Levallois technique is favoured only where suitable raw material occurs plentifully, because of the wastefulness of the technique. It was, therefore, a surprise to find it in use, at Pontnewydd, for the production of flakes, blades and points. Its use alongside discoidal and other cores suggests that selection of the technique was unrelated to the limitations imposed by the varied raw materials. The difficulties of using Levallois technique on such rocks are evidenced by the presence of unfinished, unstruck or poorly executed cores and by the occurrence both of mis-hit cores and flakes.

A programme of experimental knapping by Mark Newcomer (p.153) has shown that the range of tool-types made has probably not been influenced by the raw material. Indeed his manufacture of a Quina-style scraper (Pl.XVIIIb) shows just what was possible in such apparently intractable raw materials. Rather, the material has limited the technological refinement of the forms present.

Of some three hundred artefacts present, about half are simple flakes, many of which appear to have acquired natural chipping before or during transportation in the debris flows (p.59; p.115). This natural damage must leave some doubt over the typological identification of artefacts where minimal retouch only has taken place. There is, of course, no difficulty over the recognition of handaxes, of the products of Levallois technique, of cores, or of the naturally-backed knives which are present. The problem arises with such tool-types as scrapers, notches or denticulates. In some cases, the nature of the raw material has permitted retouch of sufficient elegance to leave no doubt as to the identification of the artefacts. This is certainly the case with some of the scrapers, the truncated blades and the fine Mousterian point.

The industries of the later Middle Pleistocene in Europe are notorious for their variability, and the traditional comparative technique of archaeology will be important to establish the likelihood – or otherwise – that the large collection of finds from Pontnewydd does indeed constitute a single industry. One cannot point to any convincing British parallels but comparable material does exist in the Upper Acheulian industries of north-western France, although these assemblages differ in detail. What one can say, however, is that the elements of the assemblage – if correctly dated at older than 225,000 years – contain no surprises and that such a collection of artefacts, if found in a single living-floor, would be accepted without reserve.

CONCLUDING REMARKS

In conclusion, therefore, we see the site as one occupied before 225,000 years ago and perhaps during the interglacial period beginning around 250,000 years ago (Oxygen Isotope Stage 7c (Fig.IX.4)), which ended in the cooler conditions of the stadial Stage 7b around 230,000 years ago (Stage 7b). It may well be, therefore, that the cool-temperate fauna of the Lower Breccia belongs to this stadial phase and that, indeed, it was at this time that the debris flow occurred which emplaced the Lower Breccia in the cave. Andrew Currant's recognition of an interglacial fauna in the Buff Intermediate layer finds support in the work of several other specialists. Collcutt has suggested that the levels of organic matter and carbonate precipitation from this complex imply "the influence of an interglacial, or at least a major interstadial" (p.71). Sand and clay mineral analysis, by David Jenkins, has in turn demonstrated the presence of the high degree of chemical weathering to be found in such a climatic phase (p.185).

We do not know the context of the human occupation of the cave, but the range of tool-types found indicates that it was likely to have been used as an encampment by hunters and cannot be regarded as any sort of 'industrial' site. The igneous, volcaniclastic and pyroclastic pebbles used for the manufacture of implements have all, with very little doubt, been picked up in or near the cave, although the flint has probably been carried a distance of some 5–10 kilometres at least (p.184 and p.190). The dimensions of the cave entrance, if as small then as now – and I am indebted to Trevor Ford for his view that this is likely to have been the case – would suggest use of the site by very few people and would suggest further that the cave was used for short periods of time, perhaps seasonally. We may see, in sum, just how far Acheulian hunters ranged over Britain from the area of densest settlement in South-Eastern England. It would be unwise to speculate on the historical context for this. From our own perspective we see the later Pleistocene as a time of rapid climatic change, but we must remember that for thousands of years at a time conditions would have been sufficiently stable for such agencies as natural population increase and pressure on resources resulting from loss of land to glacial ice or to rising sea-level, to lead to expansion of the areas settled by human populations. Indeed the history of the Pleistocene is the history of this very process. The way is open now to search for Lower Palaeolithic sites in the northern and western parts of the British Isles. Pontnewydd shows that the first place to look is in the interiors of caves infilled from their entrances by such natural processes as debris flow.

STRATEGY FOR FUTURE WORK

Our site plan (Fig.I.7) does little more than hint at the extensive archaeological and faunal deposits which survive in the cave. Progress in digging these deposits is necessarily very slow and it would be quite impracticable – even if thought desirable – to excavate more than a proportion of the site during the present research project. Successive seasons have led to an increasing refinement of our understanding of the site and the goals of the excavation are now numerous. Certain particular research aims may be mentioned:

1. The recovery of additional hominid finds. Pontnewydd is the only British site which seems likely to yield such finds in the present decade, and the opportunity cannot be lost.

2. To expand the numbers of archaeological artefacts recovered from the Lower Breccia and Intermediate. The total, so far, of not much more than a hundred is not great and fewer still are implements.

3. To seek additional dates from *in situ* material.

4. To seek dates also on burnt flint artefacts since these promise to provide our best evidence for the age of the industry.

5. To extend our study of the faunal assemblages present with the aims of identifying humanly butchered bone, of obtaining additional material for statistical comparison with other sites, and of obtaining absolute dates directly on bone.

6. To refine our understanding of the sediment stratigraphy, paying increasing attention to the textural study of the debris flows. Such a study, embracing such aspects as the size, shape and orientation of the particles in the sediments, will enable us better to understand the mechanics and nature of the flows. This will need to be undertaken in the context of the geomorphological studies now taking place.

7. To undertake more detailed studies of the petrology and mineralogy of all the deposits with a view to gaining a more detailed understanding of the relevance of the Pontnewydd sediments to glacial and interglacial Pleistocene events.

The future, then, is promising. No further report of this size is now envisaged before the final report, but individual papers, some in the new journal *Nature in Wales* published by the National Museum of Wales, will report on new developments both at Pontnewydd Cave and at other cave-sites being investigated as part of the same research programme.

BIBLIOGRAPHY

Aitken, M. J., 1978 'Radon loss evaluation by alpha counting'. A specialist seminar on thermoluminescence dating. *PACT 2*, 104–114.

Aitken, M.J., and Bowman, S.G.E., 1975 'Thermoluminescent dating: assessment of alpha particle contribution', *Archaeometry 17*, 132–138.

Aitken, M.J., Bussell, G.D. and Driver, H.S.T., 1979 'Zero-glow monitoring', *Ancient TL 9*, 13–15.

Andrews, J.T., 1983 'Short ice age 230,000 years ago' *Nature 303*, 21–22.

Atkinson, T.C., Harmon, R.S., Smart, P.L., and Waltham, A.C., 1978 'Palaeoclimatic and geomorphic implications of ^{230}Th/^{234}U dates on speleothems from Britain', *Nature 272*, 24–28.

Bevins, R.E., and Rowbotham, G., 1983 'Low-grade metamorphism within the Welsh sector of the paratectonic Caledonides', *Geol.J. 18*, ii, 141–167.

Bishop, M.J., 1982 'The Mammal Fauna of the Early Middle Pleistocene Cavern Infill Site of Westbury-sub-Mendip, Somerset'. *Spec. Pap. Palaeont. 28.*

Blatt, H., Middleton, G., and Murray, R., 1980 *Origin of Sedimentary Rocks*. Second edition (New Jersey).

Bordes, F., 1961 *Typologie du Paléolithique Ancien et Moyen* (Bordeaux).

Bordes, F., 1972 *A Tale of Two Caves* (New York).

Boswell, P.G.H., 1949 *The Middle Silurian Rocks of North Wales* (London).

Bramwell, D., 1964 'The excavations at Elder Bush Cave, Wetton, Staffs.', *N. Staffs. J. Field Studies 4*, 46–60.

Briggs, D.J., *et al.*, in prep. 'Interglacial deposits at Stanton Harcourt, Oxfordshire, England and their implications for Quaternary chronology'.

Brothwell, D.R., 1981 *Digging up Bones* (London and Oxford).

Brown, E.H., 1960 *The Relief and Drainage of Wales* (Cardiff).

Cahen, D., 1981 'Les industries préhistoriques des nappes alluviales de Petit-Spiennes et de Mesvin', *Notae Praehistoricae* (Tervuren, Belgium) *1*, 70–74.

Callow, P., 1981 *La Cotte de Saint Brelade 1881–1981* (Jersey).

Clayton, C.J., 1982 'Growth history and microstructure of Upper Cretaceous flint', *International Association of Sedimentologists, Third European Meeting (Copenhagen)*, 105–107.

Clayton, C.J., in prep. 'Petrography, structure and growth history of cherts from the Perigord region, southern France'.

Clegg, J., 1970 'Excavations at Coygan Cave, near Laugharne'. *Carmarthenshire Antiquary 5–6*, 13–20.

Collcutt, S.N., Currant, A.P., and Hawkes, C.J., 1981 'A further report on the excavations at Sun Hole, Cheddar', *Proc. Univ. Bristol Spelaeol. Soc. 16*, i, 21–38.

Collins, D., 1976 'The geography of the European Lower Palaeolithic', *Colloque X: UISPP IX Congrès, Nice*, 156–165.

Cook, S.F., 1972 *Prehistoric Demography* (Addison Wesley Module in Anthropology, 16).

Coote, G.E., and Holdaway, S., in press 'Radial profiles of fluorine in archaeological bone and teeth: a review of recent developments'.

Coote, G.E., and Sparks, R.J., 1981 'Fluorine concentration profiles in archaeological bone: an application of a nuclear microprobe', *New Zealand Jl Archaeol. 3*, 21–32.

Cordy, J. - M., 1980 'Le paléokarst de la Belle-Roche (Sprimont, Liège): premier gisement paléontologique et archéologique du Pléistocène moyen ancien en Belgique', *C.R. Acad.Sc.Paris 291 (Série D)*, 749–751.

Cronan, D. S., 1970 *Geochemistry of Recent Sediments from the central north-eastern Irish Sea* (I.G.S. Rep 70/17).

Dawkins, W.B., 1871 'On the discovery of the Glutton, (*Gulo luscus*), in Britain', *Q. Jl geol. Soc. Lond. 27*, 406–410.

Dawkins, W.B., 1874 *Cave Hunting* (London).

Dawkins, W.B., 1876 'On the mammalia and traces of man found in the Robin-Hood Cave', *Q. Jl geol. Soc. Lond. 32,* 245–258.

Dawkins, W. B., 1877 'On the mammal-fauna of the caves of Creswell Crags', *Q. Jl geol. Soc. Lond. 33,* 589–612.

Dawkins, W.B., 1880 *Early Man in Britain* (London).

Day, M.H., 1977 *Guide to Fossil Man* Third edition (London).

Debenham, N.C., Driver, H.S.T., and Walton, A.J., 1982 'Anomalies in the TL of young calcites', *PACT 6,* 555–562.

Drew, D.P., and Cohen, J.M., 1980 'Geomorphology and sediments of Aillwee Cave, Co. Clare, Ireland', *Proc. Univ. Bristol Spelaeol. Soc. 15,* iii, 227–240.

Embleton, C., 1960 'The Elwy drainage system, Denbighshire', *Geogr. Journal 126,* 318–334.

Embleton, C., 1970 'North Eastern Wales' in Lewis, C.(ed) *The Glaciations of Wales and Adjoining Areas* (London), 59–82.

Erdbrink, D.P., 1953 *A Review of fossil and recent bears of the Old World* 2 vols. (Deventer).

Falconer, H., 1868 *Palaeontological Memoirs and Notes of the late Hugh Falconer* ed. Murchison, C., 2 vols. (London).

Fisher, R. V., 1971 'Features of coarse-grained, high-concentration fluids and their deposits', *J. Sedim. Petrol. 41,* iv, 916–927.

Fladmark, K.R., 1981 'Microdebitage analysis: initial considerations,' *J. Arch. Sci. 9,* 205–220.

Frayer, D.W., 1978 *Evolution of the Dentition in Upper Paleolithic and Mesolithic Europe.* (University of Kansas Publications in Anthropology, 10).

Gascoyne, M., 1977 'Does the presence of stalagmite really indicate warm periods? New evidence from Yorkshire and Canadian caves', *Proc. 7th Internat. Speleol. Congress Sheffield* B.C.R.A., 208–210.

Gascoyne, M., 1980 *Pleistocene Climates Determined from Stable Isotopic and Geochronological Studies of Speleothem.* (Unpub. Ph-D. thesis, McMaster University, Hamilton, Ontario.)

Gascoyne, M., 1981 'Chronology and climate of the Middle and Late Pleistocene from speleothems in caves in North-West England', *Quaternary Newsletter 34,* 36–37.

Gascoyne, M., Currant, A.P., and Lord, T.C., 1981 'Ipswichian fauna of Victoria Cave and the marine palaeoclimate record', *Nature 294,* 652–654.

Gascoyne, M., Schwarcz, H.P., and Ford, D. C., 1978 'Uranium series dating and stable isotope studies of speleothems: Part I, Theory and techniques', *Trans. Br. Cave Res. Ass., 5,* 91–111.

Gladfelter, B.G., 1975 'Middle Pleistocene sedimentary sequences in East Anglia (U.K)', in Butzer, K.W., and Isaac, G.L., (eds.), *After the Australopithecines* (The Hague), 225–258.

Green, H.S., 1981a 'The first Welshman: excavations at Pontnewydd', *Antiquity 55,* 184–195.

Green H.S., 1981b 'The Lower Palaeolithic in Wales', in *Miscelanea: UISPP X Congress, Mexico* 33–43.

Green, H.S., 1981c 'A Palaeolithic handaxe from Rhossili, Gower', *Bull. Board of Celtic Studies 29,* 337–339.

Green, H.S., in press 'The Stone Age cave archaeology of South Wales', in Bull, P., and Ford, T., (eds.) *Limestones and Caves of Wales* (Norwich).

Green, H.S., and Currant, A.P., 1982 'Early man in Wales: Pontnewydd Cave (Clwyd) and its Pleistocene fauna', *Nature in Wales 1,* i, 40–43.

Green, H.S., Stringer, C.B., Collcutt, S.N., Currant, A.P., Huxtable, J., Schwarcz, H.P., Debenham, N., Embleton, C., Bull, P., Molleson, T.I., and Bevins, R.E., 1981 'Pontnewydd Cave in Wales – a new Middle Pleistocene hominid site', *Nature 294,* 707–713.

Greenly, E., 1919 *The Geology of Anglesey* (Mem. Geol. Surv. Lond., Vol.II).

Grimes, W.F., 1935 'Coygan Cave, Llansadyrnin, Carmarthenshire', *Archaeologia Cambren-*

sis 90, 95–111.

Guichard, G., 1976 'Les civilizations du Paléolithique inférieur en Périgord', in de Lumley, H., (ed.) *La Préhistoire Française I ii* (Paris), 909–928.

Harmon, R.S., Thompson, P., Schwarcz, H.P., and Ford, D.C., (1978) 'Late Pleistocene palaeoclimates of North America as inferred from stable isotope studies of speleothems', *Quaternary Research 9*, 54–70.

Haynes, G., 1982 'Utilisation and Skeletal Disturbances of North America Prey Carcases', *Arctic, 35,* 266–281.

Hedberg, H.D., (ed.), 1976 *International Stratigraphic Guide: A Guide to Stratigraphic Classifications, Terminology and Procedure* (New York).

Hendy, C. (1971) 'The isotopic geochemistry of speleothem – I. The calculation of the effects of different modes of formation on the isotopic composition of speleothems and their applicability as palaeoclimate indicators'. *Geochim.Cosmochim. Acta 35,* 801–824.

Hicks, H., 1886 'Results of some recent researches in some bone-caves in North Wales', *Q. Jl geol. Soc. Lond. 42,* 3–11.

Howells, M.F., Leveridge, B.E., and Evans, C.D.R., 1973 *Ordovician Ash-Flow Tuffs in Eastern Snowdonia* (I.G.S. Rep. 73/3).

Hubbard, R.N.L.B., 1982 'The environmental evidence from Swanscombe . . . ', in Leach, P.E., (ed.) *Archaeology in Kent to A.D.1500*. Council for British Archaeology Research Report, No.48, 3–7.

Hughes, T.McK., 1887 'On the drifts of the Vale of Clwyd and their relation to the caves and cave-deposits', *Q.Jl.geol.Soc.Lond.43,* 73–120.

Hughes, T.McK., and Thomas, D.R., 1874 'On the occurrence of felstone implements of the Le Moustier Type in Pontnewydd Cave, near Cefn, St. Asaph', *J.Anthrop. Inst. 3,* 387–390.

Huxtable, J, and Jacobi, R.M., 1982 'Thermoluminescence dating of burned flints from a British Mesolithic site: Longmoor Inclosure, East Hampshire', *Archaeometry 24,* ii, 164–169.

Institute of Geological Sciences, 1974 *IGS Boreholes, 1973,* (I.G.S. Rep. 74/7).

Jacobi, R.M., 1980 'The Upper Palaeolithic of Britain with special reference to Wales', in Taylor, J.A. (ed.) *Culture and Environment in Prehistoric Wales* (British Archaeological Reports, Oxford, no.76), 15–100.

Jahn, A., 1967 'Some features of mass movement on Spitsbergen slopes', *Geografiska Annaler 49,* 213–225.

Jaspers, M.T., and Witkop, C.J. Jr., 1980 'Taurodontism, an isolated trait associated with syndromes and X-chromosomal aneuploidy', *Am. J. Hum. Genet. 32,* 396–413.

Jefferson, G.T., 1976 'Cave faunas', in Ford, T.D., and Cullingford, C.H.D., (eds.), *The Science of Speleology* (London), 359-421.

Johnson, A.M., 1970 *Physical Processes in Geology* (San Franscisco).

Jones, P.R., 1981 'Experimental implement manufacture and use, a case study from Olduvai Gorge, Tanzania', *Phil. Trans. R. Soc. Lond. B292,* 189–195.

Kallay, J., 1963 'A radiographic study of the Neanderthal teeth from Krapina, Croatia', in Brothwell, D.R., (ed.) *Dental Anthropology* (Oxford), 75–86.

Kelly, S.F., 1967 'As good as new', *The Speleologist 2,* no.11, 20–21.

Kendall, M.G., 1948 *Rank Correlation Methods* (London).

Koenigswald, W. Von, 1973 'Veränderungen in der Kleinsäugerfauna von Mitteleuropa zwischen Cromer und Eem (Pleistozän), *Eiszeitalter und Gegenwart 23–24,* 159–167.

Kominz, M.A., Heath, G.R., Ku, J.L., and Pisias, N.G., 1979 'Brunhes time-scale and the interpretation of climatic change', *Earth and Planetary Science Letters 45,* 394–410.

Krinsley, D.H., and Doornkamp, J.C., 1973 *Atlas of Quartz Grain Textures* (Cambridge).

Kukla, G.J., 1977 'Pleistocene land-sea correlations. 1:Europe', *Earth Science Reviews, 13,* 307–374.

Kurtén, B., 1955 'Sex dimorphism and size trends in the cave bear *Ursus spelaeus,* Rosenmuller and Heinroth', *Acta Zoologica Fennica 90,* 1–48.

Lacaille, A.D., 1954 'A handaxe from Pen-y-lan, Cardiff, *Antiquaries Journal 34*, 64–7.

Leakey, M.D., 1971 *Olduvai Gorge, Vol.3: Excavations in Beds I and II, 1960–63.* (Cambridge).

Lim, C.H., Jackson, M.L., and Higashi, T., 1981 'Intercalation of soil clays with dimethylsulphoxide', *Soil Sci. Soc. Amer. Journal 45*, 423–427.

Lumley, H. de, 1972 *La Grotte Moustérienne de l'Hortus* Mémoire no. 1, Etudes Quaternaires, Université de Provence, (Marseille, France).

Lumley, H. de, (ed.), 1976 *La Préhistoire Française* Vols.I–II (Paris).

Mehra, Q.P., and Jackson, M.L., 1960 'Iron oxide removal from soils and clays by a dithionite-citrate system buffered with sodium bicarbonate', *Clays and Clay Minerals 7*, 317–327.

Mello, J.M., 1877 'The bone-caves of Creswell Crags – 3rd paper' *Q. Jl geol. Soc. Lond. 33*, 579–588.

Middleton, G.V., and Hampton, M.A., 1973 'Sediment Gravity Flows . . .' in Middleton, G.V., and Bouma, A.H., (eds.) *Turbidites and Deep-Water Sedimentation*, 1–38. (Soc. econ. Palaeontol. Mineral. Tulsa, Pacific Section Short Course).

Millward, D., Moseley, F. and Soper, N.J., 1978 'The Eycott and Borrowdale Volcanic Rocks', in Moseley, F. (ed.) *The Geology of the Lake District*, 99–120.

Miskovsky, J.-Cl., 1974 *Le Quaternaire du Midi méditerranéen* (Etudes Quaternaires, 3. Université de Provence. C.N.R.S.).

Mitchell, G.F., Penny, L.F., Shotton, F.W., & West, R.G., 1973 *A Correlation of Quaternary Geological Deposits in the British Isles* (Geol. Soc., London).

Moir, J.R., and Hopwood, A.T., 1939 'Excavations at Brundon, Suffolk (1935–7)', *Proc. Prehist. Soc. 5*, 1–32.

Molleson, T.I., 1981 'The application of the principles of bone fossilization to relative dating problems, with particular reference to the bones from La Caune de L'Arago Tautavel, France' in de Lumley, H., and Labeyrie, J., (eds), *Datations Absolues et Analyses Isotopiques en Préhistoire. Méthodes et Limites*, (C.N.R.S.), 659–676.

Molleson, T.I., and Oakley, K.P., 1966 'Relative antiquity of the Ubeidiya hominid', *Nature 209*, 1268.

Monnier, J.-L., and Texier, P.-J, 1977 'Découverte de trois hachereaux au Bois-du-Rocher (Côtes-du-Nord)', *L'Anthropologie 81*, 621–629.

Niggli, E., Overweel, C.J., and van der Vlerk, I.M., 1958 'An X-ray crystallographic application of the fluorine dating method of fossil bones', *Proc. K. Ned. Akad. Wet. B56*, 538–542.

Ninkovich, D., and Shackleton, N.J., 1975 'Distribution, stratigraphic position and age of ash layer 'L', in the Panama Basin region', *Earth and Planetary Science Letters 27*, 20–34.

Oakley, K.P., 1971 'British Isles' in Oakley, K.P., Campbell, B.G., and Molleson, T.I., *Catalogue of Fossil Hominids, Part II: Europe.*(British Museum (NH), London).

Oakley, K.P., 1980 'Relative dating of the fossil hominids of Europe', *Bull. Br. Mus. nat. Hist. (Geol.) 34*, 1–63.

Park, R.G., 1983 *Foundations of Structural Geology* (Glasgow & London).

Pettijohn, F.J., 1975 *Sedimentary Rocks* Third edition (London).

Pierson, T.C., 1980 'Erosion and deposition by debris flows at Mt. Thomas, North Canterbury, New Zealand', *Earth Surface Processes 5*, iii, 227–247.

Pierson, T.C., 1981 'Dominant particle support mechanisms in debris flows at Mt. Thomas, New Zealand, and implications for flow mobility',*Sedimentology 28*, i, 49–60.

Posnansky, M., 1963 'The Lower and Middle Palaeolithic industries of the English East Midlands', *Proc. Prehist. Soc. 29*, 357–394.

Prior, D.B., Stephens, N., and Douglas, G.R., 1970 'Some examples of modern debris flows from Northern Ireland', *Zeit. für Geomorph. 14*, 275–288.

Rapp, A., 1960 'Recent development of mountain slopes in Kärkevagge and surroundings, Northern Scandinavia', *Geografiska Annaler 42*, 65–200.

Reineck, H.-E., and Singh, I.B., 1980 *Depositional Sedimentary Environments* Second Edition (Berlin).

Rezk, M., 1976 *Studies on the Clay Mineralogy of Soils from Denbighshire, North Wales* (Unpub. Ph.D. Thesis, University of Wales).

Rodine, J.D., and Johnson, A.M., 1976 'The ability of debris, heavily freighted with coarse clastic materials, to flow on gentle slopes', *Sedimentology 23*, 213–234.

Roe, D.A., 1981 *The Lower and Middle Palaeolithic Periods in Britain* (London).

Rolland, N., 1981 'The interpretation of Middle Palaeolithic variability, *Man 16*, 15–42.

Rowlands, B.M.,1955 *The Glacial and Post-Glacial Geomorphological Evolution of the Landforms of the Vale of Clwyd* (Unpub. M.A. thesis, Univ. of Liverpool).

Rowlands, B.M. 1971 'Radiocarbon evidence of the age of an Irish Sea glaciation in the Vale of Clwyd', *Nature 230*, 9–11.

Sampson, C.G., 1978 *Palaeoecology and Archaeology of an Acheulian Site at Caddington, England* (Dallas).

Savage, D., 1969 'The visible effects of the flood of July 10th 1968 in and around G.B.Cave, Charterhouse-on-Mendip, Somerset',*Proc. Univ. Bristol Spelaeol. Soc. 12*, i, 123–126.

Schmid, E., 1969 'Cave sediments and prehistory', in Brothwell, D., and Higgs, E., (eds.), *Science in Archaeology,* Second edition (London), 151–166.

Schwarcz, H.P., 1980 'Absolute age determination of archaeological sites by Uranium series dating of travertines', *Archaeometry 22*, 3–24.

Schwarcz, H.P., 1982 'Application of U-series dating to Archaeometry', in Ivanovich, M., and Harmon, R.S., (eds.), *Uranium Series Disequilibrium* (Oxford), 302–325.

Schwarcz, H.P., Harmon, R.S., Thompson, P., and Ford, D.C., 1976 'Stable isotope studies of fluid inclusions in speleothems and their palaeoclimatic significance',*Geochimica Cosmochim. Acta 40*, 657–665.

Scott, K., 1980 'Two hunting episodes of Middle Palaeolithic Age at La Cotte de Saint-Brelade'. *World Archaeology 12*, 137–52.

Shackleton, N.J., and Opdyke, N.D., 1973 'Oxygen isotope and palaeomagnetic stratigraphy of Equatorial Pacific core V28–238, *Quaternary Res. 3*, 39–55.

Sharp, R.P., 1942 'Mudflow Levées, *Journal of Geomorphology 5*, 212–227.

Sharpe, C.F.S., 1938 *Landslides and Related Phenomena* Columbia Geomorphic Studies, 2 (New York).

Shaw, J.C., 1928 'Taurodont teeth in South African races', *J. Anat. 62*, 476–498.

Singer, R., and Wymer, J., 1982 *The Middle Stone Age at Klasies River Mouth Cave in South Africa* (Chicago).

Skinner, M.F., and Sperber, G.H., 1982 *Atlas of Radiographs of Early Man* (New York).

Smith, B., and George, T.N., 1961 *British Regional Geology – North Wales* (HMSO London).

Smith, W.E., 1960 'The siliceous consituents of chert', *Geol.Mijnb.39*, 1–8.

Smithson, F., 1953 'The micromineralogy of North Wales soils',*Jour. Soil Sci. 4*,194–210.

Sokal, R.R., and Sneath, P.H.A., 1963 *Principles of Numerical Taxonomy* (San Francisco and London).

Stanley, E., 1832 'Memoir on a cave at Cefn in Denbighshire', *Edin. New Philos. Journ. 14*, 40–53.

Statham, I., 1976 'Debris flows on vegetated screes in the Black Mountain, Carmarthenshire',*Earth Surface Processes 1*, ii,173–180.

Statham, I., 1977 *Earth Surface Sediment Transport* (Oxford).

Stringer, C.B., Howell, F.C., and Melentis, J.K., 1979 'The significance of the fossil hominid from Petralona, Greece',*J. Arch. Sci. 6*, 235–253.

Stuart, A.J., 1974 'Pleistocene history of the British vertebrate fauna', *Biol. Rev. 49*, 225–266.

Stuart, A.J., 1975 'The vertebrate fauna of the type Cromerian', *Boreas 4*, 63–76.

Stuart, A.J., 1976 'The history of the mammal fauna during the Ipswichian/Last Interglacial in England', *Phil. Trans. R. Soc. Lond. B276*, 221–250.

Stuart, A.J., 1977 'The vertebrates of the Last Cold Stage in Britain and Ireland', *Phil.*

Trans. R. Soc. Lond. B280, 295–312.

Stuart, A.J., and West, R. G., 1976 'Late Cromerian fauna and flora at Ostend, Norfolk', *Geol. Mag. 113,* 469–473.

Sutcliffe, A.J., 1960 'Joint Mitnor Cave, Buckfastleigh', *Trans. Proc. Torquay Nat. Hist. Soc. 13,* 1–26.

Sutcliffe, A.J., 1964 'The mammalian fauna', in Ovey, C.D., (ed.) *The Swanscombe Skull, Occ. Pap. R. Anthrop. Inst. London 20,* 85–111.

Sutcliffe, A.J., and Kowalski, K., 1976 'Pleistocene rodents of the British Isles', *Bull. Br. Mus. nat. Hist.(Geol.) 27,* ii, 31–147.

Szabo, B.J., and Collins, D., 1975 'Ages of fossil bones from British Interglacial Sites', *Nature 254,* 680–681.

Thompson, P., Ford, D.C., and Schwarcz, H.P., 1975 '^{234}U/^{238}U ratios in limestone cave seepage waters and speleothems from West Virginia', *Geochimica Cosmochim. Acta 39,* 661–669.

Tixier, J., Inizan, M.L., and Roche, H., 1980 *Préhistoire de la Pierre Taillée I. Terminologie et Technologie* (Valbonne, France).

Tuffreau, A., 1976a 'Acheuléen et industries apparentées dans le Nord de la France, et le Bassin de la Somme', in Combier, J., (ed.) *Colloque X: UISPP IX Congrès, Nice,* 93–109.

Tuffreau, A., 1976b 'Les civilisations du Paléolithique inférieur dans la région parisienne et en Normandie', in de Lumley, H., (ed.), *La Préhistoire Française I,* ii, Paris, 947–955.

Tuffreau, A., 1976c 'Les civilizations du Paléolithique inférieur en Artois et dans le Cambrésis', in de Lumley, H., (ed.), *La Préhistoire Française I,* ii, (Paris), 964–970.

Tuffreau, A., 1976d 'Les fouilles du gisement acheuléen supérieur des Osiers à Bapaume (Pas-de-Calais)', *Bull. Soc. Préhist. Fr. 73,* 231–243.

Tuffreau, A., 1978 'Les Fouilles du gisement paléolithique de Biache-Saint-Vaast (Pas-de-Calais): 1976–77 – premiers résultats', *Bull. Ass. Franc. Etude Quatern. 1–3,* 46–55.

Tuffreau, A., 1981 'Le Paléolithique inférieur et moyen du Pléistocène moyen récent dans la France septentrionale', *Notae Praehistoricae 1,* (Tervuren, Belgium), 97–98.

Turekian, K.K., and Nelson, E., 1976 'Uranium Series dating of the travertines of Caune de l'Arago (France)'. *Colloque I: UISPP IX Congres, Nice,* 172–179.

Ubelaker, D.H., 1978 *Human Skeletal Remains* (Chicago).

Valdemar, A.E., 1970 'A new assessment of the occupation of the Cefn Cave in relation to the Bont Newydd Cave,' *Trans. Cave Research Group of Great Britain 12,* ii, 109–112.

Vandermeersch, B., 1978 'Etude préliminaire du crâne humain du gisement paléolithique de Biache-Saint-Vaast', *Bull. Assoc. Franc. Etude Quatern. 1–3,* 65–67.

Villa, P., 1981 'Matières premières et provinces culturelles dans l'Acheuléen français', *Quaternaria 23,* 19–35.

Walton, A.J., and Debenham, N.C., 1980 'Spatial distribution studies of Thermoluminescence using a high-grain image intensifier', *Nature 284,* 42–44.

Wickham-Jones, C.R., and Collins, G.H., 1978 'The sources of flint and chert in Northern Britain', *Proc. Soc. Antiquaries of Scotland 109,* 7–21.

Wintle, A.G., 1977 'Thermoluminescence dating study of some Quaternary calcite: potential and problems', *Canad. J. Earth Sci. 15,* 1977–1986.

Wolpoff, M.H., 1979 'The Krapina dental remains', *Am. J. Phys. Anthrop. 50,* 67–114.

Wymer, J.J., 1968 *Lower Palaeolithic Archaeology in Britain* (London).

Wymer, J.J., 1982a 'The Palaeolithic period in Kent', in Leach, P.E., (ed.) *Archaeology in Kent to A.D. 1500* Council for British Archaeology Research Report no. 48, 8–11.

Wymer, J.J., 1982b *The Palaeolithic Age* (London).

Younis, M.G.A., 1983 *Mineralogical Studies on Soils in North West Wales.* (Unpub. Ph.D. thesis, University of Wales).

INDEX OF PERSONAL NAMES AND PLACES